BOOKS BY THE SAME AUTHOR

THE PASSION OF CHRIST IN SCRIPTURE AND HISTORY explains the necessity, and achievements of the Cross.

THE CHRISTIAN AND ROCK MUSIC is a timely symposium that defines biblical principles to make good musical choices.

THE SABBATH UNDER CROSSFIRE refutes the common arguments used to negate the continuity and validity of the Sabbath.

IMMORTALITY OR RESURRECTION? unmasks with compelling Biblical reasoning the oldest and the greatest deception of all time, —that human beings possess immortal souls that live on forever.

THE MARRIAGE COVENANT presents biblical principles established by God to ensure happy, lasting, marital relationships.

THE ADVENT HOPE FOR HUMAN HOPELESSNESS offers a simple, and comprehensive presentation of the biblical teachings regarding the certainty and imminence of Christ's Return.

FROM SABBATH TO SUNDAY presents the results of painstaking research done at a Vatican University in Rome on how the change came about from Saturday to Sunday in early Christianity.

THE SABBATH IN THE NEW TESTAMENT summarizes Bacchiocchi's extensive research on the history and theology of the Lord's Day and answers the most frequently asked questions on this subject.

WINE IN THE BIBLE shows convincingly that the Bible condemns the use of alcoholic beverages, irrespective of the quantity used.

CHRISTIAN DRESS AND ADORNMENT examines the Biblical teachings regarding dress, cosmetics, and jewelry. An important book designed to help Christians dress modestly, decently, and reverently.

DIVINE REST FOR HUMAN RESTLESSNESS offers a rich and stirring theological interpretation of the relevance of Sabbathkeeping for our tension-filled and restless society. Translated in 15 languages.

HAL LINDSEY'S PROPHETIC JIGSAW PUZZLE refutes with compelling logic the senselessness of the predictions made by writers like Hal Lindsey. It received the 1987 *Associated Church Press Award.*

WOMEN IN THE CHURCH shows why Scripture supports the participation of women in various church ministries but precludes their ordination to the representative role of elder or pastor.

THE TIME OF THE CRUCIFIXION AND THE RESURRECTION examines the time element of the Crucifixion/Resurrection as well as the meaning of Christ's death.

GOD'S FESTIVALS IN SCRIPTURE AND HISTORY. Vol. 1: *The Spring Festivals;* Vol. 2: *The Fall Festivals* examine the historical development and theological meaning of the ancient Feasts of Israel.

The price of each book is $25.00, mailing expenses included. You can order copies by phone (269) 471-2915 or by email at sbacchiocchi@biblicalperspectives.com, or online at http://www.biblicalperspectives.com

iblical
erspectives
9

THE MARRIAGE COVENANT

A Biblical Study on Marriage, Divorce, and Remarriage

by
Samuele Bacchiocchi

iblical
erspectives
4990 Appian Way
Berrien Springs
Michigan 49103

Cover photo
by
Daniel Brant

Sixth Printing 2006

You can purchase a copy of this book
($25.00, postpaid) online at
http://www.biblicalperspectives.com
or
by phone: (269) 471-2915
or
by email: sbacchiocchi@biblicalperspectives.com
or
by mail
BIBLICAL PERSPECTIVES
4990 Appian Way
Berrien Springs
Michigan 49103

Phone (269) 471-2915
Fax (269) 978-6898
E-mail: sbacchiocchi@biblicalperspectives.com
Web site: http://www.biblicalperspectives.com

Table

of

Contents

Introduction

INTRODUCTION

The Christian home is in trouble. There is hardly a Christian family that directly or indirectly has not known the pain of divorce. Divorce is no longer a disease contracted by Hollywood movie stars. It affects people from all walks of life, including Christians. This stark reality has been brought home to me through my itinerant ministry across North America and overseas. It has become a common but disturbing sight for me to look over congregations while I preach and see large numbers of single parents. In some congregations local pastors have told me that the number of broken homes outnumbers those which have not yet experienced the tragedy of divorce.

An important factor contributing to the alarming escalation of divorce among Christians is the growing acceptance of the societal view of marriage as a social contract governed by the laws of the land rather than a sacred covenant regulated by the higher moral law of God. Marriage is no longer seen by many people as a sacred covenant witnessed and guaranteed by God Himself, but rather as a social contract that can easily be terminated.

The "no fault" divorce law makes it possible to put asunder what God has united for less than the price of a good suit. This trend is influencing Christians to believe that divorce is a guiltless, and at times, proper procedure.

Need to Recover the Biblical view of Marriage. To counteract the secularization and easy-dissolution of marriage, it is imperative to recover the Biblical view of marriage as a sacred, life-long covenant. The recovery of this view can help Christians resist the societal trend to consider divorce as easy solution to their marital problems. To accomplish this objective we need to engage all the preaching, teaching, and counseling resources that Christian churches possess.

An important avenue that can effectively propagate the Biblical view of marriage as a sacred, permanent covenant is Christian literature. There is an urgent need for literature articulating, not the cultural, but the Biblical view of marriage, sex, divorce, and remarriage. I became aware of this urgent need while reviewing the extensive literature on this subject. To my surprise I found that most of the literature treats marriage, divorce and remarriage from purely sociological, psychological, medical, and economic perspectives. The few books written from a Christian perspective seldom offer an adequate analysis of what the Bible really teaches on this subject. There are scholarly studies dealing with problematic texts and words, but these studies are usually technical in nature and without practical application to our contemporary marriage situations.

The result is that many Christians today do not know for sure what the Bible really teaches in the area of marriage, sex, divorce, and remarriage. Many are asking important questions such as: "What is the difference between a Chrsitian and a non-Christian marriage? What guidance does the Bible offer on how to build up a strong marriage covenant relationship? Does the Bible clearly teach role distinctions between husband and wife? Does the Bible view the function of sex as exclusively procreational or also as relational? Is it Biblically right or wrong to use contraceptives? Are there Biblical grounds for divorce and remarriage? Is a Christian who remarries guilty of continuous adultery? When marital relationships become intolerable, should a Christian couple suffer the pain of divorce or the tragedy of maintaining a marriage without love? Should a minister who has divorced and remarried be allowed to continue to serve as a pastor? Should a minister marry divorced people and should remarried people be automatically accepted into church membership?"

Search for Biblical Answers. Questions such as these trouble many sincere Christians who are seeking truly Biblical answers. They want to know what guidance, if any, the Word of God offers to these perplexing questions affecting so many lives. The confusion is partly caused by the cultural transition in which we live. Old values are being challenged today inside and outside the church by secularistic and humanistic ideologies. Sometimes even pastors, teachers, and Christian writers contribute to the prevailing confusion by interpreting the Bible more in the light of their cultural values than in the light of their serious study of what the Bible actually teaches regarding these perplexing questions.

It is the awareness of the urgent need for literature to help Christians find true Biblical answers to important questions regarding marriage, divorce, and remarriage, that has motivated me to undertake this research. From the outset, my aim has been to provide a definite and concrete understanding of the Biblical teaching on marriage, divorce, and remarriage. It is my hope that this study, the fruit of months of dedicated research, will meet the expectations of the growing number of conservative Christians who are seeking truly Biblical answers to their questions. The reader must decide whether or not I have succeeded in "rightly handling the word of truth" (2 Tim 2:15).

Procedure and Style. The procedure I have followed throughout the book consists of two steps. First, I have endeavored to establish what the Bible teaches on marriage, divorce, and remarriage by examining all the relevant passages. Second, I have tried to apply Biblical teachings to concrete situations by articulating basic principles and by offering some practical examples.

Concerning the style of the book, I have attempted to write in simple, non-technical language. To facilitate the reading, each chapter is divided into major parts, and subdivided under appropriate headings. A brief summary is given at the end of each chapter. Unless otherwise specified, all Bible texts are quoted from the Revised Standard Version, copyrighted in 1946 and 1952.

An Overview of the Book. Out of consideration toward those who appreciate an overview of the structure and content of the book, I will briefly summarize the highlights of each chapter.

The study opens in chapter 1 with an examination of the Biblical view of marriage. The teachings of the prophets, Jesus, and Paul consistently show that marriage in the Scripture is a sacred and permanent covenant, witnessed and protected by God. The sacred nature of the marriage covenant is revealed especially through the use of marriage in the Old Testament to portray God's relationship with Israel, and in the New Testament to represent Christ's relationship with His church.

Chapter 2 explores the practical implications of the Biblical view of marriage as a sacred covenant by providing practical suggestions on how to live out the marriage covenant. A special effort is made to look at the obligations of the marriage covenant in the light of the Ten Commandments. The study shows how the principles of the Ten Commandments, which express our covenant commitment to God, can also serve to manifest our covenant commitment to our spouse.

Chapter 3 examines the Biblical view of the nature and function of sex. The study shows that in the Bible sex is seen as part of God's good creation. Its function is both unitive and procreative. It serves to engender a mysterious oneness of body, mind, and spirit between husband and wife, while offering them the possibility of bringing children into this world.

Chapter 4 addresses the crucial question of how to handle marital conflicts. The first part of the chapter looks into the major causes of marital conflicts. The second part proposes seven basic rules than can turn marital conflicts into opportunities for building a stronger marriage covenant.

Chapter 5 builds upon chapter 3 by examining a major cause of marital conflicts, namely, the difference in role perception between husband and wife. The study shows that role distinctions in the Bible are not cultural, but creational, that is to say, they have been established by God at creation to ensure unity and harmony in the home.

Chapter 6 investigates what the Bible teaches regarding divorce and remarriage. Truly I can say that this has been the most difficult chapter to write because I wanted to be true to the teaching of the Bible and yet compassionate toward those who have experienced the tragedy of divorce. The study reveals that both the Old and New Testaments clearly and consistently condemn divorce as a violation of God's original plan for marriage to be a lifelong union that enables a man and a woman to become "one flesh." Respect for this fundamental principle demands that a Christian couple experiencing marital conflicts should not seek to resolve them through divorce.

Chapter 7 first summarizes the fundamental principles that have emerged in chapter VI from the study of the Biblical teachings on divorce and remarriage and then discusses how the church can apply such principles to concrete situations today. To be faithful to her calling, the church must not only proclaim God's will for marriage to be a sacred, lifelong covenant, but it must also extend God's forgiving grace to those who have sinned by divorcing and remarrying.

Acknowledgments. It is most difficult for me to acknowledge my indebtedness to the many persons who have contributed to the realization of this book. Indirectly, I feel indebted to the many authors who have written valuable studies on the subject of marriage, divorce and remarriage. Through I could not accept the methodology and conclusions of certain studies, all of them have been beneficial by broadening my understanding of the complexity of certain issues.

Directly, I want to express my heartfelt gratitude to Thomas Baker, Arnie Guild, and Vicky Simmons (English teachers at Andrews University), who went beyond the call of duty by reading, correcting and reacting constructively to my manuscript.

My wife, Anna, deserves special mention. Her tender loving care, patience, and dedication to me and our three children, have made it much easier for me to understand and write on what God intends marriage to be. Truly I can say that through the years, and especially while writing this book, my wife has been a constant source of encouragement and inspiration to me. Without her role model as a loving, caring, patient, and encouraging wife and mother, it would have been very difficult for me to understand, experience, and write about how to build a happy, lifelong marriage.

Two Benefactors. A very special acknowledgment goes to two generous persons who felt impressed to contribute financially to the realization of this book. The first is Dr. John H. Friend, a medical doctor with a passion to help people physically and spiritually. I met Dr. Friend in Galt, California while presenting a seminar. His desire to help people became immediately evident when he offered to take me first to the motel and then to the Sacramento airport at 5:30 on Sunday morning. While driving along he expressed the desire to contribute to my ministry of research. His offer could not have come at a better time. I told Dr. Friend that I had been hoping to find a sponsor for this book on marriage which I had just delivered to the printer in camera-ready format. Sensing the urgent need to strengthen the Christian home through a recovery of the Biblical view of marriage as a sacred, lifelong covenant, Dr. Friend wrote a check to help toward the printing of this book, just before dropping me off at the Sacramento airport. Words are inadequate to express my deep gratitude for his generous contribution.

What impressed me most about Dr. Friend is his willingness to share not only his financial means but also *himself*. He related to me the pleasant memories of the years he spent in Ethiopia while serving as a medical missionary. He expressed the hope to be able one day to return to Ethiopia with his son, Steven, who is currently in medical school. His dream is to team up with his son in managing our Gimbie Seventh-day Adventist hospital in Ethiopia.

Dr. Friend believes that God has called him not only to heal the bodies but also to save the souls of people. He endeavors to meet the spiritual needs of his patients by offering them both words of spiritual counsel and religious literature. While driving me to the airport, he showed me a pile of tracts dealing with Biblical truths which he was planning to mail to his patients the next day. Such an example of dedication is not only praiseworthy but also of great inspiration to me.

Currently Dr. Friend resides in Galt, California with his wife Mona and their son Jerry. They enjoy country living, cultivating their vegetable garden and caring for the cattle of their small dairy farm.

The second person who has contributed financially to the realization of this book is a dear Australian lady who has requested to remain anonymous. I met her during a lecture tour in Australia. During the brief counseling session, she immediately impressed me by her desire to serve the Lord. She related to me some of the severe conflicts she had experienced in her own marriage, and then she expressed the desire to contribute toward the realization of this book on marriage to show her earnest desire to strengthen the Christian home.

Author's Hope. It is my fervent hope that this study, the fruit of dedicated research, may contribute toward strengthening the Christian home through a recovery of those Biblical principles established by God to ensure happy and lasting marital relationships.

To fight effectively against the alarming escalation of divorce among Christians which is threatening to undo the very fabric of our society, we need to recover the Biblical view of marriage as a sacred, lifelong covenant. The recovery of such a view can motivate Christians to engage all their resources toward ensuring that no one will put asunder what God has united.

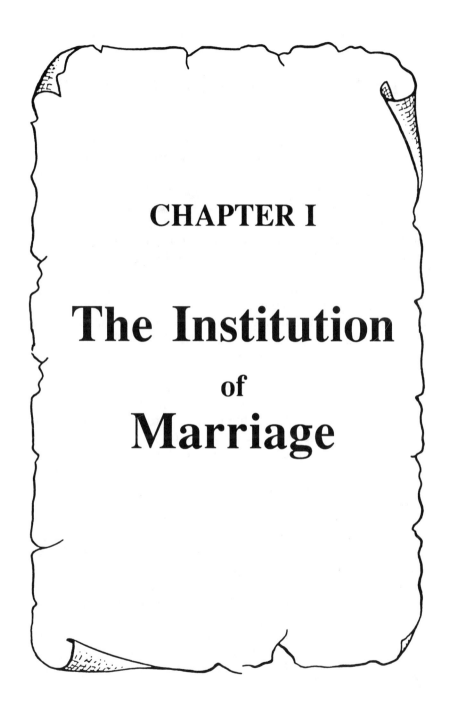

CHAPTER I

The Institution

of

Marriage

THE INSTITUTION OF MARRIAGE

Marriage is not a human institution devised in the dim past of human history as a convenient way to sort out social responsibilities. If marriage were a human invention, then different types of marriage could have equal value. Polygamy, the taking of several wives, might serve an agricultural society better than an industrialized society; polyandry, the sharing of a wife by several husbands, might prove to be more efficient and economical in a highly technological society. Monogamy, the lifelong union of one man to one woman, would have no more intrinsic value than any other type of marriage. Some could legitimately argue that monogamy has served its purpose as the ideal norm of society and should now be replaced by serial monogamy, the taking of a succession of husbands and wives. In fact, for some today the latter better satisfies the quest for greater self-fulfillment and gratification.

A Divine Institution. The Bible presents marriage as a divine institution. If marriage were of human origin, then human beings would have a right to decide the kind of marital relationships to choose. Marriage, however, began with God. It was established by God at the beginning of human history when He "created the heavens and the earth" (Gen 1:1). As the Creator of marriage, God has the right to tell us which principles should govern our marital relationships.

If God had left us no instructions about marriage after establishing it, then marriage could be regulated according to personal whims. But He has not left us in the dark. In His revelation contained in the pages of the Bible, God has revealed His will regarding the nature and function of marriage. As Christians who choose to live in accordance with God's will, we must study and respect those Biblical principles governing marriage, divorce, and remarriage. In some instances, the laws of a state regarding marriage, divorce and remarriage ignore or even violate the teachings of the Bible. In such cases, as Christians, "we must obey God rather than men" (Acts 5:29).

Objectives of Chapter. This chapter seeks to help the reader understand the Biblical view of marriage by examining three specific themes: (1) The creation of woman, (2) The institution of marriage, and (3) Marriage as a sacred covenant. The last part looks into the Old Testament teachings of the prophets and the New Testament teachings of Jesus and Paul regarding marriage. The study will show that Scripture consistently upholds marriage as a sacred and permanent covenant, established and witnessed by God Himself. The study closes urging the reader to recover the Biblical view of marriage as a sacred covenant to counteract the secularization of marriage in our society today.

PART I: THE CREATION OF WOMAN

No newspaper reporter was present to observe the creation of this universe and the celebration of the first marriage. God alone tells us how it all began in the brief account of Genesis 1-2. As the crown and culmination of His creative work, "God created man in His own image, in the image of God He created him; male and female He created them" (Gen 1:27).

This fundamental text reveals three things. *First,* the first human couple originated not from an evolutionary process, but through divine creation. *Second,* man, which, as the parallelism indicates, is the generic name inclusive of "male and female," was fashioned in the image of God. This involves moral, rational and spiritual faculties rather than gender likeness, since God transcends male/female distinctions. It may also include the capacity of a man and a woman to experience a oneness of fellowship similar to the one existing in the Trinity. *Third,* man was created as a sexual being, consisting of a male and a female counterpart. This means that though men and women are sexually and functionally different, they enjoy equal dignity and importance before God.

The Need for Companionship. In the creation account, God repeatedly recognizes that His creation was good (Gen 1:4, 10, 12, 18, 21, 25, 31). The only thing that God acknowledges to be "not good" is the incomplete creation of man as a single being: "Then God said: 'It is *not good* that the man should be alone; I will make him a helper fit for him'" (Gen 2:20).

At this point creation was still incomplete. With man alone there could be no procreation, and more important yet, no possibility for him to experience the kind of intimate relationship existing within the Godhead. To be human means more than to be male or female. It means to be able to enjoy an intimate rational and spiritual fellowship. To rectify the "not good" situation, God declares, "I will make him a helper fit for him" (Gen 2:18).

A Suitable Helper. God designed woman to be man's suitable helper, or literally, "a helper corresponding to him." Eve was created to be Adam's *other half* approximating him in every point and making the marriage union a complete whole. She was not created to be man's slave, but rather his helper. The word "helper" (*'ezer*) is used in the Bible also for God as the helper of the needy (Ps 33:20; 146:5), thus it does not imply that woman is an inferior being. She is equal in nature and worth, reflecting the same divine image (Gen 1:27). Yet she is different in function, serving as a supportive helper. We shall consider in chapter 4 the importance of respecting the creational role distinctions to ensure harmonious relationships in the home and in the church.

Woman was created to be man's counterpart, corresponding to him mentally, physically and spiritually, making him a larger person than he would have been alone, bringing into his life a new feminine perspective he would not have known otherwise. The same holds true for man. He brings to his wife a masculine perspective that enlarges her life, making her a more complete person than she could be without him. Thus, a marriage union not only fills the need for companionship, but it enables a man and a woman to become fuller, more complete persons.

The Single Life. God's evaluation of the single life as "not good" (Gen 2:18) appears to be contradicted by Christ's statement that "there are eunuchs who have been so from birth, and there are eunuchs who have been made eunuchs by men, and there are eunuchs who have made themselves eunuchs for the sake of the kingdom of heaven. He who is able to receive this, let him receive it" (Matt 19:11-12). A similar thought is expressed by Paul in 1 Corinthians 7:7 where in speaking of his single lifestyle he says: "I wish that all were as I myself am. But each has his own special gift from God, one of one kind and one of another."

These two texts (Matt 19:11-12; 1 Cor 7:7) suggest that God has singled out some people to lead lives of celibacy for the sake of His kingdom. How then can God give the gift of celibacy to some while affirming at the same time, "It is not good that the man should be alone" (Gen 2:18)? The resolution to this apparent contradiction is to be found in recognizing that God has made an exception to His own general principle. Because of the social distortions and crises brought about by sin and because of the urgent demand upon the church to advance the cause of His kingdom, God has equipped some persons with the capacity of leading fulfilling single lives.

The exact nature of the gift of celibacy is never fully explained in Scripture. Presumably it consists in the capacity to find companionship, though of a different kind, outside of marriage, by becoming deeply involved in the mission of the church in ways married persons cannot (see 1 Cor 7:32-34). According to Christ, "He who is able to receive this, let him receive it" (Matt 19:12). Those who have been granted the special gift of *single service* for Christ's kingdom must prepare for it and pursue it. To determine whether a person has the gift of leading a single life for Christ's kingdom, it is necessary to apply the two tests suggested by Matthew 19:12 and 1 Corinthians 7:8, 9: (1) Am I able to contain my sexual urges? and (2) Do I find satisfaction and companionship in the work of God's kingdom?

Single Christians who have been granted the special gift of single service for Christ's kingdom ought not to be looked down upon nor neglected by married Christians. Rather, they ought to be honored for their willingness to accept God's call to make the advancement of His kingdom the primary purpose of their lives. After all, we do not look down on Paul for choosing a single life in order to be able to serve Christ more fully and more freely.

The Provision of Woman. The way God chose to create the first bride is most significant. Unlike the rest of creation and of man himself, God formed Eve not from "the dust of the ground" (Gen 2:7) but from the very man who was to become her husband, by utilizing one of his ribs (Gen 2:21). The significance of the manner of Eve's creation, though not explicitly expressed, can hardly be missed. Eve was not made out of Adam's head to rule over him, nor out of his feet to be trampled upon by him, but out of his side to be his equal, under his arm to be protected, and near his heart to be loved.

As Adam beheld with sleepy eyes the most beautiful creature of God's creation, he declared with ecstatic excitement: "This at last is bone of my bones and flesh of my flesh; she shall be called Woman, because she was taken out of Man" (Gen 2:23). Adam's rejoicing was motivated by the discovery of the person who completed his incompleteness. His hunger for wholeness stemmed from the fact that God made him a male with the need for a female companion. God made Adam incomplete without Eve from the beginning.

The manner in which God created Adam and Eve reveals God's design that there should be male *and* female. Each of them needs the other for self-fulfillment. Each of them should accept his or her sexual and functional roles as given by God. This means that efforts to promote sexual or functional role interchangeability between men and women represent a violation of the role distinctions established by God at creation. True completeness and self-realization can be found not by transcending our sexual or functional roles but rather by fulfilling our different and yet complementary roles.

PART II: THE INSTITUTION OF MARRIAGE

After Adam expressed his excitement at the sight of Eve and exercised his authority by naming her, God united them in holy matrimony, saying: "Therefore a man leaves his father and his mother and cleaves to his wife, and they become one flesh" (Gen 2:24). This foundational statement about marriage is repeated three times in the Bible: first, by Jesus in the context of His teachings on divorce (Matt 19:5; Mark 10:7, 8) and then by Paul to illustrate the relationship of Christ to His church (Eph 5:31).

Marriage as a Covenant. The very first description of the nature of marriage in the Bible, as consisting of leaving, cleaving and becoming one flesh (Gen 2:24), reveals the Biblical under-standing of marriage as a covenant relationship. This meaning of marriage as a covenant of companionship is expressed more explicitly later in Scripture in such passages as Malachi 2:14: "The Lord was witness to the *covenant* between you and the wife of your youth, to whom you have been faithless, though she is your *companion* and your wife by *covenant*."[1] Being a sacred covenant, human marriage serves in the Old and New Testaments as the prism through which God reveals His covenant relationship with His people and Christ with His church.

To appreciate the Biblical view of marriage as a sacred cov-enant, it is helpful to distinguish between a contract and a covenant. Paul E. Palmer offers a helpful clarification of the difference between the two: "Contracts engage the services of people; covenants engage persons. Contracts are made for a stipulated period of time; covenants are forever. Contracts can be broken, with material loss to the contracting parties; covenants cannot be broken, but if violated, they result in personal loss and broken hearts. . . . Contracts are witnessed by people with the state as guarantor; covenants are witnessed by God with God as guarantor."[2] In light of this understanding of a covenant as a permanent commitment, witnessed and guaranteed by God, let us examine the three compo-nents of the marriage covenant mentioned in Genesis 2:24: leav-ing, cleaving, and becoming one flesh.

Leaving. The first step in establishing a marriage covenant is *leaving* all other relationships, including the closest ones of father and mother: "Therefore a man *leaves* his father and his mother" (Gen 2:24). Of course, leaving does not mean the abandonment of one's parents. The responsibility to "Honor your father and mother" (Ex 20:12) is applied by Jesus to adults (Mark 7:6-13). We do not evade our responsibility toward our parents as they grow old. Jesus scorned the hypocrisy of those who gave to the Temple the money they had set aside for their parents (Mark 7:9-13). As adults, however, we assume responsibility *for* our parents rather than *to* them. The Bible never suggests that married couples should sever their ties with their parents, but that they must "let go" of their former lives as sons and daughters in order to cement their rela-tionships as husbands and wives.

What "leaving" means is that all lesser relationships must give way to the newly formed marital relationship. A leaving must occur to cement a covenant relationship of husband and wife. This principle of leaving applies likewise to our covenant relationship with God. It is said of the disciples that "they *left* everything and followed Him" (Luke 5:11).[3]

Leaving is not always easy. It is often hard for a baby to leave his mother's womb. It may look cruel to see a doctor cut the umbilical cord which binds the baby to the mother. Yet, it is necessary for the growth and development of the baby. It is also hard for children to leave their parents and for parents to let their children go, for example, to a school away from home. Just as babies cannot grow physically unless they leave their mother's womb and just as children cannot receive an education unless they leave home to go to school, similarly a marriage cannot mature unless both partners are willing to leave their parents in order to cement a new marital relationship and establish a new family.

Aspects of Leaving. There are men and women who fail to build strong covenant marriages because they are still "tied to their mother's apron strings," or they are not willing to "leave" their attachment to their parents, jobs, advanced education, sports, past lives, friends, or even church work, in order to establish strong marital relationships.

Leaving involves not only leaving behind our positions as dependent children, but also ending our financial dependence upon our parents. The couple who never learns to stand financially on their own feet will have difficulty in developing their future plans independently. We must also leave behind our parental authority. Possessive, interfering parents can threaten the best marriages. While parental counsel must always be respected, parents' efforts to interfere in the private lives of their married children must be firmly resisted.

Leaving also involves learning to abandon some of our parents' attitudes and influences. This is not always easy since we are largely the product of our upbringing. The process of adjustment to a new marital relationship requires that we learn to distinguish between what is fundamental and what is incidental to our past upbringing, being willing to leave behind the latter where necessary for the health and growth of our marriages.

Perhaps the most difficult things to leave behind are the inner wounds and hurts of our childhoods. We come to our marriages with the good and bad emotional experiences of the first two decades of our lives. Through the healing power of the Holy Spirit, we can be delivered from the past wounds that can infect our marital relationships. The love of Jesus and the encouragement of our spouses can set us free from our pasts and enable us to be the understanding partners God wants us to be. So the first principle we derive from the divine institution of marriage recorded in Genesis 2:24 is as follows: *To establish a thrilling "one flesh" marriage covenant, we must be willing to leave all lesser relationships.*

Cleaving. The second essential component of a marriage covenant is *cleaving*: "Therefore a man leaves his father and mother and *cleaves* to his wife" (Gen 2:24). A leaving must occur before a cleaving can take place. This process reveals divine wisdom. A man and a woman must leave all lesser relationships for the purpose of cleaving, that is, cementing their new relationship and establishing a new home.

"Cleaving" reflects the central concept of covenant-fidelity. The Hebrew word for "cleave," *dabaq*, suggests the idea of being permanently glued or joined together. It is one of the words frequently used to express the covenant commitment of the people to God: "You shall fear the Lord your God; you shall serve him and *cleave to Him*" (Deut 10:20; cf. 11:22; 13:4; 30:20). The word is used to describe Ruth's refusal to leave her mother-in-law Naomi: "Ruth clave unto her" (Ruth 1:14 AV).

In the sight of God, cleaving means wholehearted commitment which spills over to every area of our being. It means to be permanently glued together rather than temporarily taped together. You can separate two pieces of wood taped together, but you cannot separate without great damage two pieces of wood glued together. In fact, two pieces of wood glued together become not only inseparable, but also much stronger than if they were taped together.

Cleaving involves unswerving loyalty to one's marital partner. Note that man is to cleave to "his wife." This excludes marital unfaithfulness. A man cannot be glued to his wife and flirt or engage in sexual intercourse with another woman. The two are mutually exclusive.

In a marriage covenant, cleaving does not allow the "freedom to leave" when the relationship is no longer satisfying. If the "freedom to leave" is retained as a real option, it will hinder the total effort to develop a marital relationship characterized by covenant faithfulness. As marriage counselor Ed Wheat observes, "Keeping divorce as an escape clause indicates a flaw in your commitment to each other, even as a tiny crack that can be fatally widened by the many forces working to destroy homes and families."[4]

Accepting the Biblical standard of cleaving means asking ourselves when contemplating marriage: Am I prepared to make a lifetime commitment to my prospective spouse, for better or for worse, till death do us part? Once married, cleaving means to ask ourselves: Will this action, word, decision, or attitude draw us closer together or farther apart? Will it build up or tear down our relationship? For a Christian committed to living by the principles of God's word, any course of action which weakens the cleaving must be regarded as contrary to God's design for a marriage covenant.

Many today scorn the idea of developing a close dependent relationship between husband and wife. They claim that it restricts their freedom and stifles their personal growth. What they advocate can be characterized as a "married singles" lifestyle where both partners continue to follow their independent lives while sharing the same roof and bed. It is not surprising that such marriages often fail, since there is no willingness to leave selfish considerations in order to cleave to each other "for better or for worse, for richer or for poorer, in sickness and in health."

Summing up, we can state the second principle derived from the divine institution of marriage recorded in Genesis 2:24 as follows: *To maintain a thrilling "one flesh" marriage covenant we must be willing to cleave to our marital partners, avoiding any thought, word, or action that could weaken our loyalty and commitment to them.*

Becoming One Flesh. The third essential ingredient of a marriage covenant is that "they become *one flesh*" (Gen 2:24). Note the progression: leaving, cleaving, becoming one flesh. As husband and wife leave lesser relationships and learn to cleave to one another, they become a new entity, "one flesh."

The phrase "one flesh" needs some explanation because it is frequently misunderstood to refer primarily to the sexual union. The phrase is closely parallel to our English compound word *everybody*. When we speak of every*body* we do not think of *bodies* only. Rather, we mean every *person*. Or when God speaks of destroying *all flesh* (Gen 6:17; 7:21), obviously He does not mean all the flesh without the bones, but every *person*. Similarly, to become "one flesh" (Gen 2:24) means *to become one functioning unit*. H. C. Leupold explains that becoming one flesh "involves the complete identification of one personality with the other in a community of interests and pursuits, a union consummated in intercourse."[5]

No theologian or scientist has ever yet explained how two people are able to so interpenetrate one another's lives that they become "one flesh," that is, one functioning unit. Yet we know that it happens! Couples who have been married for many years start to think, act, and feel as one; they become one in mind, heart and spirit. This is why divorce is so devastating. It leaves not two persons, but two fractions of one.

The phrase "one flesh" does also refer to the physical or sexual aspect of marriage. Paul explicitly uses the phrase in this way when speaking of sexual intercourse between a man and a harlot (1 Cor 6:16). Sexual intercourse per se, however, does not automatically assure that a man and a woman become *one* in a mystical, emotional, and spiritual unity. Genital intercourse without spiritual communion often leaves people divided, alienated, and bitter toward each other. Thus, sexual intercourse itself does not bring about *real* oneness.

To achieve the Biblical "one flesh" union, sexual intercourse in marriage must be the natural fruit of love, the crowning act of marital union. If sex is not the expression of genuine love, respect, and commitment, then it offers only a physical contact while keeping the partners mentally and spiritually apart. Sexual desire must become the desire for the total union and oneness of body, soul, and spirit between marital partners.

Gradual Process. A man and a woman who come together in marriage do not automatically become "one flesh" when they exchange their marriage vows. Their personalities are still free, independent and assertive of their respective wills. But as they live together as husband and wife, they realize that they must safeguard their individuality while striving to become one. They must not allow their differences to divide them but must learn to accept their differences, viewing them not as antagonistic but as complementary. They can still be themselves and yet come into unity. The husband learns to accept his wife as she is because he needs to be accepted as he is. Their differences contribute to achieving their oneness because they are accepted as being complementary and not contradictory.

The becoming of "one flesh" is beautifully exemplified in the children of a married couple. In their children, husband and wife are indissolubly united into one person. Our three children, Loretta, Daniel and Gianluca, possess both my features and those of my wife. There is no way I could retrieve my features from any of my children nor could my wife retrieve hers. They are my flesh and my wife's. Something marvelous and permanent happened when they were born: they became the sum total of what we both are. What happens biologically in children occurs psychologically in a husband/wife relationship as the two gradually become "one flesh," a new functioning unity. This is why extra-marital sexual relationships are not only immoral but also destructive to the one-flesh relationship.

Continuity. Becoming "one flesh" also implies continuity. We cannot become one flesh with a succession of husbands and wives. This is why the modern practice of serial monogamy must be rejected as immoral: it defeats the Biblical purpose of marriage which is to develop a permanent "one flesh" relationship. The "one flesh" principle excludes polygamy and extra-marital relationships of all kinds, because no man can become "one flesh" with more than one woman. The Old Testament persons who violated the "one flesh" principle by taking more than one wife paid the price for their transgressions. Problems of all kinds developed in their families as their wives became jealous or felt exploited, degraded, or hated.

Summing up, the third principle we derive from the divine institution of marriage recorded in Genesis 2:24 is as follows: *To become a "one flesh" functioning unit, husband and wife must learn to accept their differences as complementing their oneness and must reserve their sexual expressions exclusively for each other.*

PART III: MARRIAGE: A SACRED COVENANT

The preceding study of the divine institution of marriage has shown that God intended marriage to be a sacred and permanent covenant. To appreciate more fully the Biblical view of marriage as a sacred and permanent covenant, we shall now consider briefly the teachings of the prophets, of Jesus and of Paul.

The Covenant Concept. The concept of the covenant stands out in Scripture among all the signs and symbols used by God to reveal His saving grace. In His mercy, God chose to enter into a solemn covenant of love, not only with individuals such as Abraham, but also with the whole household of Israel. They did not deserve His love which He freely manifested toward them. God's covenant of love, though not always reciprocated, is everlasting, extending from generation to generation: "The Lord your God is God; He is the faithful God, keeping His covenant of love to a thousand generations of those who love Him and keep His commands" (Deut 7:7-9 NIV).

To help His people understand and accept the unrelenting nature of His covenant of love, in the Old Testament God often used the metaphor of the husband/wife relationship. The obvious reason is that the marriage covenant, characterized by love, compassion, and faithfulness, fittingly exemplifies God's covenant relationship with His people. A few examples will serve to illustrate this point.

Hosea's Marriage. In the final days of the kingdoms of Israel and Judah, when they were threatened with extinction by the expansionist policies of the neighboring nations, God appealed to His wayward people through a succession of prophets. Among these was Hosea, who was told by God to marry a prostitute, Gomer, and raise a family by her. Through this experience, Hosea

was to act out God's unrelenting covenant of love to His people.
When Gomer went after her lovers, Hosea was sent to take her back
and love her again.

Through Hosea's marital experiences, God revealed Himself to
Israel as a compassionate, forgiving husband: "In that day, says the
Lord, you will call me, 'my husband,' . . . And I will betroth you to
come to me in righteousness and in justice, in steadfast love, and in
mercy. I will betroth you to me in faithfulness; and you shall know
the Lord" (Hos 2:16, 19-20). By revealing Himself as a faithful,
compassionate and unrelenting husband, God sets a pattern for the
husband/wife relationship. What God does on a larger scale as
Israel's husband, a human husband is called to do on a smaller scale
in his relationship with his wife.

Later Prophets. The imagery of the marriage covenant is used
by later prophets to remind the people of their covenant relationship
with God. For example, Jeremiah reminded the people that God
had entered into a covenant with them and had become their
husband: "my covenant . . . they broke, though I was their husband"
(Jer 31:32). Even though they had broken the covenant, God
remained a faithful husband who would make a new covenant with
His people, working to transform their hearts (Jer 33:33). The
implication is clear. Marriage is a sacred covenant in which the
husband and wife must be faithful to their commitment as God is
faithful to his promise.

Jeremiah's message was ignored. Eventually Judah was cap-
tured by the Babylonians and all her leading citizens were taken
into exile. There in exile, Ezekiel graphically portrays God's
unfailing love as that of a husband wooing and winning back an
unfaithful wife: "When I looked upon you, behold, you were at the
age for love; and I spread my skirt over you, and covered your
nakedness; yea, I plighted my troth to you and entered into a
covenant with you, says the Lord God, and you became mine. . . .
But you trusted in your beauty, and played the harlot . . . Wherefore
. . . I will judge you as women who break wedlock . . . I will deal
with you as you have done, who have despised the oath in breaking
the covenant, yet I will remember my covenant with you in the days
of your youth, and I will establish with you an everlasting covenant" (Ez 16:8, 15, 38, 59).

In a similar vein Isaiah describes the final restoration of Israel in terms of a loving husband forgiving and restoring his unfaithful wife: "Your Maker is your husband.... For the Lord has called you like a wife forsaken and grieved in spirit, like a wife of youth when she is cast off, says your God. For a brief moment I forsook you, but with great compassion I will gather you. . . With everlasting love I will have compassion on you, says the Lord, your Redeemer" (Is 54:5-8).

The above examples suffice to show how the Old Testament prophets often describe God's covenant relationship with His people in terms of an ever-loving, faithful husband who never tires of wooing back an unfaithful wife. This example of God as a faithful and loving husband reveals what God intends marriage to be: a sacred covenant where love and faithfulness prevail.

Malachi's Teaching. Malachi, one of the last Old Testament prophets, fittingly sums up the Old Testament view regarding the sacred and inviolable nature of the marriage covenant. In his time, the Jews were languishing in a ruined Jerusalem and lamenting that God no longer accepted their offerings. Malachi responded by pointing out that the cause of their suffering was to be found in their unfaithfulness to God manifested especially through their unfaithfulness to their wives: "You cover the Lord's altar with tears, with weeping and groaning because He no longer regards the offering or accepts it with favor at your hand. You ask, 'Why does he not?' Because the Lord was witness to the covenant between you and the wife of your youth, to whom you have been faithless, though she is your companion and your wife by covenant" (Mal 2:13-14).

Here Scripture tells us explicitly that marriage is a covenant to which God is a witness.[6] Since God does not break covenants (Lev. 26:40-45), the marriage covenant is all the more binding. This means that what we do to our marital partner we do also to the Lord. Christian commitment and marital commitment are two sides of the same covenant. For this reason, Malachi admonishes the people, saying: "So take heed to yourselves, and let none be faithless to the wife of his youth. 'For I hate divorce, says the Lord God of Israel, and covering one's garment with violence, says the Lord of hosts'" (Mal 2:15-16).

Note that God hates *divorce*, not the *divorced*. As Christians we should reflect Christ's attitude of loving concern toward those who have suffered marital disaster (John 4:6-26) while at the same time upholding the Biblical imperative of the sacred and inviolable nature of the marriage covenant.

Malachi admonishes the people that in the best interest of their families and communities they should not violate their marriage covenant by divorcing their wives. The reason is that divorce violates not only God's original plan for marriage but also the marriage covenant to which the Lord is a witness. Divorce betrays life's most intimate companion and as such is a grievous sin which God hates.

Christ's Teaching. Malachi's teaching on the sacred nature of the marriage covenant was reiterated and expanded four centuries later by Christ Himself. In response to the Pharisees' question about the concession of Moses regarding divorce, Christ pointed back to the institution of marriage, saying: "For your hardness of heart he [Moses] wrote you this commandment. But from the beginning of creation 'God made them male and female.' 'For this reason a man shall leave his father and mother and be joined to his wife, and the two shall become one flesh.' So they are no longer two but one flesh. What therefore God has joined together, let no man put asunder" (Mark 10:5-9).

In this memorable statement Christ appeals to the divine institution of marriage (Gen 2:24) to point out that marriage is the strongest human bond that transforms two people into "one flesh." Moreover, Jesus affirms that God Himself is the one who actually joins a couple in marriage. This means that when Christian couples exchange their marital vows in the presence of witnesses, they are in actual fact uttering their vows of mutual commitment to God Himself. At the deepest level, marriage is a covenant between a couple and God, because God is not only the witness but also the author of the marriage covenant.

A man and a woman marry by their own choice; but when they do, God joins them together into one permanent union. Because marriage is God's indissoluble union of the couple, no human court or individual has the right to put it asunder. It is evident that for Jesus marriage is not a mere civil contract, but a divinely ordained union which God alone has power to establish and terminate. The full force of this truth was explained by Christ privately to His disciples in these terms: "Whoever divorces his wife and marries another, commits adultery against her; and if she divorces her husband and marries another, she commits adultery" (Mark 10:11-12).

By this statement, Jesus declares unambiguously that the marriage covenant must not be violated by divorce and remarriage because it is a sacred inviolable bond. To do otherwise is to "commit adultery," a sin clearly condemned by God's moral law (Ex 20:14; Deut. 5:18). With a few simple words Jesus refutes the view that divorce is a viable option for a married couple. The covenant structure of marriage makes divorce an act of covenant breaking, a failure to keep a moral obligation.

Paul's Teaching. Following the teaching of Jesus, Paul affirms in different words that marriage is a lifelong and indissoluble covenant. In Romans 7:1-3, Paul sets forth the principle that death ends the dominion of the law and then illustrates the principle through the marriage relationship. The point of the illustration is that death and death alone releases a person from the bond of marriage: "A married woman is bound by law to her husband as long as he lives; but if her husband dies she is discharged from the law concerning the husband. Accordingly, she will be called an adulteress if she lives with another man while her husband is alive. But if her husband dies she is free from the law, and if she marries another man she is not an adulteress" (Rom 7:2-3).

Paul's illustration sheds light on his view of marriage as a lifelong covenant which can be terminated only by death. The same teaching is presented by Paul again in 1 Corinthians 7:39 where he declares: "A wife is bound to her husband as long as he lives."

The covenantal nature of the marriage relationship is expressed by Paul again in Ephesians 5:31-32 where he uses the marriage union to illustrate the covenant relationship between Christ and His bride, the church: "'For this reason a man shall leave his father and mother and be joined to his wife, and the two shall become one.' This is a great mystery, and I take it to mean Christ and the church."

Just as the prophets in the Old Testament used the marriage covenant to portray the relationship between God and Israel, so

Paul in the New Testament uses the marriage union to represent Christ's covenant of sacrificial love and oneness with the church. Just as marriage unites two people when they commit their lives to each other, so the Gospel joins the believer to Christ as he trusts Him for his salvation. Since the marriage covenant represents the permanent relationship between Christ and His church, it must be permanent; otherwise it would be an inaccurate representation of the indissoluble relationship between Christ and His church.

The use of marriage in the Old and New Testaments to reveal God's covenant relationship with His people serves also to demonstrate what marriage today should be like. We may call this "reciprocal illumination." By revealing through human marriage His covenant of salvation, God has simultaneously revealed to us the unique meaning of marriage as a sacred and permanent covenant.

CONCLUSION

Our study of the divine institution of marriage and of the teachings of the prophets, Jesus and Paul, regarding marriage, has shown us how Scripture consistently upholds marriage as a sacred and permanent covenant, witnessed and protected by God. We have found that as a sacred covenant, marriage was effectively used in the Old Testament to portray God's relationship with Israel and in the New Testament to represent Christ's relationship with His church. If God used marriage as a metaphor to represent His commitment to His people, He must surely have thought of it as a sacred, permanent covenant.

The recovery of the Biblical view of marriage as a sacred and permanent covenant, witnessed and guaranteed by God Himself, is indispensable in counteracting the secularization of marriage. This trend has influenced many Christians to view marriage as a temporary social contract governed by civil laws, rather than as a permanent covenant, witnessed and guaranteed by God Himself. To counteract this trend, it is essential for Christians to recover and accept the Biblical view of marriage as a sacred covenant. The conviction that it is God Who has united our lives in holy matrimony and Who will help us to stay together will motivate us to persevere in preserving the unity of the marriage covenant.

NOTES TO CHAPTER I

1. Emphasis supplied. See also Proverbs 2:17; Ezekiel 16:8.

2. Paul E. Palmer, "Christian Marriage: Contract or Covenant?" *Theological Studies,* vol. 33, no. 4 (December 1972): 639.

3. Emphasis supplied.

4. Ed Wheat, *Love Life for Every Married Couple* (Grand Rapids, 1980), p. 38.

5. H. C. Leupold, *Exposition of Genesis,* 2 vols. (Grand Rapids, 1942), vol. 1, p. 137.

6. See also Proverbs 2:17.

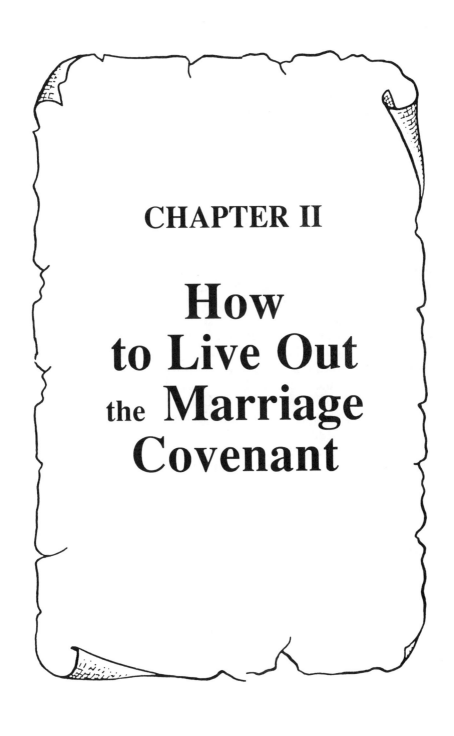

CHAPTER II

How
to Live Out
the Marriage
Covenant

HOW TO LIVE OUT
THE MARRIAGE COVENANT

The concept of the marriage covenant is central to the Biblical view of the relationship between God and His people and between marital partners. From Genesis to Revelation, the Bible intertwines God's marriage covenant with His people and our marriage covenant with our spouses.

Human marriages are meant to be like God's marriage covenant with His people in purpose and permanence. In Jesus Christ, God says to us, "I take you." We are free to consent to become covenant partners by responding, "We take You." In a sense our salvation is nuptial. It begins when we say "I do" to Christ's marriage proposal. By accepting Christ's marriage proposal, we become engaged or betrothed to Him in this present life. "I betrothed you to Christ," Paul says, "to present you as a pure bride to her one husband" (2 Cor 11:2). At the end of history, we will experience the complete union with Christ seen in Scripture as the consummation of marriage celebrated with the "marriage supper of the lamb" (Rev 19:9).

The marriage covenant provides us with a clue to understanding the heart of God. It helps us understand what God has done, is doing, and will do for us. It tells us that God's covenant love is a love "that will not let us go." By helping us understand the purpose and permanence of God's relationship with us, the metaphor of the marriage covenant helps us also to understand the purpose and permanence of our marital relationships. The fact that human marriages have a divine pattern provides us with a holy help in understanding how to live out our marriage covenant.

Objective of Chapter. This chapter explores the practical implications of the Biblical view of marriage as a sacred and permanent covenant witnessed and guaranteed by God. In the first part of the chapter, we shall see how the concept of marriage as a sacred covenant is not just an abstract Biblical truth or principle but the only real and solid foundation upon which a permanent and happy marriage can be built. In the second part, we shall examine the kind of commitment that characterizes a marriage covenant: namely, a *total*, *exclusive*, *continuing* and *growing* commitment. In the third part we shall take a closer look at the obligations of the marriage covenant in the light of the Ten Commandments. We shall see that the principles of the Ten Commandments which express our covenant commitment to God can also serve to manifest our covenant commitment to our spouses. The overall objective of the chapter is to provide practical suggestions on how to live out the marriage covenant.

PART ONE:
THE IMPORTANCE OF A MARRIAGE COVENANT

The Foundation of Marriage. Marriage is like a house. If it is to last, it needs a solid foundation. The bedrock upon which the foundation of marriage must rest is an unconditional, mutual covenant that allows no external or internal circumstances to "put asunder" the marital union that God Himself has established. This covenantal commitment and conviction that God has united our lives in holy matrimony gives us reason to believe that He will enable us to stay together, even when our marriages appear to be "for worse." It is this covenant foundation that will motivate us to seek God's help in trying again to make successes of our marriages, even when our needs are unfulfilled and our relationships seem to be sterile or sour.

This covenantal foundation is often lacking in Christian marriages today. "What is missing in most marriages today," perceptively observes Paul Stevens, "is what the Bible identifies as the heart of marriage: a covenant. Everything is superstructure. Understanding expectations, developing good communication (especially sexual), gaining skills in conflict resolution, discovering appropriate roles or creating new ones, making our marriages fun and free, becoming spiritual friends and sharing a ministry–these are the walls, the roof, the wiring, the plumbing and the heating. They are essential to the whole. But if there is no foundation, they will collapse with the whole building."[1]

The foundation ensuring the stability and permanence of marriage is the mutual commitment of a couple to cleave to one another "for better, for worse." The Biblical concept of a lifelong, permanent bond between husband and wife is quickly becoming an outdated, foreign concept. More and more couples enter the marriage relationship believing that it is terminable. They interpret the promise "Till death do us part" as meaning "Till disagreement or other interests do us part."

To resist this societal trend which is undermining the foundation of marriage, we must recover and reaffirm the Biblical view of marriage as a sacred and permanent covenant. Declaring our permanent commitment to each other not only on the wedding day, but periodically throughout our lives (especially on the wedding anniversary and each other's birthday) will help us to preserve our marriage covenant.

A covenant marriage is not a relational prison locking a man and a woman into a permanent relationship. It is rather, to quote Paul Stevens again, "an elastic link between two hearts. When they move apart, a tug reminds them they belong. Or, a covenant is a net beneath two trapeze artists. It is a risky business, this high-wire stunt, and they will undoubtedly fall sometime. But the safety net beneath them holds."[2]

A Covenant of Faith. A marriage covenant is a covenant of faith because no Christian spouse knows for sure how the marriages is going to work out. What spouses *can* know for sure is whether or not they have solemnly committed themselves before God to a lifelong covenantal partnership in which they shall belong together as long as they both shall live. This covenant can only be made by those who share a common faith in God and in His ability to work out His purpose in their marriage. Sharing this common faith provides the courage to believe that God will help us to make our marriages work, even when they seem hopelessly doomed.

A Christian couple contemplating marriage needs to determine whether or not they are prepared fully and freely to enter into a lifelong marriage covenant. Discerning covenantal compatibility is more important even than determining personal compatibility. When a mutual and strong covenant commitment exists, the possibility of resolving conflicts within marriage also exists. A covenantal marriage is not completely without conflicts. Total commitment to your mate does not eliminate the possibility of tensions, tears, disagreements, impatience, and conflicts. That is the bad news. But the good news is that by the grace of God, no marital conflict is beyond solution. A couple fully committed to God and to one another can rest in the assurance that God will provide the enabling power of His Spirit to resolve conflicts and restore harmony.

There are many people legally married today who have never made a covenantal commitment to their spouses. At the time of their legal marriage, some of them were not emotionally mature enough to solemnly make before God that lifelong covenant commitment. Others may have chosen to retain the idea of divorce in their minds as a last-ditch option. Instead of promising faithfulness to each other "till death do us part," they pledge to remain together "as long as we both shall love."

Whatever the original reason may have been for failing to enter into a marriage covenant, now is the time to make such a covenant, even if you are experiencing a good marriage. A refusal to make a marriage covenant indicates a flaw in your commitment to your spouse. That flaw is like a tiny crack that can be fatally widened by sinister forces working to destroy marriage. To avoid such a risk, we must recover and reaffirm the Biblical understanding of marriage as a lifelong sacred covenant, witnessed and guaranteed by God Himself.

A Covenant Under Attack. Four major social forces today are conspiring to undermine the Biblical view of marriage as a sacred covenant, reducing it instead to a temporary social contract governed by civil laws and terminated when it no longer meets the expectations of one or both spouses.

Secularism has caused the loss of the sense of the sacred in various realms of life, including marriage. For example, the Lord's Day is no longer viewed by many Christians as a "holy day" but rather as a "holiday," a day to seek for personal pleasure and profit, rather than for the presence and peace of God. Life is no longer sacred for many people, as over 1,500,000 induced abortions are performed every year in the United States alone, besides the countless number of persons killed everywhere by senseless crimes, drugs and violence. Similarly, marriage is no longer regarded by many as a lifelong, sacred covenant witnessed and guaranteed by God Himself, but rather as a temporary social contract, governed solely by civil laws.

Humanism teaches that marriage is a human and not a divine institution. Its function is to meet a person's needs: social, sexual, emotional, and financial. Accordingly, when such needs are no longer met, the marriage contract can be legitimately terminated.

Selfism tells us that we have the right to reach self-fulfillment, self-sufficiency, and self-development. If marriage becomes a stumbling block to self-actualization, it must be dissolved. Fritz Perls expresses it in this way: "I do my thing, and you do your thing. I am not in this world to live up to your expectations, and you are not in this world to live up to mine. And if by some chance we meet, it's beautiful."[3]

Relativism in moral issues facilitates the breaking up of marital relationships and the establishing of new ones. A child of humanism and relativism is the "no fault" divorce law which makes the dissolution of marriage so easy that some lawyers advertise their divorce services for less than $100.00: "All legal fees and services included in one low price." What a sad commentary on the cheapness of marriage today! What God has united many will put asunder for less than the price of a good suit.

To resist the various social forces which are conspiring to break apart the marriage covenant, reducing it to a temporary relationship of convenience, Christians must recover and reaffirm the Biblical understanding of marriage as a lifelong, sacred covenant, witnessed and guaranteed by God Himself. To help us understand more fully how to live out the marriage covenant, we shall examine first the nature of its commitment and then the ten commandments of the marriage covenant.

PART II:
THE COMMITMENT OF A MARRIAGE COVENANT

A marriage covenant is characterized by *total, exclusive, continuing* and *growing commitment.* We shall take a brief look at each of these four basic characteristics.

Total Commitment. To accept marriage as a sacred covenant means first of all to be willing to make a *total commitment* of ourselves to our marriage partners. This is why Paul in Ephesians compares marriage to the relationship of Christ with His church (Eph 5:25-26). Christ's commitment to us, the church, is so total that He loved us while we were yet unfaithful (Rom 5:8) and gave up His life that we may live (Eph 5:25).

Christ's total commitment to us, to be with us in life and death, shows us the kind of total commitment upon which Christian marriage is to be founded. It is a commitment based on unrelenting love. It is a love which is "patient and kind; . . . not jealous or boastful; . . . not arrogant or rude; . . . it does not rejoice at wrong, but rejoices in the right. [It is a love that] bears all things, believes all things, hopes all things, endures all things" (1 Cor 13: 4-7). It is this loving commitment which makes Christian marriage a sacred and permanent covenant. A Christian married couple is called to enter intimately into the kind of total commitment existing between Christ and His church. Such a commitment makes possible the blending of two lives into an existential union of marital interrelationship where they grow together in loving unity and fidelity.

When Christian couples enter into a marriage covenant, they are committing themselves to maintaining their marital union, no matter what. This total commitment is set forth in the marriage vows: "for better, for worse, for richer, for poorer, in sickness and in health."

By taking the marriage vows, Christian mates promise to each other what is well expressed by Elizabeth Achtemeier: "I will be with you, no matter what happens to us and between us. If you should become blind tomorrow, I will be there. If you achieve no success and attain no status in our society, I will be there. When we argue and are angry, as we inevitably will, I will work to bring us together. When we seem totally at odds and neither of us is having needs fulfilled, I will persist in trying to understand and in trying to restore our relationship. When our marriage seems utterly sterile and going nowhere at all, I will believe that it can work and I will want it to work and I will do my part to make it work. And when all is wonderful and we are happy, I will rejoice over our life together, and continue to strive to keep our relationship growing and strong."[4]

Such a total commitment is possible only by divine grace. It is God who gives us power to hold fast to our commitment. This is the unseen factor often ignored in marriage manuals. What is true for salvation is also true for a committed marriage: there is both a divine initiative and a human response. As Paul puts it, "work out your own salvation with fear and trembling; for God is at work in you, both to will and to work for his good pleasure" (Phil 2:12-13). We must work to achieve total and permanent commitment in our marriages and yet recognize that it is God who is at work in and through us to make this goal possible.

A most marvellous thing about a totally committed marriage is the fact that it is solely a relationship of grace, a relationship in which I do not have to earn my wife's love constantly because she gives it to me as a gift. Love is seldom deserved because most of the time we are not lovable. Yet it is given to me, and this gives me acceptance, security, and freedom to act and to plumb all my creativity. This manifestation of unconditional love challenges us to respond by being more loving and lovable.

Exclusive Commitment. To accept marriage as a sacred covenant means also to be willing to make an *exclusive commit-ment* of ourselves to our marital partners. It means, as the marriage vows put it, "to forsake all others" and "to keep thee only unto her [or him], so long as ye both shall live." This understanding of the marriage covenant is under severe attack in our sexually permissive society where immoral connotations of illicit sexual acts have been eliminated through the introduction of new "softer" terms. Forni-cation is now referred to as "premarital sex," with the emphasis on the "pre" rather than on the "marital." Adultery is now called "extramarital sex," implying an additional experience, like an extraprofessional activity.

A landmark survey of 100,000 women conducted by *Redbook Magazine* and supervised by sociologist Robert Bell of Temple University, indicates that about one third of all married women and almost half (47%) of wage-earning wives reported "having sexual relations with men other than their husbands."[5] Considering that men tend to be more promiscuous than women, we can safely assume that the percentage of married men having extramarital relations is even higher.

The prevailing unfaithfulness to marriage vows has led some Christians, including some pastors, to adopt a "live and let live" attitude toward divorce and remarriage. Some Christians assume that God will accept them despite their infidelity to their wives or husbands in divorcing and marrying someone else. To such persons, the church must declare that God is not mocked. Their unfaithfulness to their marriage vows stands under the judgment of the Lord who tells us that the ultimate destiny of the faithless will be eternal destruction: "But as for the cowardly, the *faithless*, the polluted, as for murderers, *fornicators*, sorcerers, idolaters, and all liars, their lot shall be in the lake that burns with fire and brimstone, which is the second death" (Rev 21:8).[6]

In view of the prevailing violation of marital vows, as Christians we face today an unprecedented challenge to maintain by God's grace our exclusive commitment to our marriage partners. Exclusive commitment extends beyond the sexual sphere and includes forming relationships with friends or relatives closer than those with our spouses. By taking third parties into the confidences of our marital life, we undermine the exclusiveness of our marital commitments. Ellen White warns that "When a woman relates her family troubles or complains of her husband to another man, she violates her marriage vows; she dishonors her husband and breaks down the wall erected to preserve the sanctity of the marriage relation; she throws wide open the door and invites Satan to enter with his insidious temptations. This is just as Satan would have it."[7]

Continuing Commitment. To accept marriage as a sacred covenant also means to be willing to make a *continuing commit-*

ment to one's marital partner. Time changes things, including our looks and our feelings. When my fiancée accepted my marriage proposal, I was rather thin with nice wavy hair. Thirty years later I find myself considerably heavier with a shining top. I am thankful to God that the change in my looks has not caused my wife to change her commitment to me. Marital commitment must continue through the changing seasons of our lives. With each change in our lives, our marital commitments must be renewed.

To speak today of a continuing commitment may seem naive when the number of divorces or annulments each year in America is equivalent to about one half of the new marriages.[8] Yet, to approach marriage with an openness to divorce is to deny the Biblical meaning of the one-flesh, permanent covenantal relationship. In His response to the question raised over divorce, Jesus was unequivocal in affirming that marriage is a continuing, lasting commitment: "What therefore God has joined together, let not man put asunder" (Matt 19:6; Mark 10:9).

A young couple contemplating marriage needs to consider whether or not both are prepared to make a continuing commitment to one another. But a continuing commitment to our marriage partners is not accomplished once and for all. It must be reaffirmed each day, when we are healthy or sick, wealthy or poor, happy or sad, successful or failing. In all the changing moods of life, we must determine by God's grace to reaffirm our marriage commitments until death doth us part.

Some time ago, a woman told me that she had filed for divorce because her feelings toward her husband had changed. She did not feel in love with him anymore. The counsel of Ellen White to such people is to change their dispositions, not their marriage partners: "If your dispositions are not congenial, would it not be for the glory of God for you to change these dispositions?"[9] The good news of the Gospel is that our feelings and dispositions can be changed through Christ's enabling power (Phil 4:13). Divine grace makes a continuing commitment to marriage not a possibility, but a reality.

Our continuing commitment to our marital partners must rest on our covenantal commitments and not on feelings. David Phypers points out that "when Paul commanded husbands to love their wives as Christ loved the church, he understood that love was a decision and not a feeling. No feeling of romantic love could have taken Jesus to the cross, yet he went because he loved us. In the same way we are to love each other whether we like it or not, and in so doing, to fulfill our consent to each other, to be husbands and wives together as long as we both shall live."[10]

Growing Commitment. To accept marriage as a sacred covenant means also to experience a *growing commitment* which deepens and matures through life's experiences. The Christian life is a call to grow "to the measure of the stature of the fullness of Christ" (Eph 4:13), until we love with the fulness of His love. The same call applies to our marriage relationships. There must be a maturing and deepening of our commitment to each other. When marriage commitment stops growing, it begins to wither away.

Growth in commitment to marriage is not achieved overnight. It is a continuous daily process lasting through the whole course of our married lives. It involves, among other things, following the model of Christ's love for His church by being willing to sacrifice selfish wants for the good of the other, being willing to love even when love is not reciprocated. It involves also accepting unsuspected flaws in the character of the partners and working together to resolve misunderstandings, tensions, or hostilities.

Growth in our marital commitment often takes place through deaths and resurrections. There are times in our marital relationship when communication becomes very difficult, if not impossible. Hurt, hostility, and resentment seem to prevail. Yet, as we learn by God's grace to put to death and to bury all such ill-feeling, out of that dying, new life comes in our relationship. "If a marriage is growing," writes Thomas N. Hart, "it is growing through deaths and resurrections. If it is not growing, it might be because there is a refusal to die the deaths that have to be died and seek in them the direction in which new life is breaking. If Jesus for fear, had refused to die, he would not know the kind of life he now knows as risen Lord, nor would we have the gift of his Spirit."[11]

The sad reality is that many marriages do not grow in maturity and love. Rather than expending energy to keep their relationships improving, some marriage partners settle down into a dull routine. To find a way out of such dullness, some partners seek for excitement and growth in extramarital relationships. In so doing, however, they only add misery to their lives by violating their marriage covenant and by putting asunder the marital unity formed by God.

The solution to a dull marriage is to be found not by seeking excitement outside marriage, but by working together to enrich the relationship. This involves improving our communication skills by learning to express inner feelings, by listening to the thoughts, desires and wishes of our partner, by leaving the cares and concerns of our work behind when we go home, and by watching for opportunities to manifest tenderness and affection.

Conclusion. To live out marriage as a sacred covenant means to be willing to make a *total, exclusive, continuing* and *growing* commitment to our marriage partner. Such a committed Christian marriage is not easy or trouble free. Commitment to a marriage covenant, like our commitment to the Lord, may result in some forms of cruficixion. But there is no other way to enter into the joys of Christian marriage. When we commit ourselves to honor by God's grace our marriage covenant of mutual faithfulness until death, then we will experience how God is able mysteriously to unite two lives into "one flesh."

PART III:
THE TEN COMMANDMENTS OF
A MARRIAGE COVENANT

Both the covenant between God and His people and the covenant between marital partners entail privileges and obligations. The privileges of the old covenant included God's choice of the Israelites as His special people, His promise to bless them, to give them the land of Canaan, to send them a Redeemer, to reveal to them His will and to make them His chosen instruments for the conversion of the world. The obligations consisted of the commitment of the people to obey the principles of conduct God gave to them in the form of commandments (Ex 24:3). God's choice of the Hebrew slaves as His own people was unconditional: "The Lord your God has chosen you to be a people for his own possession, out of all the people that are on the face of the earth. It was not because you were more in number than any other people that the Lord set his love upon you and chose you, for you were the fewest of all peoples; but it was because the Lord loves you . . ." (Deut 7:6-8).

While God's covenantal commitment to Israel was unconditional, the blessings of the covenant were conditional. If the people obeyed God's commandments, then "the Lord your God will keep with you the covenant . . . he will love you, bless you, and multiply you . . ." (Deut 7:12-13). God spelled out the obligations of the covenant in terms of commandments. These included the Ten Commandments as well as other regulations governing their social and religious life.

A Double Concept of the Law. The terms "law" and "commandments" are almost dirty words today. They are generally associated with the Old Covenant in which the Israelites allegedly had to earn their salvation through strict obedience. Many Christians believe that in the New Covenant they do not need to be concerned about obeying the law because they are "justified by faith apart from works of law" (Rom 3:28). Such reasoning creates a false antithesis by assuming that salvation was offered on the basis of human obedience in the Old Covenant and is now offered on the basis of divine grace in the New Covenant. Why would God offer salvation in two mutually exclusive ways? The truth of the matter is that salvation has always been a divine gift and never a human achievement.

Those who appeal to Paul to negate the role of the law in the New Covenant fail to realize that Paul does not attack the validity and value of the law as a moral guide to Christian conduct. On the contrary, Paul emphatically affirms that Christ specifically came "in order that the just requirements of the law might be fulfilled in us" (Rom 8:4). What Paul criticizes is the soteriological understanding of the law, that is, the law viewed as a method of salvation.

When Paul speaks of the law in the context of the *method of salvation* (justification—right standing before God), he clearly affirms that law-keeping is of no avail (Rom 3:20). On the other hand, when Paul speaks of the law in the context of the *standard of Christian conduct* (sanctification—right living before God), then he maintains the value and validity of God's law (Rom 7:12; 13:8-10; 1 Cor 7:9).

Law as a Loving Response. Many Christians fail to realize that the Old Covenant made at Sinai contained not only *principles of conduct* (commandments to be obeyed—Ex 20-23), but also *provisions of grace and forgiveness* (instructions on how to receive atonement for sin through the typological services of the tabernacle—Ex 25:40). God's biddings are accompanied by His enablings.

The commandments of the covenant were given not to restrict the Israelites' delight and joy in belonging to God, but to enable them to experience the blessings of the covenant. The Psalmist declares as "blessed" or "happy" the man whose "delight is in the law of the Lord, and on his law he meditates day and night" (Ps 1:1-2). The function of the commandments was not to enable the Israelites to become God's covenant people, but to respond to God's unconditional choice of them as His covenant people. The law is designed to spell out the lifestyle of those who already belong to God.

The relationship between covenant and commandments appears to be a *vicious circle*: God chooses us to be His people but in order really to belong to Him we must obey His commandments. In reality, however, as Gordon Wenham points out, what looks like a vicious circle is a *gracious circle*, because "law both presupposes and is a means of grace."[12] It presupposes God's unconditional election and it provides a means for the reception of the blessings of the covenant.

Obedience to God's commandments is our love response to God's unconditional choosing of us. It is because God showed "his love for us . . . while we were yet sinners" (Rom 5:8) that He commands us to love Him by living according to the principles of conduct He has graciously revealed to us (John 14:15).

Our love response to God's covenantal commitment to us is shown through worship and law. Through worship we bless God for His goodness to us. Through the law we love God by living in harmony with the principles He has revealed for our well being. Both worship and law find their parallel in the marriage covenant. As Paul Stevens rightly explains: "The first, worship, has its parallel in marriage in the different languages of love. The second, the law, is paralleled in marriage by its own 'laws'—without which the full blessing of the covenant cannot be appropriated. These are not the conditions of the marriage relationship but conditions of blessings within the relationship. They are lifestyle statements for persons in covenant. These marriage 'laws' are the structure of the marriage house, which is built on a covenant foundation."[13]

Sinai Covenant and Marriage Covenant. It is an enlightening exercise to compare the Sinai covenant with the marriage covenant by interpreting the Ten Commandments as ten principles of conduct for married people. Paul Stevens has produced a most perceptive comparison between the two covenants by means of the following table:

Covenant Between Israel and Yahweh	Covenant Between Wife and Husband
1. No other Gods	1. Exclusive loyalty to my spouse
2. No graven image	2. Truthfulness and faithfulness
3. Not taking the Lord's name in vain	3. Honoring my spouse in public and private
4. Remembering the sabbath day	4. Giving my spouse time and rest
5. Honoring father and mother	5. Rightly relating to parents and parents-in-law
6. No murder	6. Freedom from hatred, destructive anger and uncontrolled emotions
7. No adultery	7. Sexual faithfulness; controlled appetites
8. No stealing	8. True community of property with the gift of privacy
9. No false testimony	9. Truthful communication
10. No coveting	10. Contentment: freedom from demands[14]

This table shows that the implications of the Ten Commandments for the marriage covenant are profound. To appreciate these more fully, we shall briefly reflect on how each of the Ten Commandments apply to the marriage covenant. These reflections are an expansion and modification of Paul Stevens' exercise called "marital meditations based on the commandments."[15]

The First Commandment of the Sinai covenant summons the Israelites to worship only Yahweh who delivered them from Egyptian bondage: "You shall have no other gods before me" (Ex. 20:3). In this commandment God appeals to us to put Him first in our affections, in harmony with Christ's injunction to seek first God's kingdom and His righteousness (Matt 6:33). We can violate the spirit of the first commandment by putting our trust and confidence in such human resources as knowledge, wealth, position and people.

Applied to the marriage covenant, *the first commandment calls us to give exclusive loyalty to our spouse.* In practice, this means making our spouse the most important person in our life after God. It means not allowing such matters as professional pursuits, parents, children, friends, hobbies, and possessions to become our first love and thus take the first place in our affections which is to be reserved for our spouse. It also means not amending the commandment by making our loyalty to our spouse contingent on other factors, as when people say: "I am prepared to give priority to my spouse *as long as* it does not hinder my professional pursuits." The first commandment, then, calls us to give unconditional and exlusive loyalty to our spouse.

The Second Commandment of the Sinai covenant emphasizes God's spiritual nature (John 4:24) by prohibiting idolatry: "You shall not make for yourself a graven image . . . you shall not bow down to them or serve them" (Ex 20:4-5). The commandment does not necessarily prohibit the use of illustrative material for religious instruction. Pictorial representations were employed in the sanctuary (Ex 25:17-22), in Solomon's Temple (1 Kings 6:23-26) and in the bronze serpent (Num 21:8-9; 2 Kings 18:4). What the commandment condemns is the veneration or adoration of religious images or pictures since these are human creations and not the Divine Creator.

Applied to the marriage covenant, *the second commandment enjoins us to be truthful and faithful to our spouse.* Just as we can be unfaithful to God, we can also be unfaithful to our spouse by having false images of her/him in our mind. In practice, this may mean trying to shape our partner into our own image of an "ideal spouse" by nagging or manipulative threats or rewards. It may mean clinging to false images of love relationships with real or fantasy partners. It may also mean making an idol of social relationships outside marriage. This would include forming relationships with friends or relatives that are closer than those with one's spouse. The second commandment, then, summons us to be truthful and faithful to our spouse by not making idols of anything that can weaken our marriage covenant.

The Third Commandment builds upon the preceding two commandments by inculcating reverence for God: "You shall not take the name of the Lord your God in vain" (Ex 20:7). Those who serve only the true God and serve Him not through false images or idols but in spirit and truth will show reverence to God by avoiding any pprofane, careless or unnecessary use of His holy name.

Applied to the marriage covenant, *the third commandment summons us to respect and honor our spouses in public and private.* In practice, this means respecting our spouses by showing them deference and courtesy both in public and private. It means avoiding belittling our spouses, or cutting them off in front of the children or on social occasions. It also means not taking our spouses' presence for granted as though they were just another person. The third commandment, then, enjoins us to show respect toward our spouses by avoiding words or actions that can belittle them and thus weaken our marriage covenants.

The Fourth Commandment calls us to honor God by consecrating the Sabbath time to Him: "Remember the sabbath day, to keep it holy. Six days you shall labor, and do all your work; but the seventh day is a sabbath to the Lord your God" (Ex 20:8-10). The first three commandments are designed to remove obstacles to the true worship of God: the worship of other gods, the worship of God through false images, and the lack of reverence for God. Now that the obstacles have been removed, the fourth commandment invites us to truly worship God, not through the veneration or adoration of objects, but through the consecration of the Sabbath time to God. Time is the essence of our lives. The way we use our time is indicative of our priorities. By consecrating our Sabbath time to God we show that our covenant commitment to Him is real. We are willing to offer Him not mere lip-service, but the service of our total being.

Applied to the marriage covenant, *the fourth commandment invites us to show our love to our spouses by setting aside a regular and special time for them.* In practice, this means learning to put aside our work or personal pleasures on a regular basis, in order to listen to, to enjoy, to celebrate and to cultivate the friendship of our spouses. It means, especially, using the climate of peace and tranquillity of the Sabbath day as an opportunity to draw closer to God and to our marital partners. It means taking time, especially on the Sabbath, to walk together, to relax together, to read together, to appreciate good music together, to meditate together, to pray together, to visit together, to bless our spouses in every way they need to be blessed.

The celebration of the Sabbath, the sign of our covenant commitment to God (Ex 31:13; Ez 20:12), can strengthen the marriage covenant in two ways: theologically and practically. *Theologically,* the Sabbath being a sign of our sacred covenantal commitment to God, serves to remind us as marital partners of the sanctity of our covenant commitment to our spouses. *Practically,* the Sabbath offers time and opportunities to Christian couples to strengthen their marriage covenants by coming closer to one another. The Fourth Commandment, then, calls us to show in a concrete way our covenantal commitment to our marriage partners by setting aside a regular and special time for them.

The Fifth Commandment enjoins us to honor and respect our parents: "Honor your father and your mother" (Ex 20:12). The first four commandments tell us how to show our covenantal commitment to God while the last six commandments teach us how to love our fellow beings. Since parents stand as the representatives of God to their children, it is logical and fitting that the second table of the law begins with our duties toward our parents. The way we respect and obey our parents is indicative of our obedience and respect for God and for those placed in authority over us.

Applied to the marriage covenant, *the fifth commandment calls us to rightly relate to our parents and to our spouses' parents.* We do not evade our responsibility toward our parents as they grow old. As married persons, we assume responsibility *for* our parents rather than *to* them. In practice, this involves welcoming our respective parents to our home without allowing them to control our home. It involves working out with our spouse how to honor our respective parents in their old age or when ill. It involves seeking our parents' counsel, without allowing them to dictate their ideas. It involves honoring our spouse's parents by not making constant jokes about our in-laws. The fifth commandment, then, enjoins us to rightly relate to the parents of each spouse by respecting and supporting them without allowing them to interfere in our marital relationship and thus weaken our marriage covenant.

The Sixth Commandment orders us to respect others by not taking their lives: "You shall not kill" (Ex 20:13). Jesus magnified the meaning of this commandment to include anger and hate (Matt 5:21, 22; cf. 1 John 3:14, 15). This commandment forbids not only physical violence to the body, but also moral injury to the soul. We break it when, by our example, words, or actions, we lead others to sin, thus contributing to the destruction of their souls (Matt 10:28).

Applied to the marriage covenant, *the sixth commandment calls us to renounce hatred and destructive anger.* In practice, this commandment forbids abusing our spouses verbally or physically. It forbids provoking them to anger by criticising their appearance, speech, actions, or decisions. It forbids nourishing hostile feelings toward them and attempting through words or actions to destroy their integrity. It forbids harping on at past offenses which have been confessed and forgiven. It challenges us to offer our spouses constructive and not destructive criticism. The sixth commandment, then, calls us to renounce any form of hatred or hostility that can hurt our spousse and thus weaken our marriage covenants.

The Seventh Commandment explicitly enjoins sexual faith-fulness: "You shall not commit adultery" (Ex 20:14). Jesus magnified this commandment to include not only the physical act of adultery but also any kind of impure act, word or thought (Matt 5:27, 28). *The seventh commandment summons us to be faithful to our marriage covenant by refraining from illicit sexual acts or thoughts.*

In practice, this commandment calls us to be faithful to our spouse in our body as well as in our mind (Matt 5:27-30). Such fidelity involves among other things: not seeking sexual experiences outside marriage; not allowing the attractiveness of members of the opposite sex to become deliberate fantasies of intimacy in our minds; repulsing thoughts of sexual lust or perversion and refusing to be sexually stimulated by erotic books, films or magazines; treating our spouse as the object of our love and romance rather than as the means of sexual gratification; viewing sex as a good gift of our Creator and as an expression of mutual and total self-giving to a love relationship. The seventh commandment, then, calls us to honor our marriage covenants by being sexually faithful to our spouses both mentally and physically.

The Eighth Commandment enjoins us to respect others by not stealing what rightfully belongs to them: "You shall not steal" (Ex 20:15). This commandment forbids any act by which we dishonestly obtain the goods or services of others. We may steal from others in many subtle ways: withholding or appropriating what rightfully belongs to others, taking credit for the work done by others, robbing others of their reputation through slanderous gossip, or by depriving others of the renumeration or consideration they have a right to expect.

Applied to the marriage covenant, *the eighth commandment summons us to live in true community, without taking from our partners the right of privacy and self-determination.* In practice, this means that we must not deprive our spouses of the right to make their decisions by demanding a complete community of property. It means that one spouse must not control the finances so that the other feels dispossessed. It means that we must not hold back any security from our partners as a safety measure or bargaining chip.

It means that no sacrificial demands must be made of our partners in order to please our personal desires or whims. It means that we must not "steal" the individuality, dignity, and power of our spouses, by making decisions for them. It means that, like Zacchaeus, we must be willing to give back what we have taken from our spouses: freedom, money, dignity, power, goods. The eighth commandment, then, calls us to honor our marriage covenants by living in a true community, without "stealing" from our partners their freedom, dignity, money, power, or goods.

The Ninth Commandment enjoins us to respect others by speaking truthfully about them: "You shall not bear false witness against your neighbor" (Ex 20:16). This commandment is violated by speaking evil of others, misrepresenting their motives, misquoting their words, judging their motives, and criticising their efforts. This commandment may also be broken by remaining silent when hearing an innocent person unjustly maligned. We are guilty of bearing "false witness" whenever we tamper with truth in order to benefit ourselves or a cause that we espouse.

Applied to the marriage covenant, *the ninth commandment enjoins us to be faithful communicators with our spouses.* In practice, this involves respecting our spouses' integrity by not "hitting them below the belt," or by not exaggerating the truth about them, saying, for example, "You *never* take my feelings into consideration" or "You *always* do what you like." It involves learning to understand not only the words but also the feelings behind the words of our spouses. This enables us to interpret their thoughts and feelings more accurately. We can bear false witness against our spouses by projecting onto them what we think they say or mean by certain actions. We can bear false witness also by quoting our spouses out of context or by suppressing information that would give more accurate pictures of them. The ninth commandment, then, enjoins us to be faithful communicators with our spouses by learning to accurately understand, interpret and represent their words, actions and feelings.

The Tenth Commandment supplements the eighth by attacking the root from which theft grows, namely, coveteousness: "You shall not covet . . ." (Ex 20:17). This commandment differs from the other nine by prohibiting not only the outward act but also the inner thought from which the action springs. It establishes the important principle that we are accountable before God not only for our actions but also for our intentions. It also reveals the profound truth that we need not be controlled by our natural desire to covet what belongs to others, because by divine grace we can control our unlawful desires and passions (Phil 2:13).

Applied to the marriage covenant, *the tenth commandment enjoins us to be content with and grateful for our spouses.* In practice, this contentment is expressed in different ways: refraining from comparing our spouses' talents or performances with those of others; welcoming and rejoicing over our spouses' achievements, gifts, and experiences without coveting them for ourselves; learning to express gratitude to God every day for giving us the spouses we have; maintaining the proper reserve toward persons of the opposite sex and reserving expressions of special affection for our spouses; avoiding making unreasonable demands on our spouses to force them to become like real or fictitious spouses we covet. The tenth commandment, then, enjoins us to be content with and for our spouses, by resisting the temptation to look for "greener grass on the other side of the fence."

CONCLUSION

Christian marriage, to be stable and permanent, needs to be built upon the foundation of an unconditional, mutual covenant commitment that will not allow anything or anyone "to put asunder" the marital union established by God. To accept this Biblical view of marriage as a sacred covenant means to be willing to make *total, exclusive, continuing,* and *growing* commitments to our marriage partners. Such commitments are not easy or trouble free. Just as our covenantal commitment to God requires obedience to the principles embodied in the Ten Commandments, so our covenantal commitments to our marriage partners demand obedience to the principles of the Ten Commandments which are applicable to our marriage relationships.

There is no other way to enter into the joys of Christian marriage than by assuming its covenantal obligations. When we commit ourselves to honor our marriage covenants of mutual faithfulness "till death do us part," then we experience how God is able mysteriously to unite two lives into "one flesh." Honoring our marriage covenant is fundamental to the stability of our family, church and society.

NOTES TO CHAPTER II

1. R. Paul Stevens, *Married for Good* (Downers Grove, Illinois, 1986), p. 17.

2. Ibid., p. 20.

3. Quoted in E. A. Griffin, *The Mind Changers* (Wheaton, Illinois, 1983), p. 32.

4. Elizabeth Achtemeier, *The Committed Marriage* (Philadelphia, 1976), p. 41.

5. "The Redbook Report on Premarital and Extramarital Sex," *Redbook Magazine* (October 1975): 38.

6. Emphasis supplied.

7. Ellen G. White, *The Adventist Home* (Mountain View, California, 1951), p. 338.

8. According to the *National Center for Health Statistics* in 1986 there were in the United States 2,400,000 marriages and 1,159,000 divorces (*Monthly Vital Statistics*, vol. 35, n. 13 (August 1987): 3. This means that the divorce rate is slightly less than 50 percent. Considering, however, that some divorce more than once, the actual divorce rate is somewhat lower.

9. Ellen G. White (n. 7), p. 345.

10. David Phypers, *Christian Marriage in Crisis* (Bromley, Kent, England, 1986), p. 59.

11. Thomas N. Hart, *Living Happily Ever After* (New York, 1979), p. 31.

12. Gordon Wenham, "Grace and Law in the Old Testament," in Bruce Kaye and Gordon Wenham, eds., *Law, Morality and the Bible* (Downers Grove, Illinois, 1978), p. 17.

13. R. Paul Stevens (n.1), pp. 87-88.

14. Ibid., p. 86.

15. Ibid., p. 88-94.

CHAPTER III

Marriage
and
Sex

MARRIAGE AND SEX

During much of Christian history, sex in marriage has been condoned as a necessary evil for producing children. Before the sexual revolution of our times, calling a woman "sexy" would have been insulting. Nowadays many woman would accept that adjective as a prized compliment. "The Victorian person," writes Rollo May, "sought to have love without falling into sex; the modern person seeks to have sex without falling into love."[1]

The attitude of society toward sex has truly swung from one extreme to another. From the Puritan view of sex as a necessary evil for *procreation*, we have come to the popular *Playboy* view of sex as a necessary thing for *recreation*. From the age of warning "Beware of sex," we have come to the age of shouting "Hurrah for sex." *Homo sapiens* has become *homo sexualis*, packed with sexual drives and techniques.

Both extremes are wrong and fail to fulfill God's intended function of sex. The past negative view of sex made married people feel guilty about their sexual relations; the present permissive view of sex turns people into robots, capable of engaging in much sex but with little meaning or even satisfaction in it. In spite of the increasing number of books on the techniques of love-making, more and more people are telling marriage counselors: "We make much love, but it isn't much good. We find little meaning or even fun in it!"

Objective of the Chapter. This chapter examines the Biblical view of sex. We shall consider various aspects of sex within and without marriage in the light of the Biblical teaching. The chapter is divided into three parts. The first part surveys past attitudes toward sex, from ancient Israel to modern times. The second part examines the Biblical view of the nature and function of sex. Attention will also be given to the morality or immorality of contraception. The third part addresses the question of whether or not there will be marital relationships in the world to come. The overall objective of the chapter is to counteract the secular and hedonistic view of sex by helping Christians understand and experience sex as God intended it to be.

PART I: PAST ATTITUDES TOWARD SEX

Ancient Israel. The Hebrew people understood and interpreted human sexuality as a positive gift from God. They were not affected by the later Greek dualism between spirit and matter which considered sexual intercourse an evil "fleshy" activity to be shunned if possible. Such thinking was foreign to the Hebrews who saw sex within marriage as beautiful and enjoyable. A wedding was a time of great celebration, partly because it marked the beginning of the sexual life of the couple.

The bridal pair retired to a nuptial tent or chamber at the end of the wedding festivities to make love together while lying on a clean, white sheet. Blood on the sheet indicated that the bride had been a virgin and provided evidence of the consummation of marriage (Deut 22:13-19). A newly betrothed man was even excused from participating in war in order to be able to enjoy his bride (Deut 20:7)!

This indicates that the ancient Hebrews had a healthy attitude toward sex. They saw it as a divine gift which gave pleasure to the persons involved while providing the means for the propagation of the race. The classic example of the Bible's exaltation of human sexuality is found in the Song of Songs. This book has often been a source of embarrassment to Jews and Christians alike. Some interpreters, like Sebastian Castellio, have viewed the Song of Songs as an obscene description of human love which does not belong in the Biblical canon. Others, like Calvin, have defended the inclusion of the book in the canon by interpreting it as an allegory symbolizing the love of God for His people. The book, however, is not an allegory. It is a romantic celebration of human sexuality. According to some traditions, portions of the book were sung during wedding processionals and wedding feasts.

When the Hebrews came to the land of Canaan, they were exposed to the evil and excesses of the fertility cults associated with the worship of Baal, which included sacred prostitution. To correct these evils, several regulations were given. There were strict prohibitions, for example, against revealing in public one's "private parts" (Gen 9:21; 2 Sam 6:20), incest (Lev 18:6-18; 20:11-12, 14, 20; Deut 27:20, 22), bestiality (Lev 18:23; 20:15-16), homosexuality (Lev 18:22; 20:13), and various kinds of sexual "irregularities" (Ex 22:16; Lev 19:20, 29; 15:24; 18:19; 20:18; Deut 25:11). Overall, however, the Jews had a positive view of sex, although they saw it primarily in terms of its reproductive function.

New Testament Times. In New Testament times, we find the beginning of two extreme attitudes toward sex: licentiousness and celibacy. Some interpreted the freedom of the Gospel as freedom to engage freely in sexual relations outside marriage. Jude speaks of "ungodly persons who pervert the grace of our God into licentiousness" (Jude 4). Peter warns against the enticement of false teachers who had "eyes full of adultery, insatiable for sin" (2 Pet 2:14). The problem of sexual permissiveness and perversion had become so noticeable in the Corinthian church that Paul openly rebuked those who engaged in incestuous and adulterous sexual relations (1 Cor 5:1, 6:16-18).

Other Christians were influenced by Greek philosophical ideas which viewed anything related to the physical aspect of life as evil. Since the sexual act involves "fleshly" contact and pleasure, it was viewed as inherently evil. This thinking prevailed in the Greco-Roman world and exercised considerable influence among some Christians. In Corinth, for example, there were some Christians who maintained that unmarried people should remain single and those who were married should refrain from sexual activity (1 Cor 7:1-5, 8-11, 25-28).

Paul responded to these "ascetic" believers by affirming that it was right and proper for married persons to engage in sexual activities: "The husband should give to his wife her conjugal rights, and likewise the wife to her husband. . . . Do not refuse one another except perhaps by agreement for a season . . . lest Satan tempt you through lack of self-control" (1 Cor 7:3, 5). Paul counsels the unmarried and the widows to remain single (1 Cor 7:8, 25-26). His reason, however, is based not on theological but on practical considerations, namely, on the need to avoid the added burdens of a family during the end-time persecution which Paul believed would soon break out (1 Cor 7:26-31). Paul's counsel does not reflect a negative view of sexuality because his advice was predicated solely on practical considerations. This is indicated by his counsel, "It is better to marry than to be aflame with passion. . . . If you marry, you do not sin, and if a girl marries she does not sin" (1 Cor 7:9, 28).

Christian Church. The negative view of sexuality, already present in embryonic form during apostolic times among some Christians, developed fully during the early church, shaping the sexual attitudes of Christians up to modern times. This view can be traced back to Greek philosophy, especially to Platonic thought, which saw man as having two parts: the soul, which is good, and the body, which is bad. Such dualistic thinking influenced Christianity through a movement known as Gnosticism. This heretical movement taught that all matter, including the human body, was evil. Only the spark of the divine in man (soul) is good and through special knowledge (*gnosis*) such a spark could be released from the human body and returned to the divine realm. Thus, salvation was perceived as the liberation of the soul from the prison-house of the body.

This dualistic teaching greatly influenced Christian thought through the centuries to the point that gradually many Christians abandoned the Biblical view of the resurrection of the body, replacing it with the Greek concept of the immortality of the soul. The fundamental error of this view, which an increasing number of scholars are rejecting as unBiblical, is its assumption that matter is evil and must be destroyed. Such a view is clearly discredited by those Biblical texts which teach that matter, including the human body, is the product of God's good creation (Gen 1:4, 10, 12, 18, 21, 25, 31). The Psalmist declares: "For thou didst form my inward parts, thou didst knit me together in my mother's womb. I praise thee, for thou art fearful and wonderful. Wonderful are thy works" (Ps 139:13-14).

The adoption of the unBiblical Greek notion of the human body as intrinsically evil has led many Christians through the centuries into a warped attitude toward sex. Its effect still lingers, as many today are still uneasy about their marital sexual relations, viewing them as something tainted with sin.

Augustine's Role. The church father who has molded the negative Christian attitudes toward sex more than any other person is Augustine (354-430).[2] He regarded the sexual drives and excitement which cannot always be rationally controlled to be the result of sin. He speculated that if sin had not come in, marital intercourse would be without the excitement of sexual desire. The male semen could be introduced into the womb of the wife without the heat of passion, in a natural way similar to the natural menstrual flow of blood emitted from the womb.

As a result of sin, the sexual act is now accompanied by powerful drives which Augustine called concupiscence, or lust. In his view, the satisfaction of lust through intercourse was a necessary evil to bring children into this world.

In effect, Augustine equated original sin with the sexual act and its lustful desires since the act is the channel through which he thought the guilt of Adam's first transgression is transmitted from parent to child. By making the sexual act the means whereby original sin is transmitted, Augustine made sex for pleasure a sinful activity. This view necessitated the administration of baptism immediately after birth to remove the stain of the original sin from the soul of the newborn baby.

The major fallacy of this view is its reduction of original sin to a *biological factor* which can be transmitted like an infectious disease through sexual intercourse. In Scripture, however, sin is *volitional* and *not biological*. It is a willful transgression of a divine moral principle (1 John 3:4), and not a biological infection transmitted through sexual contact.

What can be transmitted is not the guilt of sin, as Augustine believed, but its punishment. Guilt is the personal transgression of a divine principle, which cannot be imputed upon a third party. The punishment of our wrong doings, however, can be passed on in terms of sickness and/or evil hereditary tendencies. Scripture tells us that God visits "the iniquity of the fathers upon the children and the children's children, to the third and fourth generation" (Ex 34:7). In the case of Adam's sin, what has been passed on to mankind are the consequences of its punishment, which include evil inclinations and death. These consequences cannot be mechanically removed through infant baptism.

Original Sin. The notion of original sin is derived primarily from Romans 5:12 where Paul says that "sin came into the world through one man and death through sin, and so death spread to all men because all men sinned." In this statement the apostle simply affirms the fact that mankind shares in Adam's sin and death. He makes no attempt to explain how this happens. He makes no allusion to sexual procreation as the channel through which mankind has become partakers of Adam's sin and death. The context clearly indicates that Paul's concern is to affirm the fundamental truth that Adam's disobedience has made us sinners and Christ's obedience has made us righteous: "For as by one man's disobedience many were made sinners, so by one man's obedience many will be made righteous" (Rom 5:19).

The concept to which Paul alludes to establish the connection between the sin of Adam and that of mankind is not that of biological transmission of sin through sexual procreation, but that of corporate solidarity. As Achan's sin became the sin of his household because its members shared in a corporate solidarity with him (Josh 7:24), so Adam's sin has become the sin of mankind because its members share in a corporate solidarity with him. This Pauline argument provides no support for the Augustinian attempt to equate original sin with sexual excitement and intercourse.

Augustine's association of original sin with sex has been widely accepted throughout Christian history, conditioning the sexual attitudes not only of Roman Catholics but also of Christians in general. As Derrick Baily notes, "Augustine must bear no small measure of responsibility for the insinuation into our culture of the idea, still widely current, that Christianity regards sexuality as something peculiarly tainted with evil."[3]

Partly as a reaction to this negative view of sex as a necessary evil for the propagation of the human race, a completely different and pleasure-oriented (hedonistic) view of sex has emerged. The sexual revolution of our time has glamorized sexual profligacy and prowess, ridiculing sexual chastity as a prudish superstition. The catastrophic consequences of the sexual revolution can be seen in the ever-increasing number of divorces, abortions, incidents of incest, sexual abuse of children, and the loss of the true meaning and function of sex. In the light of this painful reality, it is imperative for Christians to understand the Biblical meaning and function of sex.

PART II: THE BIBLICAL VIEW OF SEX

Image of God. The book of Genesis is the logical starting point for our quest into the Biblical view of sex. The first statement relating to human sexuality is found in Genesis 1:27: "So God created man in his own image, in the image of God he created him; male and female he created them." It is noteworthy that while after every previous act of creation, Scripture says that God saw that "it was good" (Gen 1:12, 18, 21, 25), after the creation of mankind as male and female, it says that God saw that "it was *very* good" (Gen 1:31). This initial divine appraisal of human sexuality as "*very* good" shows that Scripture sees the male/female sexual distinction as part of the goodness and perfection of God's original creation.

It is important to note also that human sexual duality as male and female is related explicitly to God's own image. Theologians have long debated the possible nature of this relation. Since Scripture distinguishes human beings from other creatures, theologians have usually thought that the image of God in humanity refers to the rational, moral and spiritual faculties God has given to men and women. This is a valid interpretation since these faculties distinguish human maleness and femaleness from that of lower creatures.

There is, however, another possible way in which human maleness and femaleness reflect the image of God, namely in the capacity of a man and a woman to experience a oneness of fellowship similar to the one existing in the Trinity. The God of Biblical revelation is not a *solitary* single Being who lives in eternal *aloofness* but is a *fellowship* of three Beings so intimately and mysteriously united that we worship them as one God. This mysterious oneness-in-relationship of the Trinity is reflected as a divine image in man, not as a single individual but as a sexual duality of maleness and femaleness, mysteriously united in marriage as "one flesh." The love uniting husband and wife points to the love that eternally unites the three Beings of the Trinity. In this sense, it constitutes a reflection of the image of God in humanity.

A "Unisex" God? Some theologians interpret the image of God, not in terms of a similarity of oneness-in-fellowship, but in terms of a correspondence in sexual distinctions within each person of the Godhead. Paul Jewett articulates this view saying: "If we are to think of God as sexual, we have to think of the divine as both feminine and masculine *if this symbolization of God is to convey a personal wholeness.* God becomes he/she. Otherwise the attribution of personality to God would be skewed or out of balance. A purely masculine God would be as intolerable as a purely masculine human, and the same could be said for the purely feminine."[4]

The attempt to make God into a unisex Being consisting of both feminine and masculine characteristics, if not properly qualified, can lead to a disastrous misrepresentation of the God of Biblical revelation. While it is true that God possesses not only masculine but also feminine qualities, since He compares His love, for example, to that of a woman's for her sucking child (Is 49:15), the fact remains that the possession of feminine qualities does not make God into a "he/she" androgynous Being. We recognize varying degrees of masculinity and femininity in every person , yet we do not regard a man who possesses unusual feminine gentleness as a he/she person.

The fact that the Bible sometimes presents God as our Father (Jer 31:9; Matt 23:9), while at other times compares God to a crying or compassionate mother (Is 42:14; 49:15), does not mean that God is an androgynous he/she Being. It is important to see the distinction between those statements which describe the *person of God* (God *is* our Father) and those which describe the *qualities of God* (God is *like* a crying or compassionate mother). The former identifies the person of God, the latter compares the compassion of God to that of a mother.

Today, both liberal and evangelical feminists are clamoring for a re-symbolization of the Godhead based on impersonal or unisex categories. This is seen as the first indispensable step to clearing the way for the elimination of sexual and functional role distinctions in the home and in the church. To achieve this, they advocate dropping the masculine names of God, adopting, instead, non-personal names such as "parent, Benefactor, Almighty" or androgynous names such as "Father-Mother" for God and "Son-

Daughter" for Christ. The ultimate result of such efforts is not merely switching labels on the same product, but rather introducing new labels for an entirely different product. Biblical faith knows nothing of an androgynous Godhead, partly masculine and partly feminine. Any attempt to introduce a female counterpart in the person of God means to reject the God of Biblical revelation, accepting, instead, the one fabricated by feminist speculations.

In light of the foregoing considerations, we reject as unBiblical the attempts to interpret the image of God in human maleness and femaleness as indicative of sexual distinctions within the persons of the Godhead. God transcends human sexual distinctions, yet He has chosen to reveal Himself predominantly through male terms and imageries because the male role within the family and church best represents the role that He sustains toward the human family. The image of God in humanity must rather be seen, as discussed earlier, in the rational, moral and spiritual faculties God has given to men and women, as well as in the capacity of a man and a woman to experience a oneness of fellowship similar to the one existing within the Trinity.

Becoming "One Flesh." The oneness of intimate fellowship between a man and a woman is expressed in Genesis 2:24 by the phrase *"one flesh:"* "Therefore a man leaves his father and mother and cleaves to his wife, and *they become one flesh."* The phrase *"one flesh,"* as already shown in chapter 1, refers to the total union of body, soul, and spirit between marital partners. This total union can be experienced especially through sexual intercourse when the act is the expression of genuine love, respect, and commitment. On the other hand, the merely physical or sexual meaning of the phrase "one flesh" is clearly found in 1 Corinthians 6:16 where Paul applies it to the sexual intercourse between a man and a harlot.

The phrase *becoming one flesh* sheds considerable light on God's estimate of sex within a marital relationship. It tells us that God sees sex as a means through which a husband and a wife can achieve a new unity. It is noteworthy that the "one flesh" imagery is never used to describe a child's relationship to his father and mother. A man must "leave" his father and mother to become "one flesh" with his wife. His relationship to his wife transcends the one to his parents because it consists of a new oneness consummated by the sexual union.

Becoming one flesh also implies that the purpose of the sexual act is not only *procreational*, that is, to produce children, but also *psychological*, that is, fulfilling the emotional need to consummate a new oneness-relationship. Oneness implies the willingness to reveal one's most intimate physical, emotional and intellectual self to the other. As they come to know each other in the most intimate way, the couple experiences the meaning of becoming one flesh. Sexual intercourse does not automatically ensure this oneness intimacy. Rather it consummates the intimacy of perfect sharing which has already developed.

Sex as "Knowing." Sexual relations within marriage enable a couple to come to know each other in a way which cannot be experienced in any other way. To participate in sexual intercourse means not only to uncover one's body but also one's inner being to another. This is why Scripture often describes sexual intercourse as "knowing," the same verb used in Hebrew to refer to knowing God. Genesis 4:1 says: "And Adam knew Eve his wife and she conceived."[5]

Obviously Adam had come to know Eve before their sexual intercourse, but through the latter he came to know her more intimately than ever before. Dwight H. Small aptly remarks: "Self-disclosure through sexual intercourse invites self-disclosure at all levels of personal existence. This is an exclusive revelation unique to the couple. They know each other as they know no other person. This unique knowledge is tantamount to laying claim to another in genuine belonging . . . the nakedness and physical coupling is symbolic of the fact that nothing is hidden or withheld between them."[6]

The process which leads to sexual intercourse is one of growing knowledge. From the initial casual acquaintance to dating, courtship, marriage, and sexual intercourse, the couple grows in the knowledge of each other and this makes greater intimacy possible. Sexual intercourse represents the culmination of this growth in reciprocal knowledge and intimacy. As Elizabeth Achtemeier puts it: "We feel as if the most hidden inner depths of our beings are brought to the surface and revealed and offered to each other as the most intimate expression of our love."[7]

Sex as Pleasure. A revolution has taken place in Christian thinking about sex within the last hundred years. Until the beginning of our century, Christians generally believed that the primary function of sex was procreative, that is, to produce children. Other considerations, such as the unitive, relational and pleasurable aspects of sex were seen as secondary and usually tainted with sin. In the twentieth century the order has been reversed. Christians place the relational and pleasurable aspects of sex first and the conception of children last.

From a Biblical perspective, sexual activity is both unitive and procreative, or we might say, recreative and reproductive. God's command, "Be fruitful and multiply" (Gen 1:28), is a command to be sexual. When we obey it, we fulfill God's purpose by becoming one flesh and producing children. So sex in marriage is both unitive and procreative. "During the Middle Ages," writes David Phypers, "Christians stressed the procreative aspect of sex while neglecting and sometimes despising its unitive purpose. Today, we stress its unitive role, and may ignore the command to be fruitful and increase in number."[8]

As Christians we need to recover and maintain the Biblical balance between the relational and procreational functions of sex. Sexual intercourse is a relational act of perfect sharing that engenders a sense of oneness while offering the possibility of bringing a new life into this world. We need to recognize that sex is a divine gift that can be legitimately enjoyed within marriage. Like all other divine gifts, sex is to be partaken of with thankfulness and moderation.

Sex as a Divine Gift. It is noteworthy that the wise man Solomon mentions together bread, wine, clothing and marital love as the good gifts that God has approved for our enjoyment: "Go, eat your bread with enjoyment, and drink your wine with a merry heart; for God has already approved what you do. Let your garments be always white; let not oil be lacking on your head. Enjoy life with the wife whom you love, all the days of your life which He has given you under the sun, because that is your portion in life and in your toil at which you toil under the sun" (Eccl 9:7-9).

Sexual activity is generally more important to humans than it is to animals. It is significant that among the mammals, only the human female is capable of enjoying sexual orgasm as well as the male. It is recognized that this experience binds a woman to her partner emotionally as well as physically. The fact that both the human male and female can share together in the pleasure of sexual intercourse indicates that God intended marital sex to be enjoyed by both partners.

In the Song of Songs, the celebration of sexual love between the bride and bridegroom is expressed in suggestive romantic words: "I am my beloved's, and his desire is for me. Come, my beloved, let us go forth into the fields and lodge in the villages; let us go out early to the vineyards .... There I will give you my love" (Song of Songs 7:10-12).

The same positive view of marital sex is found in the New Testament. In his letter to the Corinthians, Paul urges husbands and wives to fulfill their marital duties together, because their bodies do not belong to themselves alone but to each other. Therefore they should not deprive each other of sex, except by mutual agreement for a time to devote themselves to prayer. Then they should come together again lest Satan tempt them through lack of self-control (1 Cor 7:2-5).

In Ephesians Paul speaks of the physical union of a man and a woman as a profound "mystery" reflecting Christ's love for His church. Therefore, we should not be uneasy about marital sex, because when we come together we are experiencing something of the mysterious redemptive love of Christ for the world.

The author of Hebrews admonishes that "Marriage should be honoured by all, and the marriage bed kept pure" (Heb 13:4 NIV). Here, marital sex is extolled as honorable, something not to be embarrassed about. But the same writer adds, "God will judge the adulterer and all the sexually immoral" (Heb 13:4 NIV).

Bible writers are unanimous in commending sex within marriage and in condemning all forms of sexual activity outside marriage. Paul warns the Corinthians, "Do not be deceived: Neither the sexually immoral . . . nor adulterers, nor male prostitutes, nor homosexual offenders . . . will inherit the kingdom of God" (1 Cor. 6:9, 10 NIV). The book of Revelation places the "fornicators" among those whose "lot shall be in the lake that burns with fire and sulphur" (Rev 21:8).

Sex as Procreation. In the Bible the function of sex, as noted earlier, is not only unitive but also procreative. It not only serves to engender a mysterious oneness of spirit, but it also offers the possibility of bringing children into this world. God's command "Be fruitful and multiply" (Gen 1:28) expresses God's original intent for the purpose of sex. Through marital sex and the birth of children, God enables men and women to reflect His image by sharing in His creative activity. This means that sex in marriage without the intention of having children fails to fulfill a fundamental divine purpose for sex. The lengths to which some married couples will go in order to have children reveals the deep creative urge God has placed within us.

Of course, not all couples are able to have or are justified in having children. Old age, infertility, and genetic diseases are but some of the factors that make childbearing impossible or inadvisable. For the vast majority of couples, however, sex in marriage should include the desire to have children. As sex consummates the act of marriage, so children consummate the sexual act. This does not mean that every act of sexual union should result in conception, but rather that the desire for having children should be part of the overall intent of sexual relations.

Various contraceptive techniques make it possible today to separate sexual activity from childbearing. A growing number of couples choose to enjoy a lifetime of sexual activity without desiring or planning for children. They are not simply concerned about delaying the arrival of children but in avoiding them altogether. Children are seen as a threat to their high standard of living associated with two incomes and two careers.

"We are not meant to separate sex from childbearing" writes David Phypers, "and those who do, totally and finally, purely for personal reasons, are surely falling short of God's purpose for their lives. They run the risk that their marriage and sexual activity may become self-indulgent. They will only look inwards to their own self-satisfaction, rather than outwards to the creative experiences of bringing new life into the world and nurturing it to maturity."[9]

The life-begetting function of sex enables a married couple to further God's creative work by becoming procreators with Him. It is altogether consistent with God's creative work that the sexual life-begetting experience should be joyous. Did not God's angels shout for joy when He created (Job 38:7)? Bringing into life a new person in God's image is a joyful and solemn privilege delegated by God to married couples. In this sense, they become workers together with God in furthering His creation.

Importance of Children. Children are a fundamental part of our marriage and sexual relationships. They represent God's blessings upon the marital union. The Psalmist expresses this truth, saying: "Sons are a heritage from the Lord, children a reward from Him. Like the arrows in the hands of a warrior are the sons born in one's youth. Blessed is the man whose quiver is full of them" (Ps 127:3-5 NIV).

The population explosion has not rescinded God's command to be fruitful and multiply. World famine is not so much the result of too many people as much as the result of greed, exploitation, irresponsible governments, misuse of natural resources, and un-willingness to adopt more effective methods of agriculture and to teach people responsible family planning. While a number of developing countries are facing population explosions, most Western countries are experiencing population stagnation or decline. West-ern societies are aging, and unless the current trend is reversed, it will soon become increasingly difficult for them to support their ever-growing numbers of elderly people.

We no longer need large families, but we still need families. The church needs Christian families that can share with the world the love of God experienced in the home. Society needs the service and moral influence of Christian families. Most Western societies live today in what social analysts call the "Post-Christian era." This is the era in which social values and practices are influenced no longer by Christian principles but rather by humanistic ideologies. The latter promote a secular view of marriage and a hedonistic view of sex. Marriage has become a dissolvable social contract rather than a permanent sacred covenant, and sex is regarded primarily as a recreational activity rather than as a procreational responsibility.

As Christians, we are called not to conform to the world (Rom 12:2) but to transform the world through God's given principles and power. In the area of marriage and sex, we must show to the world that we obey God's command to "Be fruitful and multiply" (Gen 1:22) and not to "put asunder what God has united" (Matt 19:6).

The Use of Contraception. It is a fact that today most couples in the Western world use contraceptives to delay the start of their families, to space the arrival of subsequent children, and to limit their numbers. This practice is followed by most Christians, often unthinkingly. Is this right? Does Scripture allow us to limit and time our children's births? Or does the command to be fruitful and multiply mean that we should leave the issue of family planning to the mercies of God? No explicit answer can be found in the Bible because the subject of contraception was not an issue in Bible times. In those days, larger families were needed and welcomed to meet the demand for helping hands in that agricultural society.

In seeking for Biblical guidance on the subject of contraception, we need to ask two fundamental questions: (1) What is the purpose of sexual intercourse? and (2) Do we have the right to interfere with the reproductive cycle established by God?

We have discussed earlier, at great length, the first question. We have seen that the function of sexual intercourse is both relational and procreational. It is a relational act of perfect sharing that engenders a mysterious sense of oneness and offers the possibility of bringing children into this world. The fact that the function of sex in marriage is not only to produce children but also to express and experience mutual love and commitment, implies the need for certain limitations on the reproductive function of sex. If a couple were to risk a new conception each time they made love, they would soon forfeit sexual intercourse as a means of giving themselves totally to each other. This means that the relational function of sex can only remain a viable dynamic experience if its reproductive function is controlled.

Natural or "Unnatural" Contraception? This leads us to consider the manner of controlling the reproductive cycle. This issue is addressed by the second question, namely, do we have the right to interfere with the reproductive cycle established by God? The historic answer of the Roman Catholic Church has been a resounding "NO!" In December 1930, Pius XI reaffirmed the traditional Catholic position against contraceptives in his encyclical *Casti Connubii*: "Since therefore the conjugal act is destined primarily by nature for the begetting of children, those who in exercising it deliberately frustrate its natural effect and purpose, sin against nature, and commit a deed which is shameful and intrinsically vicious."[10]

The unyielding historical Catholic position has been tempered by Pope Paul VI's encyclical *Humanae Vitae* (July 29, 1968) which acknowledges the morality of the sexual union between husband and wife, even if not directed to the procreation of children.[11] Moreover, the encyclical, while condemning artificial contraceptives, allows for a natural method of birth control, known as the "rhythm method." This method consists of confining intercourse to the infertile periods in the wife's menstrual cycle.[12]

The attempt of *Humanae Vitae* to distinguish between "artificial" and "natural" contraceptives, making the former immoral and the latter moral, itself smacks of artificiality. Why is it "artificial" to block the flow of the sperm in the uterus and yet not "artificial" to time the placement of the sperm so that it does not fertilize an egg? In either case, the fertilization of the egg is prevented by human intelligence. Moreover, to reject as immoral the use of artificial contraceptives can lead to rejecting as immoral the use of any artificial vaccine, hormone or medication which is not produced naturally by the human body.

The morality or immorality of contraception is determined not by the *kinds* of contraceptives we use, but by the *reasons* for their use. "Like most other human inventions," writes David Phypers, "contraception is morally neutral; it is what we do with it that counts. If we use it to practice sex outside marriage or selfishly within marriage, or if through it we invade the privacy of others' marriages, we may indeed be guilty of disobeying the will of God and of distorting the marriage relationship. But if we use it with a proper regard for the health and well-being of our partners and our families, then it can enhance and strengthen our marriages. Through contraception we can protect our marriage from the physical, emotional, economic, and psychological strains they might suffer through further pregnancies, while at the same time we can use the act of marriage, reverently and lovingly, as it was intended, to bind us together in lasting union."[13]

Contraception and Sin. To ban contraception, as the Catholic Church has done historically, means to ignore the effects of sin on marriage, sex and childbirth. If sin had not entered into this world, there would have been no need for contraception. The menstrual cycle and the fertility rate would have been regular in all women. Childbirth would have been easy and painless. The abundant provisions of the earth would have amply satisfied the need for food and shelter. The socio-political structures of a perfect society would have provided to any child unlimited educational and professional opportunities.

But sin has spoiled our world. Both the human and sub-human creation has been marred by sin. Some women are very fertile while others totally infertile. Childbirth is a great source of pain to most women. Thorns, thistles, pests, and droughts destroy our crops. The socio-political systems of many developing countries are unable to provide adequate housing, education, employment, and medical services to most members of their societies. Christians are not spared the results of sin. Christian mothers may not be able to give birth without Caesarean delivery, and many suffer from various health problems. These and many other reasons may cause couples to delay, to space, or to limit the size of their families. In situations such as the ones mentioned above, contraception becomes a responsible way to respect human life and resources.

It is significant to note that the command, "Be fruitful and multiply" (Gen 1:28), is immediately followed by the command to subdue and have domination "over every living thing." This implies that God is calling us to be responsible stewards of His creation, controlling any destabilizing factor such as the threat of population explosion.

To be responsible stewards of God's creation means that under normal circumstances Christians have no right to avoid children altogether by using natural or "unnatural" means of contraception. We have a duty before God to become responsible parents, by bringing up children in the love, "discipline and instruction of the Lord" (Eph 6:4). The way we fulfill this duty will vary from couple to couple as we prayerfully seek divine guidance regarding the timing of our children's births and the methods we use to this end.

Sex Outside Marriage. Nowhere has Christian morality come under greater attack than in the whole area of sex outside marriage. The Biblical teaching that sex is *only* for marriage does not even enter the thinking of most people today. The Biblical condemnation of illicit sexual acts has become for many a license for sexual experimentation.

As we mentioned earlier, the popular acceptance of sexual permissiveness is evidenced by the introduction and use of "softer terms." Fornication, for example, is referred to as "pre-marital sex" with the accent on the "pre" rather than on the "marital." Adultery is now called "extra-marital sex," implying an additional experience like some extra-professional activities. Homosexuality has gradually been softened from serious perversion through "deviation" to "gay variation." Pornographic literature and films are now available to "mature audiences" or "adults."

More and more, Christians are giving in to the specious argument that "love makes it right." If a man and a woman are deeply and genuinely in love, it is claimed, they have the right to express their love through sexual union without marriage. Some contend that pre-marital sex releases people from their inhibitions and moral hangups, giving them a sense of emotional freedom. The truth of the matter is that pre-marital sex adds emotional pressure because it reduces sexual love to a purely physical level without the total commitment of two married people.

Biblical Condemnation. The Biblical condemnation of sexual relations before or outside of marriage is abundantly clear. Adultery, or sexual intercourse between married persons and someone other than their marital partners, is condemned as a serious sin. Not only is adultery forbidden in both versions of the Decalogue (Ex

20:14; Deut 5:18), but it was also punishable by death in ancient Israel: "If a man commits adultery with the wife of his neighbor, both the adulterer and the adulteress shall be put to death" (Lev 20:10; cf. 18:20; Deut 22:22-24). The same punishment was meted out to a man or a woman who engaged in pre-marital sex (Deut 22:13-21, 23-27).

The New Testament goes beyond the Old Testament by internalizing the whole sexuality of a person and placing it within the context of motivation. Jesus emphasized that to entertain lustful desires toward a person of the opposite sex outside marriage means to be guilty of adultery (Matt 5:27-28). The reason for this is that defilement comes not only from outward acts but also from inward thoughts, which in Biblical symbology derive from the heart: "Out of the heart come evil thoughts, murder, adultery, fornication, theft, false witness, slander. These are what defile a man" (Matt 15:19-20).

Sexual laxness was pervasive in the Greco-Roman world of New Testament times. Hence, one of the conditions the Jerusalem council made for the inclusion of the Gentiles in the Christian Church was that they should abstain from all forms of "unchastity" (Acts 15:20, 29).

Paul's letters reveal the difficulties the apostle had in leading Gentile converts away from sexual immorality. To the Thessalonians he wrote: "For you know what instructions we gave you through the Lord Jesus. For this is the will of God, your sanctification: that you abstain from unchastity; that each of you know how to take a wife for himself in holiness and honor, not in the passion of lust like heathen who do not know God" (1 Thess 4:2-5). Here Paul admonishes those who had sexual urges to satisfy them by entering not into temporary relationships "in the passion of lust like the heathen who do not know God," but into permanent marital relationships. Such relationships are to be characterized by "holiness and honor."

Paul is most explicit in his condemnation of prostitution. He asks the Corinthians who lived in the celebrated sex center of the Mediterranean world: "Do you not know that he who joins himself to a prostitute becomes one body with her? For, as it is written, 'The two shall become one flesh.' But he who is unified to the Lord becomes one spirit with Him. Shun immorality. Every other sin which a man commits is outside the body; but the immoral man sins against his own body. Do you not know that your body is a temple of the Holy Spirit within you, which you have from God? You are not your own; you were bought with a price. So glorify God in your body" (1 Cor 6:16-20).

Reasons for Condemnation. In this passage, Paul helps us to see why the Bible strongly condemns sex outside marriage. Sex represents the most intimate of all interpersonal relationships, expressing a "one-flesh" unity of total commitment. Such a unity of commitment cannot be expressed or experienced in a casual sexual union with a prostitute where the concern is purely commercial and recreational. The only oneness experienced in such sexual unions is the oneness of sexual immorality.

Sexual immorality is serious because it affects the individual more deeply and permanently than any other sin. Paul describes it as a sin committed inside the body: "Every other sin which a man commits is outside the body; but the immoral man sins against his own body" (1 Cor 6:18). It might be objected that all sins of sensuality such as gluttony or drunkenness affect a person inside the body. Yet they do not have the same permanent effect on the personality as the sin of fornication. Indulgence in eating or drinking can be overcome, stolen goods can be returned, lies can be retracted and replaced by the truth. But the sexual act, once committed with another person, cannot be undone. A radical change has taken place in the interpersonal relationship of the couple involved that can never be undone. Something indelible has been stamped on them both forever. Even with a prostitute, sexual union leaves its permanent mark. It is a spot in the consciousness that cannot be removed.

"The immoral man sins against his own body." This truth is openly rejected by those who regard pre-marital sex not as sinful, but as helpful to a satisfactory sexual adjustment in marriage. Some even believe that sexual relations with the person one intends to marry are necessary to guarantee sexual compatibility. Such attitudes fail to recognize that sexual intercourse before marriage is the worst possible preparation for marriage. The reasons for this are not difficult to discover.

Sex without Commitment. To begin with, sex before marriage is sex without commitment. If we do not like our partners, we can change and find somebody else. Such casual relationships destroy the integrity of the person by reducing him or her to an object to be used for personal gratification. Some who feel hurt and used after sexual encounters may withdraw altogether from sexual activity for fear of being used again or may decide to use their bodies selfishly, without regard to the feeling of others. Either way, our sexuality is distorted because we have destroyed the possibility of using it to relate genuinely and intimately toward the one we love. Sex cannot be used as a means for fun with one partner at one time and as a way to express genuine love and commitment with another partner at another time. Those who become accustomed to a variety of sexual partners will find it difficult, if not impossible, to express through sex their total commitment and final intimacy with their marital partners.

Engaged couples will probably deny the charge that when they sleep together they are not expressing genuine commitment to one another. But if they were fully and finally committed to each other, they would be married. Engagement is the preparation for marriage, but it is not marriage. Until the wedding vows are taken, the possibility of breaking up a relationship exists. If a couple has had intercourse together, they have compromised their relationship. Any subsequent break up will leave permanent emotional scars. It is only when we are willing to become one, not only verbally but also legally by assuming responsibility for our partners, that we can seal our relationships through sexual intercourse. In this setting, sex fittingly expresses the ultimate commitment and the final intimacy.

Marriage licenses and wedding ceremonies are not mere formalities but serve to formalize the marriage commitment. As Elizabeth Achtemeier explains: "Just the fact that such young people [living together] are hesitant legally to seal their union is evidence that their commitment to one another is not total. Marriage licenses and ceremonies are not only legal formalities; they are also symbols of responsibility. They say publicly, what is affirmed privately, without reservation, that I am responsible for my mate—responsible not only in all those lovely emotional and spiritual areas of married life, but responsible also in the down-to-earth areas that have to do with grubby things like money, health insurance, and property. For example, two people just living together have no obligation for each other when the tax form comes up for an audit, or the other is involved in a car accident and legal suit; but persons holding a marriage license do have such responsibility, and commitment to a marriage involves accepting that public responsibility too. It is a matter of accepting the full obligations that society imposes on its adult members in order to ensure the common good."[14]

PART III: MARRIAGE IN THE WORLD TO COME

Will there be marital relations in the world to come? The answer of many sincere Christians is "NO!" They believe that at the resurrection the redeemed will receive some kind of "unisex" spiritual bodies which will replace our present physical and heterosexual bodies . Their belief is derived primarily from a misunderstanding of the words of Jesus found in Matthew 22:30: "For in the resurrection they neither marry nor are given in marriage but are like angels in heaven." Does this text imply that at the resurrection all sexual distinctions will be abolished and that our bodies will no longer be physical? If this interpretation were correct, it would mean that, contrary to what the Scripture says, the original creation of humanity as physical, heterosexual beings was not really "very good" (Gen 1:31). To remove the "bugs" from His original creation, God would find it necessary in the new world to create a new type of human being, presumably made up of "non-physical, unisex" bodies.

Change Implies Imperfection. To say the least, this reasoning is absurd for anyone who believes in God's omniscience and immutability. It is normal for human beings to introduce new models and structures to eliminate existing deficiencies. For God, however, this would be abnormal and incoherent since He knows the end from the beginning.

If at the resurrection God were to change our present physical, heterosexual bodies into "non-physical, unisex" bodies, then as

Anthony A. Hoekema rightly observes: "The devil would have won a great victory since God would then have been compelled to change human beings with physical bodies such as he had created into creatures of a different sort, without physical bodies (like the angels). Then it would indeed seem that matter had become intrinsically evil so that it had to be banished. And then, in a sense, the Greek philosophers would have been proved right. But matter is not evil; it is part of God's good creation."[15]

Like Angels. A study of Jesus' statement in its own context provides no support to the view that at the resurrection the redeemed will receive non-physical, unisex, angelic bodies. The context is a hypothetical situation created by the Sadducees in which six brothers married in succession the widow of their brother. The purpose of such successive, levirate marriages was not relational but procreational, namely to "raise up children for his [their] brother" (Matt 22:24). The testing question posed by the Sadducees was, "In the resurrection to which of the seven will she be wife?" (Matt 22:28).

In answering this hypothetical situation, Jesus affirmed, "You are wrong, because you know neither the scripture nor the power of God. For in the resurrection they neither marry nor are given in marriage, but are like angels in heaven" (Matt 22:30). In the context of the hypothetical situation of seven brothers marrying the same woman to give her an offspring, Christ's reference to not marrying or giving in marriage but being like angels, most likely means that marriage as a means of procreation will no longer exist in the world to come. It is evident that if no new children are born, there will be no possibility of marrying a son or of giving a daughter in marriage. The cessation of the procreational function of marriage will make the redeemed "like angels" who do not reproduce after their own likeness.

In His answer, Jesus did not deal with the immediate question of the marital status of a woman married seven times, but with the larger question of the procreational function of marriage, which, after all, was the reason the six brothers married the same woman. This indirect method of answering questions is not unusual in the teachings of Jesus. For example, when asked by the Pharisees, "Is it lawful for a man to divorce his wife?" (Mark 10:2), Jesus chose to ignore the immediate question, emphasizing instead the original creational design for marriage to be a lifelong commitment, without divorce (Mark 10:5-9).

Single in Heaven? Does the cessation of the procreational function of marriage imply the termination also of its relational function? Not necessarily so. If God created human beings at the beginning as male and female, with the capacity to experience a oneness of intimate fellowship, there is no reason to suppose that He will recreate them at the end as unisex beings, who will live as single persons without the capacity to experience the oneness of fellowship existing in a man/woman relationship.

The doctrine of the First Things, known as etiology, should illuminate the doctrine of the Last Things, known as escatology. If God found His creation of human beings as male and female *very good* (Gen 1:31) at the *beginning*, would He discover it to be *not so good* at the end? We have reason to believe that what was "very good" for God at the beginning will also be "very good" for Him at the end.

Christians who believe that human life originated not perfectly by divine *choice* but imperfectly by *chance* through spontaneous generation may find it rational to believe in a radical restructuring of human beings from physical and heterosexual to non-physical and unisexual. They could explain this transformation as part of the evolutionary process used by God. But for Christians like myself who believe in an original perfect creation and who celebrate through the Sabbath the perfection of God's original creation, it is impossible to imagine that at the end God will radically change the structure and nature of the human body.

Cessation of Procreation. The cessation of the human reproductive capacity in the world to come, as implied by the statement of Jesus in Matthew 22:30, could be seen as a change in God's original design of the function of human sexuality. But this is not necessarily true. Scripture suggests that God had already contemplated such a change in His original plan, when He said: "Be fruitful and multiply, and *fill the earth*" (Gen 1:28).

The command to *"fill the earth"* presupposes that God had intended to terminate the reproductive cycle once the earth had been filled by an ideal number of persons. In a perfect world, without the presence of death, the ecological balance between land and people would have been reached in a relatively short time. At that time God would have interrupted the reproductive cycle of human and sub-human creatures, to protect the ecosystem of this planet.

It is reasonable to presume that the resurrection and translation of the saints constitute the post-Fall fulfillment of God's original plan for the "filling" of the earth. In a sense, the redeemed represent the ideal number of inhabitants which this renewed earth will be able to support adequately. This is suggested by the reference to *names* "written before the foundation of the world in the book of life" (Rev 13:8; see 17:8; 21:27; Dan 13:1; Phil 4:3). The mention of names suggests the existence of an original divine plan for an ideal number of righteous to inhabit this earth. Had sin not arisen, God in His providence would have interrupted the reproductive cycle once the ideal number of people had been reached. But the cessation of the procreative function of marriage before or after the Fall does not necessitate the cessation of its relational function.

Continuity of Relationships. Jesus' reference to our being "like angels" (Matt 22:30) at the resurrection does not necessarily imply the termination of the relational function of marriage. Nowhere does Scripture suggest that the angels are "unisex" beings, unable to engage in an intimate relationships similar to that of human marriage. The fact that angels are often mentioned in the Bible in pairs (Gen 19:1; Ex 25:18; 1 King 6:23) suggests that they may enjoy intimate relationships as couples.

We noted earlier that God has revealed Himself, not as a *solitary* Being who lives in eternal aloofness, but as a *fellowship* of three Beings so intimately united that we worship Them as one God. If God Himself lives in a most intimate relationship with the other members of the Trinity, there is no reason to believe that He would abolish at the end the unitive function of marriage that He, Himself, established at creation.

Support for this conclusion is provided also by the fact, already noted, that the sexual distinctions of maleness and femaleness are presented in Scripture as reflecting the "image of God" (Gen 1:27). One aspect of the "image of God" in humanity is the capacity given by God to a man and a woman to experience through marriage a oneness of fellowship similar to the one existing in the Trinity. If human maleness and femaleness reflected the image of God at creation, we have reason to believe that they will continue to reflect God's image at the final restoration of all things. The purpose of redemption was not the destruction of God's original creation but its restoration to its original perfection. This is why Scripture speaks of the resurrection of the body and not of the creation of new beings.

CONCLUSION

Sex is seen in the Bible as part of God's good creation. Its function is both unitive and procreative. It serves to engender a mysterious oneness of body, mind, and spirit between husband and wife while offering them the possibility of bringing children into this world.

Scripture strongly condemns sex outside marriage because it is a sin affecting a person more deeply and permanently than other sins (1 Cor 6:18). It leaves a permanent mark in the consciousness that cannot be removed. Sex outside of marriage is sin because it is sex without commitment. It reduces a person to an object to be used for personal gratification. Such a selfish use of sex impairs, if not totally destroys, the possibility of using it to express and experience genuine love and commitment toward one's marital partner. At a time when sexual permissiveness and promiscuity prevails, it is imperative for Christians to reaffirm their commitment to the Biblical view of sex as a divine gift to be enjoyed only within marriage.

NOTES TO CHAPTER III

1. Rollo May, "Reflecting on the New Puritanism," in *Sex Thoughts for Contemporary Christians*, ed. Michael J. Taylor, S.J. (New York, 1972), p. 171.

2. For a discussion of the attitude of the early church, including Augustine, toward sex, see Derrick Sherwin Bailey, *Common Sense About Sexual Ethics: A Christian View* (New York, 1962); Donald F. Winslow, "Sex and Anti-sex in the Early Church Fathers," in *Male and Female: Christian Approaches Sexuality,* eds. Ruth Tiffany Barnhouse and Urban T. Holmes III (New York, 1956).

3. As quoted by William E. Phipps, *Was Jesus Married?* (New York, 1970), p. 175.

4. Paul Jewett, *Man as Male and Female* (Grand Rapids, 1975), p. 261.

5. See also Genesis 4:17, 25.

6. Dwight H. Small, *Christian: Celebrate Your Sexuality* (Old Tappan, New Jersey, 1974), p. 186.

7. Elizabeth Achtemeier, *The Committed Marriage* (Philadelphia, 1976), p. 162.

8. David Phypers, *Christian Marriage in Crisis* (Kent, England, 1986), p. 38.

9. Ibid., p. 39.

10. Cited in Norman St. John-Stevas, *The Agonizing Choice: Birth Control, Religion and Law* (Bloomington, Indiana, 1971), p. 84.

11. *Humanae Vitae,* paragraph 11.

12. *Humanae Vitae*, paragraph 10.

13. David Phypers (n. 8), p. 44.

14. Elizabeth Achtemeier (n. 7), p. 40.

15. A. A. Hoekema, *The Bible and the Future* (Grand Rapids, 1979), p. 250.

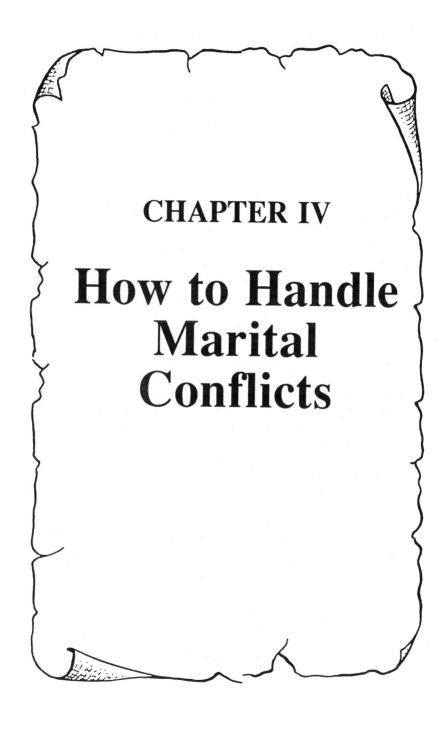

CHAPTER IV

How to Handle Marital Conflicts

HOW TO HANDLE
MARITAL CONFLICTS

In a relationship as intimate as marriage, some conflicts are inevitable. The more intimate the marriage relationship is, the more likely it is for conflicting views and desires to surface. No two normal intelligent persons want the same things all the time or see issues in exactly the same way. The fact that each of us is a unique person will lead to conflicts in relationships.

We have to be realistic and recognize that disagreements are part of marriage. Two strong, independent personalities will not flow together without causing some turbulence. This is true for both Christian and non-Christian couples, whether educated or uneducated.

Marital conflicts assume different forms. Occasionally, they deteriorate into an all-out war. Most often, however, they are skirmishes fought in subtle ways: verbal abuse, stoic silence, public criticism, sarcastic remarks, intimidation, demeaning remarks, indifference. Such common tactics are wrong and they tend to weaken a marriage.

Conflict in marriage is not necessarily bad or sinful. The determinative factor is how the conflict is handled. If a conflict is used constructively to enhance communication and deepen understanding, then it can strengthen and solidify a marriage covenant.

When a married couple tells me that they have never had an argument or conflict during their 30 or 40 years of marriage, I assume that one of two things must be true of them: (1) they are not telling the truth, (2) their relationship must be rather superficial and boring.

The Bible warns us against pretending that everything is well when in reality there are problems in our lives or in our society. Jeremiah and Ezekiel sternly condemn those false prophets who misled the people into believing that all was well with their lives when in reality, they were living in open opposition to the will of

God: "They have healed the wound of my people lightly, saying, 'Peace, peace,' when there is no peace" (Jer 6:14; cf. 8:11; Ez 13:10-11, 14-16).

God is against a phony acceptance of the *status quo* because healing can only take place when wrongs are acknowledged, forgiven, and truth comes to light. This applies to conflict in marriage as well. Marital relationships can be healed and strengthened not by burying all the differences, but by facing and resolving them.

Maintaining a phony peace at any price when there is no peace only serves to weaken the marriage covenant. The Christian couple committed to live out their marriage covenant must be prepared to seek divine grace and wisdom to honestly face and resolve their differences. To the degree a couple succeeds in developing the ability to openly discuss and resolve their differences, they will deepen their marital commitment and intimacy.

Objective of this Chapter. This chapter is divided into two parts. In the first part, we shall examine nine major causes of marital conflicts, namely (1) personality differences, (2) intellectual differences, (3) spiritual differences, (4) vocational tensions, (5) role conflicts, (6) family crises, (7) in-law difficulties, (8) sexual adjustments, and (9) the use of money. In the second part, we shall consider seven basic rules on how to handle conflicts in marriage constructively: (1) be committed to preserving your marriage covenant, (2) be honest and fair in handling the conflict, (3) keep your anger under control, (4) choose an appropriate time to discuss a problem, (5) stick to the issue at hand, (6) listen carefully and speak tactfully, and (7) be willing to forgive and to forget. The ultimate aim of this chapter is to help a Christian couple turn conflicts into opportunities to build a stronger marriage covenant.

PART I: CAUSES OF MARITAL CONFLICTS

When a couple marries, two cultures come together. Each brings to marriage its different upbringing, values, habits, temperament, and expectations. The way these differences are handled determines to a large extent the success of the marriage.

The areas of differences which cause marital conflicts are many. For the sake of brevity, we shall limit our study to nine of the major causes of marital conflicts.

1. Personality Differences

Frequently, in dating and courtship, a couple fails to see or chooses to ignore the extent of their differences in taste, habits, values, and temperament. In their desire to establish real friendship and trust, both the man and woman tend to show acceptance and tolerance of each other. They put their best foot forward and act as though they like those things which, in reality, they do not.

After marriage, however, men and women sometimes react with intolerance to differences in taste, habits, and values. For example, before marriage, a girl who hates fishing may be willing to get up at 3:30 in the morning to go fishing for the whole day with her guy. After being married, however, if her husband invites her to go fishing, she may say, "Forget it! I can't stand fishing." "How can you hate fishing when you were so glad to go fishing with me before we got married?" the husband may reply. Gong! The fight begins.

The problems of adjustments become evident when the honeymoon is over. "It comes as something of a shock to most young couples," writes Cecil Osborne, "to discover that marriages are not 'consummated,' they are worked at, hammered out, prayed through, suffered through."[1] The extent of adjustments in marriage is largely determined by the depth of difference between the personalities of the spouses. An aggressive, outgoing spouse will need to make a lot of adjustment to a partner who is calm and withdrawn. Some marriages fail because couples are psychologically incompatible and will not adjust to the demands of living together in intimate marital relationships.

An unbelieving couple may find it impossible to adjust to radical differences in their personalities. A Christian couple, however, can overcome incompatibilities with God's help. If they are sincerely seeking divine wisdom and strength in making the necessary changes, they will gradually learn how to adjust to each other. Sometimes God will give them the wisdom to become creative by drawing out the positive aspects of each other's character traits. Christian spouses who claim that they cannot adjust to each other are saying that God's grace is unable to help them make the necessary personality changes.

2. Intellectual Differences

Another area of potential conflicts is intellectual and/or educational differences. A man with a graduate degree and a high IQ marrying a woman with a high school diploma and a lower IQ may be tempted to think he is "stuck" with an intellectual weakling who is unable to engage in a meaningful intellectual discussion. Such an attitude would diminish his respect for her and increase the possibility of verbal abuse.

The conflict can readily intensify if the husband or wife is interested in participating in educational programs or pursuits while the spouse prefers to attend social functions or entertainment. Christian couples committed to preserving their marriage covenants will seek creative ways to reconcile their differences. They will recognize that God did not make a mistake after all by creating them so differently. Instead of rejecting one another because of their differences, they will seek ways to appreciate each other's strengths.

The husband will need to recognize the difference between being knowledgeable and being intelligent or wise. The fact that his wife has not earned graduate degrees does not make her less intelligent or wise. It is not uncommon to meet an educated person unable to deal with simple practical problems easily resolved by a less educates person. Moreover, the husband may need the help of his wife in developing intellectual and cultural aspects of his personality. For her part, the wife may need to develop an interest in her husband's intellectual and professional pursuits. She may do this by asking questions of her husband, listening to him with interest, and reading literature related to his field of endeavors. Rather than being critical of their intellectual and/or educational differences, a Christian couple can work creatively to turn such differences into complementary strengths.

3. Spiritual Differences

A subtle area of potential marital conflict is that of spiritual and religious differences between spouses. A deeply spiritual wife who enjoys family worship and church services will resent the fact that her husband fails to lead out in family worship and in the religious instruction of the children. She will be tempted to view her husband as spiritually immature, unable to fulfill his role as the spiritual leader of their home.

If the wife makes her husband feel like a loser in the area of spiritual leadership, it will make it harder for him to take an aggressive spiritual role because by doing so, he might prove his wife right. By judging her husband as a loser in the spiritual realm, she gives him a reason to become antagonistic toward her and her God.

It will not help for the wife to say to her husband, "I fervently hope and pray that you will become the kind of spiritual leader God is expecting you to be." That may sound spiritual, but it will only serve to make the husband feel inadequate at that moment. Judgmental criticism, even when expressed with pious-sounding rhetoric, antagonizes and alienates.

A creative alternative could be for the wife to ask her husband, for example, "What can we do to enhance our family worship? Would you like me to look for some devotional reading at a Christian bookstore? You have been so busy lately; would you like me to plan for family worship for the next few days? Is there something that makes it hard for you to pray, read the Bible or go to church? Is there anything I can do to help you?" Questions such as these, asked in the right spirit, will make the husband feel accepted and respected. This in turn will motivate him to live up to his wife's expectations by taking a more active role in the religious life of his family.

Most marital conflicts can be resolved when husband and wife enjoy a healthy fellowship with God. If one or both partners lose this fellowship, then the possibility of resolving conflicts is greatly reduced because they are no longer able to bring their problems together to the Lord in prayer and seek His solution.

4. Vocational Tensions

Happiness in a marriage relationship is closely tied to professional success and productivity. A man who is successful in his work will enjoy the respect of his wife. On the other hand, a man who performs poorly in his work and is frequently laid off can lose the respect of his wife and children.

At a time of increased automation in industry, even highly skilled workers are laid off and unable to secure new jobs. In other instances, there are good workers employed in industries plagued by frequent strikes that use up all their family savings. Experiences such as these can create conflicts in the home because when a man is unable to fulfill his role as bread winner, he is apt to become discouraged, irritable, and take his frustrations out on his wife and children.

There are also situations in which a man is embarrassed by his low-paying job which does not satisfy his wife's or his own financial expectations. This causes him to feel unhappy at work and defeated at home. To meet the financial needs of the home, it may become necessary for the wife and mother to seek employment, even though she enjoys being at home. The family may have to accept a reduction in their standard of living.

Conflicts can also develop when the husband fails to understand and to lighten the overwhelming burden his wife carries as a housewife at home and wage-earner at the office or factory. Men who are critical of their wives' contribution will weaken the self-image of their wives. A woman needs the same support in her vocation as a wife and wage-earner that a man needs in his profession. To support each other vocationally, a couple needs to recognize the unique gifts or talents each of them has received from God. 1 Corinthians 12:11 tells us that the Holy Spirit "apportions [gifts] to each one individually as he wills."

Since no couple can totally avoid vocational and/or financial stress, it is important that both spouses be strongly committed to support each other in times of distress. Their faith in God's promise to supply their needs (Phil 4:19) gives them reason to do their best in planning prudently for the future while leaving the rest in the care of Him who holds their future in His hands.

5. Role Conflicts

Closely related to vocational tensions is the inability or unwillingness on the part of the husband or the wife to fulfill their respective roles. Conflicts develop, for example, when the husband insists that the Bible gives him the right to boss his wife and children and the wife resents the domineering and tyrannical behavior of her husband. Such role conflicts, if not properly resolved, will almost inevitably lead to marital break-ups.

In view of the importance of respecting the proper role distinctions taught in the Bible in order to ensure the happiness and stability of the marriage covenant, we shall devote the whole following chapter to this question. We shall examine what it means from a Biblical perspective for the husband to be the "head" and for the wife to be the "helper." We shall see that practicing headship does not mean lording over the wife and children, but rather providing a caring leadership that will ensure their physical, spiritual, and social wellbeing. Similarly, practicing submission does not mean serving the husband as a slave, but rather willingly and joyfully accepting the husband's loving leadership.

6. Family Crises

Another source of marital conflicts is the unexpected crises in the family. When a spouse is suddenly or gradually incapacitated by a crippling disease, the other spouse may have difficulty in coping with the new situation. When a woman goes through menopause, the husband may develop a subconscious alienation and hostility toward her.

Conflicts may also arise from the death of a child or a loved one. Death is never easy to accept, but it can be especially devastating when a loved one is suddenly snatched by an untimely death through accident or illness. Some parents are unable to accept the loss of a child and to adjust to the new reality. Their repressed anger and pain can make them nervous, irritable, and hostile toward each other.

Sudden changes can severely test the inner strengths of a couple. A husband and wife's ability to cope with changes is largely determined by the depth of their faith in God and their commitment to one another. As Christians, we must learn to accept sudden illness or loss of a loved one as permitted by a loving God who has our best interest at heart. Many times it is impossible for us to understand why a faithful Christian or an innocent child should suffer or suddenly die. Paul himself tells us that three times he besought the Lord to remove from him the "thorn in the flesh," whatever affliction that may have been. But the Lord told him, "My grace is sufficient for you, for my power is made perfect in weakness" (2 Cor 12:9).

Sudden changes in family life caused by sickness and death have served to draw countless couples closer together as they have sought greater divine strength and grace to meet the crisis. Christians can endure sorrow better than those who have no hope (1 Thess 4:13-18) because they have inner spiritual resources enabling them to hope in the face of despair.

7. In-Law Difficulties

Relationships with in-laws can severely test marital relationships. Problems arise when husband and wife do not break away sufficiently from their parental families or when they go to the other extreme by ignoring them altogether.

The mother-in-law is often blamed for many marital conflicts and has been the butt of more jokes than has any other kinship member. But even though the mother-in-law stereotype is well entrenched in our culture, most couples have no problems relating to their mother-in-law. There are situations, however, where either mother-in-law can create real problems in the marital relationships of their children. For example, a domineering mother who has always made decisions for her daughter may try to make them for her even after marriage. She may tell her what to cook, what furniture or drapes to purchase and how to relate to her husband. The same can be true of a domineering father who insists that the son purchase a certain kind of car or home.

In such cases, either of the spouses may object to their in-laws' interference in their own personal decisions. A conflict can easily arise if spouses feel obligated to follow the advice of their own parents rather than the advice of their mates. It is important for a couple to recognize that advice from parents may be helpful, but it is not binding upon them. They must have the right and freedom to make their own decisions.

Marital conflicts can also be caused by the inability of spouses to accept their in-laws for no apparent reason other than incompatible personalities. They may be members of the same church and belong to the same social class and yet feel an open dislike for each other. In such a case, it is virtually impossible to enjoy social interaction between the young couple and their parental family. Placing the blame on the mate will only serve to make matters worse. If efforts to change the situation fail, couples must learn to accept it, showing proper respect to their in-laws and drawing closer to one another to compensate for the missing friendship of their in-laws.

8. Sexual Adjustments

The failure to attain a satisfactory sexual relationship is often a major cause of marital conflicts and breakups. We have seen in chapter 2 that from a Biblical perspective, the function of sex within marriage is both unitive and procreative, or, we might say, relational and procreational. Sexual intercourse is a relational act that engenders a sense of oneness while allowing the possibility of bringing a new life into this world.

Unitive Function of Sex. The Bible recognizes that one of the reasons for marriage is to enable husband and wife to fulfill each other's sexual needs. In 1 Corinthians 7:3-5, Paul writes: "The husband should give to his wife her conjugal rights, and likewise the wife to her husband. For the wife does not rule over her own body, but the husband does; likewise the husband does not rule over his own body, but the wife does. Do not refuse one another except perhaps by agreement for a season, that you may devote yourselves to prayer; but then come together again, lest Satan tempt you through lack of self-control." What this means is that a Christian couple should seek to meet each other's sexual needs. A satisfactory sexual relationship is very important to the success of the total relationship between husband and wife.

Psychological Factors. Conflicts in the sexual relationship often reflect the attitudes, tensions, and mood of the total relationship. Some couples blame poor sexual adjustment for the breakup of their marriages, when the real cause of their inadequate sexual relationship is disharmony in their total relationship. A couple who has been arguing during the day about money, their children's education, their in-laws, or vacation travel, can hardly be in the mood for making love when they retire at night. This is particularly true for the wife.

James Jauncey notes that "it is important for a husband to realize that a wife's sexual ardor is highly sensitive to psychological factors. If he has been criticizing her or has been unpleasant to her in any way, she will be cold as ice. Generally, he will have to put these matters right first before she will consent to his arms."[2] Couples experiencing problems in their sexual relationships must examine their total marital relationships to determine whether or not differences in other areas affect their sex life.

Fatigue. Several other factors can cause problems in sexual relationships. Fatigue on the part of one or both partners is one of them. Dwight H. Small rightly points out that "Many Christian couples are guilty of being so occupied with living as to leave no time for loving."[3] A young mother who is exhausted after caring for her young children the whole day may not have any energy or desire left for a sexual relationship. The same may be true of young spouses working and studying hard to finish their education. The stress of their studies and work can adversely affect their sexual functioning. This may cause additional stress if the husband or wife becomes upset at being unable to function sexually. In such cases, the thoughtful partner needs to provide closeness and intimacy to the stressed partner without demanding sexual participation.

Difference in Male-Female Sexual Needs. At a more general level, conflicts in sexual relationships may result from failing to understand the difference between a woman's and a man's sexual needs. Simply stated, women tend to be stimulated more by the emotional and romantic aspect of the sexual relationship while men are more stimulated by the physical aspect. The absence of romantic tenderness can inhibit the sexual response of a woman, but not necessarily that of a man. This means that when a husband insists on having sex without preparing his wife emotionally for the experience, she may resent "being used" rather than being loved.

Women also tend to be more cyclical than men in their sexual desire. After a sexual experience, a woman may not desire to have sex again for several days. Instead, a man's sexual drive is more constant. In the book *The Act of Marriage*, Tim LaHaye explains that a man's sex drive is connected to his ability "to be the aggressor, provider, and leader of his family. The woman who resents her husband's sex drive while enjoying his aggressive leadership had better face the fact that she cannot have one without the other."[4]

A man experiences immediate release during sexual intercourse while a woman enjoys the tenderness before, during, and after intercourse. Understanding these differences can help a couple avoid conflicts and resentment in their sexual relationships. Above all, it is important for husband and wife to maintain an attitude of love, care and concern for one another. The Biblical principle that "it is more blessed to give than to receive" (Acts 20:35) applies to every phase of the marital relationship, including the sex life.

Lack of Trust. Conflicts in the sexual relationship may also result from a lack of trust. Unless husband and wife fully trust each other, they cannot experience physical intimacy. The reason is simple. Physical intimacy depends upon emotional and psychological intimacy. When there is a lack of mutual trust, emotional intimacy is destroyed, and physical intimacy is impossible.

Struggle for dominance can also affect a sexual relationship. When the husband or the wife is struggling to dominate the other, they may use sex as a weapon in their power struggle. This may happen when one partner refuses to respond sexually to the other or when one uses sex to obtain concessions.

Poor Communication. At the root of many conflicts in sexual relationships is the failure to communicate. One partner cannot know what is pleasing or annoying to the other without being told. If a husband and wife want to have a satisfying sexual life, they need to discuss their needs and desires openly. A husband may expect to see his wife come to bed in an attractive nightgown and not in flannel pajamas with curlers in her hair. For her part, the wife may wish to see her husband come to bed shaved and showered. Unless expectations such as these are properly communicated, one or both partners will most likely not be sexually responsive.

Sex in marriage can be a source of frustration and conflicts or of satisfaction and intimacy. A couple who wants their sex life to be what God intends it to be must live in accordance with God's principles for the marriage covenant: being faithful, caring, and maintaining open and honest communication.

9. The Use of Money

Marriage counselors report that the chief cause of marital conflicts in both Christian and non-Christian families is the use of money.[5] Lloyd Saxton summarizes recent research, saying, "All recent studies indicate that married couples quarrel over money more than anything else, that economic factors are closely related to marital stability and critical to marital adjustment, and that economic stress is a major cause of marital failure."[6]

In the average family, there is never enough money left over after the bills are paid to supply all the desires of the husband and wife. The result is that many couples spend restless nights arguing over financial matters.

Money as Power. Marital disputes over money often are not really over dollars and cents but over who controls the spending. A couple may fight over certain expenditures, not so much because they really care about the money that was spent, but because the money was spent without previous approval of one of the partners. To retaliate over the fact that the husband bought a chain saw without consulting her, a wife may buy a sewing machine or something equally expensive.

The balance of power in a family is often tipped in favor of the partner earning more money. In most cases, it is the husband who exercises the right to make major decisions because of his greater income. On the other hand, as the wife's income and contribution to the family budget increases, so her share of influence in the major decisions in the family is likely to increase. Changes in the balance of earning power are likely to cause tensions and conflicts.

In a Christian home, money should be seen as a shared resource and not as a source of power. When money is used as a source of power, it becomes a cause of problems. It is, therefore, important for Christian couples to examine their attitudes toward money. If husbands or wives recognize that they use money as a tool to control the other, they must deal with the problem. Each must ask God for grace to learn to use money not to control but to serve each other.

The question of who handles the money should be resolved on the basis of competence and not on the basis of gender. Ultimately, it does not make any difference whether the husband or the wife handles the money, so long as it is the most capable person who does it. Some men feel that their masculinity is threatened if they allow the wife to manage the family finances. In most cases, the husband may be the one to assume such a responsibility, if this arrangement is mutually agreeable. But if the husband, or the wife for that matter, is a compulsive spender, it is wise to let the most responsible and competent partner assume the role of money manager.

Some couples choose to divide the financial responsibilities. In my home, for example, my wife is responsible for buying clothing, groceries, household goods, and for paying the children's tuition. On my part, I assume responsibility for such items as taxes, insurance, car and house payments and repairs.

Money as Status. People are often judged by how much money they make. Since we do not wear our financial statements on our foreheads or sleeves, we reveal our financial status by the things we purchase. These are known as *status symbols.* They include such items as cars, clothes, club memberships, exotic vacations, and homes. Disagreements over the purchase of items such as these may in fact be disagreements over status. The wife may wish to increase her status by moving into a better neighborhood or by buying more expensive furniture. The husband, on the other hand, may be indifferent toward such status symbols or may wish to show his status by buying a Mercedes and parking it in the driveway.

The attempt to "shore up one's ego" by purchasing expensive items causes conflicts when a husband and wife desire different status symbols. Moreover, a couple that needs to buy something newer and better than do the neighbors to reassure themselves that they are important, reveals their inner insecurity and immaturity because only "children depend upon others for their self regard. Those who reach adulthood and still depend upon others for their feelings about themselves have never grown up."[7]

Money as Love. Love toward a person is often expressed by giving presents. A man and a woman often give presents to each other when dating and later when married. The presents which cost money or consist of money may be seen as expressions of love. This could mean that if the husband or wife stops giving presents, he or she may be seen as withholding love.

A wife may feel that her husband does not love her any more because he does not bring her presents as he did before they were married. Such a feeling can cause frustration, resentment and conflict. The reason a husband may temporarily suspend the practice of bringing presents to his wife may not necessarily stem from lack of love and concern for her, but from a tight financial situation which does not allow extra money for presents. A love relationship based on money or things money can buy is essentially a selfish relationship.

Scripture reminds us that "the love of money is the root of all evil; it is through this craving that some have wandered away from the faith and pierced their hearts with many pangs" (1 Tim 4:10). This warning applies to marital relationships. When marriage partners condition their love to each other upon the economic or material benefits to be derived from the other, they will eventually pierce "their hearts with many pangs." The reason for this fact is that it is difficult to satisfy a partner who constantly craves for money or goods.

Money as Independence. A good income offers a sense of security and independence. For a Christian, however, real security is to be found not in the uncertainty of riches but in the assurance of God's promise to provide for our daily needs (Matt 6:25-34). The rich man of Christ's parable who thought to ensure his future financial security by building larger barns to store his abundant harvest was told by God: "Fool! This night your soul is required of you; and the things you have prepared, whose will they be?" (Luke 12:20). Paul charges Timothy to "command those who are rich in this present world not to be arrogant nor to put their hope in wealth, which is so uncertain, but to put their hope in God, who richly provides us with everything for our enjoyment" (1 Tim 6:17).

The sense of financial independence can harm a marriage relationship when an independent income by the husband or the wife produces an independent spirit. There are working couples who wish to maintain their economic independence by controlling their respective incomes. Such an independent spirit can harm a marriage relationship since the husband and wife will often argue about who is responsible for what.

An independent income may produce an independent spirit in the wife. Tim LaHaye says, "I am convinced that one of the reasons young married couples divorce so readily today is because the wife is not economically dependent upon her husband; whenever difficulties and pressures arise, she can say, as a young lady said to me, 'I don't have to take this kind of thing; I can live by myself.'"[8]

A Christian couple must seek by God's grace to resist the temptation to undermine the "one flesh" union by developing feelings of independence from one another. As a successful Christian life can only be lived by being constantly dependent upon God's enabling grace, so a successful marriage relationship can only be maintained when a husband and wife learn constantly to depend upon one another.

As we have seen, money is not only a medium enabling us to meet our various needs, but it also represents power, status, love, and independence. It is no wonder that money can be a major cause of marital conflicts. That is why it is important for a couple to develop proper attitudes toward money, using it responsibly, not as a weapon of power to make decisions, but as a shared resource to meet common needs.

PART II: HOW TO HANDLE MARITAL CONFLICTS

Some conflicts, as we have just seen, are inevitable in every marriage because no two persons have exactly the same personalities, attitudes, and values. Some of the differences do not come to light until the couple has been married for some time. When the differences appear, some conflicts are bound to arise.

There is nothing wrong with conflicts, provided they serve a constructive purpose by improving communication and strengthening marital relationships. Sometimes conflicts can bring smoldering resentments to surface, which, left unresolved, can destroy a marriage or at least cost the psychological health of one or both partners.

Conflicts, per se, are not necessarily bad or sinful. It is the *way* conflicts are handled that determines their impact on the marriage relationship. Conflicts may destroy a marriage, but they may also strengthen it. A successful Christian marriage is not necessarily one in which there are no conflicts, but rather one in which the partners have learned to resolve their differences openly, honestly, and constructively.

Unfortunately, in many instances, conflicts are detrimental to the marriage relationship because they become a way to attack, wound, and diminish the other partner. When a couple engages in name-calling, ridiculing, and belittling of each other, the result will only widen the gap between them. To prevent conflicts from deteriorating into an all-out war, it is important to observe the seven basic rules outlined below. These rules, if obeyed, will enable a Christian couple to handle their conflicts constructively, turning them into opportunities for removing obstacles to a stronger marriage.

1. Be Committed to Preserving Your Marriage Covenant

The first rule in handling marital conflicts successfully is *to be totally committed to preserving your marriage covenant.* It is only within the context of a loving and irrevocable commitment that marital conflicts can be successfully resolved. When couples are determined not to let anything or anyone put asunder the marital unions established by God (Matt 19:6), they can risk being honest and open in discussing their differences.

If we are deeply committed to preserving our marriage covenants, we will not allow any issue to divide us. We will not permit any argument to degenerate into a hostile confrontation. We will not waste our time quarreling over things we cannot change.

There are many differences in marriage that by God's grace can be overcome, but there are also inherited or acquired characteristics which we cannot change. There is no point in my wife's criticizing me for my baldness or for my heavy Italian accent. Similarly, there is no point my criticizing my wife for the shape of her nose or for thefew extra pounds she has gained since we got married almost thirty years ago. Being committed to preserving our marriage covenant means to ask God to make us willing to accept what we cannot change, to give us courage to change what needs to be changed, and to give us wisdom to know the difference.

A total commitment is only possible by divine grace. It is God who gives us the power to hold fast to our commitments. God is interested in our marriages. He not only joins our lives together, but He is helping us stay together when conflicts arise. He wants us to enjoy happy, harmonious marriage relationships. He will move heaven and earth, if necessary, to resolve any conflicts that may arise in our relationships. But He needs our cooperation.

We must take God as our partner into our marriage relationships by keeping the fire ever burning on the altar of our daily worship. We must begin and close each day praying together, renewing our commitment to God and to each other. We must ask God daily for the enabling power of the Holy Spirit to be truthful, kind, patient and understanding toward each other. The couple that prays together stays together. As our love for God increases, our love for one another will grow stronger and our capacity to resolve conflicts will become greater.

2. Be Honest and Fair in Handling Conflicts

A second important rule in handling marital conflicts is *to be honest and fair*. Couples who are committed to preserving their marriage covenants will not engage in "dirty fighting," hitting below the belt, or lying to win the argument. Paul alludes to this principle in Ephesians 4:25 where he says: "Therefore, putting away falsehood, let everyone speak the truth with his neighbor, for we are members one of another." The verses that follow contain other significant principles to be considered. The particular tense used in Greek for "putting away falsehood" (aorist participle) conveys the idea of something already done at a specific point in time. Thus, a literal translation would read: "*Having* put away falsehood, let everyone speak truthfully with his neighbor."

Applied to a marriage relationship, this text challenges husbands and wives who have laid aside falsehood from their lives to speak truthfully to one another when conflicts arise. It is essential for a couple to commit themselves to an honest relationship so that when conflicts develop, they will not fall into the trap of lying to each other just to win the argument. From the very beginning of their relationship, a couple should commit themselves to being totally honest with each other. They need to say: "Let us not try to kid one another by playing games. I promise to be honest with you and I want you to be honest with me. If a conflict occurs, let us not resort to unfair practices to win."

The object of conflict should not be not to find fault or to assess blame but to resolve problems. Marriage is not a competitive sport but a cooperative endeavor. When a problem occurs, the goal should not be to determine who is right and who is wrong, but to find a satisfactory solution. "The attitude of partners," as Stephen Grunlan puts it, "should not be a win/lose approach; that is, every solution involving a winner and a loser. Rather, the attitude of partners should be a win/win approach. The couple faces the problem together and when a solution is found, they both win."[9]

When the concern of spouses is for each to win the argument, ultimately, they both become losers: first, because they will often resort to unfair tactics to win, and second, because the outcome of the conflict will be a weaker relationship where feelings of resentment and bitterness remain and eventually lead to new confrontations. Thus, it is most important for a couple to handle conflicts with honesty and fairness, seeking the best solution to a problem, regardless of whose idea it is.

3. Keep Your Anger Under Control

Besides being committed to honesty and fairness in handling conflicts in marriage, the third rule is *to keep your anger under control*. Paul alludes to this principle in Ephesians 4:26 where he says: "Be angry but do not sin." We noticed that in the preceding verse Paul exhorts us to speak truthfully to one another. This does not mean that a Christian should never feel or express anger. Rather it means that truthful persons will not allow their anger to become undisciplined and uncontrolled.

Something essential would be missing in a marital partner who is unable to feel or express anger. Obviously, there must be a right kind of anger. There are situations where a partner will be aroused to the point of indignation by overt wrongs committed by the other partner. A marriage covenant would lose its meaning if, for example, spouses would not become angry at the infidelity of their partners. This verse tells us that there is a place in the Christian life for righteous indignation. God says: "I permit you to be angry, but don't let your anger lead you to sin."

We all know that anger becomes sinful when is expressed through outbursts of temper, profane or insulting language, or physical violence. Uncontrolled anger can become a deadly weapon which must be banished from the Christian life. But the anger which is disciplined, selfless, and pure, can be a great moral force in the world. This world would have lost much without the righteous indignation of Jesus against human hypocrisy (Mark 3:5; John 2:13-17).

As sinful creatures, we are all subject to feelings of pride, selfishness, fatigue, and anxiety which sometimes break out in uncontrolled outbursts of anger and irritation. This ugly side of our nature is revealed especially in marriage, when we treat it as the place for blowing off our steam and releasing our frustrations. At home, we think we can safely unload our temper, anger, and tensions. Our angry outbursts, offensive remarks, and sharp retorts wound our partners who may also reveal their ugly nature by retaliating with similar outbursts of rancor.

Angry words, once spoken even unintentionally, are deadly weapons that can wound and crush our mates permanently. Just as

God's word does not return empty but accomplishes its purpose (Is 55:11), so our words will accomplish their purpose, even when we wish that they would not. A man who in a moment of anger tells his wife, "Let's face it, I do not feel like loving you anymore," will inflict upon her a permanent wound. So do cutting remarks such as, "No wonder you act so irresponsibly. Your father died in a mental hospital." Such cutting words cannot be easily forgotten. Your mate may later say, "I forgive you," but deep inside, the hurt caused by those words may never be healed. Angry words can gradually break that inner covenant bond that holds marriages together. It is therefore essential to learn by divine grace to keep our anger under control.

If a conflict gets out of control in a marriage, the only way to still the storm is for the more spiritually mature partner to break the cycle of mutual attack by refusing to retaliate for the hurt received. This is the only way to bring to an end a marital fight.

4. Choose an Appropriate Time to Discuss a Problem

This leads us to consider a fourth rule which is *to choose an appropriate time to discuss a problem.* The wise man Solomon notes that there is "a time to keep silence, and a time to speak . . . a time for war, and a time for peace" (Eccl 3:7-8). This is certainly true of marital conflicts. Marriage counselors agree that *timing* is critical to constructive resolution of conflicts. George Bach and Peder Wyden write: "Far too many fights become needlessly aggravated because the complaint opens fire when his partner really is in an inappropriate frame of mind or is trying to dash off to work or trying to concentrate on some long-delayed chore that he has finally buckled down to. Indeed there are times when failure to delay—or to advance—the timing of a fight can have cataclysmic consequences."[10]

There may be times when an issue has to be resolved immediately. In most cases, however, conflicts develop over a period of time and can be temporarily put off until an appropriate time. This is the procedure followed in most organizations, and it should be followed in marriage.

A basic rule to remember regarding the timing for discussing problems is to avoid raising them *just before* anything that will not provide adequate time to satisfactorily deal with them. For example, the time just before a meal, just before going to bed, just before making love, just before going to work, or just before going to church, is inappropriate for dealing with unpleasant disagreements.

The best time to discuss sensitive issues or serious differences is when both husband and wife are well rested, wide awake and feeling at ease. At such favorable times one can be more rational, considerate, and accommodating. A wise husband or wife who knows the importance of proper timing for discussing serious and disagreeable things will say, "I don't think this is the best time to discuss this matter. Why don't we deal with it later on when the children are in bed or after we have rested!" Having said this, we must set a time and keep the appointment.

Another important rule regarding timing is not to delay the discussion unduly. Anger, conflicts, and negative feelings must be resolved as soon as possible because the longer we postpone mending a conflict, the more difficult it will be to resolve it later. Paul emphasizes this important rule in Ephesians 4:26-27, saying: "Do not let the sun go down on your anger, and give no opportunity to the devil." This means that we must never go to sleep with bitter feelings or thoughts against our partners. If there has been a conflict during the day or in the evening, we must make peace and banish any lingering negative feelings before we go to sleep. The longer we allow bitter feelings to flourish, the more difficult it will be to eradicate them later.

5. Stick to the Issue at Hand

A fifth important rule to remember in handling marital conflicts is *to stick to the issue at hand.* When a couple chooses an appropriate time to discuss a certain problem (rule four), they should use that time to address that particular issue and not to bring up all their past problems.

Stephen Grunlan relates the story of a woman who complained to her friend that her husband became historical every time they had an argument. "Her friend corrected her by saying, 'You mean he becomes *hysterical.*' 'No,' replied the woman, 'I mean *historical.* Whenever we have an argument, he brings up every related problem since we have been married.'"[11]

Marriage counselors emphasize the importance of sticking to the issue at hand. Dragging past grievances into the matter under discussion will hinder the resolution of the immediate conflict. It may also open old wounds and thus aggravate the situation.

Sticking to the issue also involves avoiding sweeping generalization and accusation. The following argument will serve to illustrate this point:

Husband: You left the lawn mower out in the backyard yesterday and now the motor is soaked from last night's rain. When will you ever learn to put things away in the proper place.

Wife: Look who is talking. You leave your shoes all over the house, and I have to pick them up and put them away all the time.

In this argument, the lawn mower is generalized and used as a pretext to launch a sweeping accusation. The wife defends herself by launching a counterattack totally unrelated to the issue involved. The end result is that a minor incident can turn into a hostile confrontation. How different the outcome would have been if the husband had stuck to the original issue and the wife had been willing to accept responsibility. Imagine the conversation going something like this:

Husband: Honey, did you know that you left the lawn mower out in the backyard yesterday, and the motor got soaked with rain last night?

Wife: Oh no! I completely forgot to bring in the lawn mower. I'm sorry. Will you be able to get the motor started now?

Husband: I think so, but I will have to pull out the spark plug and dry it. I hope you won't leave the lawn mower out again.

Wife: No, I'll be sure to bring it in next time. I'm sorry for causing you extra work.

Husband: No problem. Just remember it next time.

This conversation brings a happy ending to the incident of the lawn mower, leaving the question of the shoes for another discussion. The husband disciplines himself by sticking to the issue of the lawn mower while the wife acknowledges her responsibility. An apology and forgiveness settles the issue. Minor incidents such as this can be easily resolved when partners stick to the issue and acknowledge responsibility. Failure to do so can cause minor problems to balloon into serious altercations.

6. Listen Carefully and Speak Tactfully

Closely related to a responsible attitude of sticking to the issue at hand (rule five) is rule six: *listen carefully to the words of your mate and speak tactfully.* Conflicts in marriage should serve to improve communication by helping partners know better how each feels and thinks about an issue.

Communication presupposes listening. Learning to listen carefully to the words of a mate is essential in handling conflicts. Yet this rule of effective listening is most difficult to implement because in a conflict situation when a person is talking, the other is not listening but is thinking about how to respond. The louder our voices and the uglier our words, the less our spouses will listen and the poorer will be our communication.

It is important to listen carefully to understand what the real issue is. For example, a husband may complain over the fact that his wife bought a new vacuum cleaner rather than having the old one repaired. In reality, what he may be complaining about is the fact that his wife did not consult him. He may fear that his wife does not think that he is responsible for the home. Or a wife may complain that her husband spends little time with her when what she really means is that her husband does not seem to care enough for her.

When a couple argues and fights, they need to make sure that they understand what they are really fighting about. This is possible only by learning to listen carefully to each other and to ask questions that may help uncover those hidden feelings which are the cause of the conflict.

Understanding the issue through careful listening and questioning is the first important step. Equally important is the next step of speaking tactfully and graciously. Paul expresses this principle in Ephesians 4:29, saying: "Let no evil talk come out of your mouths, but only such as is good for edifying, as fits the occasion, that it may impart grace to those who hear."

A Christian is called upon to refrain from harsh, evil speaking and to engage instead in edifying speech which imparts grace and encouragement to others. This requires learning how to be courteous and tactful in our speaking. Tact involves being sincere and open while at the same time showing respect for the other person's feelings, and being careful not to hurt them unnecessarily. Christ is our perfect example of tactfulness and courtesy even toward His persecutors. As His followers we should manifest the same attitude, especially toward our family members.

True courtesy and tactfulness in speech is not learned merely by practising a few rules of etiquette, but through a renewal of the heart. It is only when the heart has been touched by the love of Christ that people will feel motivated to listen carefully and to speak tactfully to all, especially to their marital partners.

7. Be Willing to Forgive and to Forget

The success of the preceding six rules in resolving marital conflicts is largely dependent upon the seventh rule which is *to be willing to forgive and to forget the wrongs of your mate.* Ideally, marital conflicts should always be handled in a controlled and rational way, leading to greater communication between mates. Realistically, however, in every marriage there are times when conflicts become uncontrolled and irrational. There are situations when, because of fatigue, pride, selfishness, or anxiety, the ugly side of our nature breaks out in angry outbursts, cutting remarks, abusive language, or irrational accusations. Such behavior awakens the equally ugly side in our mates who may retaliate similarly with angry and abusive language.

The only way to bring a conflict which has gotten out of control to a satisfactory end is for one partner to break the retaliation cycle by forgiving the other partner for the hurt received. In Christian marriages forgiveness must be patterned after the forgiveness Christ offers us. He forgives us in spite of the pain and sorrow we have caused Him. On the cross, Christ forgave those who crucified Him, saying: "Father, forgive them; for they know not what they do" (Luke 23:34). When we forgive, we acknowledge that we have suffered a real wrong which by God's grace we choose to forget.

In a covenant marriage, we recognize the sin that our mates have committed against us. We do not explain away the sinful behaviour of our mate by saying, "He did not mean what he said," or "Probably I deserve what he did to me," or "I do not feel really hurt by what he did to me." Rather, we realistically recognize that we have suffered wrong, but we do not allow such wrongs to weaken our mutual commitment. Why? First, because we recognize that we are sinful beings who sometimes hurt each other terribly. We violate the deepest trust of our mates. We trample upon their unconditional love. Second, because we realize that since God can forgive our mates, so can we.

Forgiveness in a marriage covenant must be as unconditional as is Christ's forgiveness to us. In Ephesians 4:32, Paul writes: "And be kind to one another, tenderhearted, forgiving one another, as God in Christ forgave you." God forgave us in Christ, not after we promised to reform and obey, but "while we were yet sinners" (Rom 5:8). In the same way, we must forgive our mates not only if they promise never to wrong us again, but simply because God in Christ has forgiven us.

This means that when we forgive, we must be willing to forget the wrong we have suffered. The Scripture reassures us that God's forgiveness involves forgetting our sinful actions: "I, I am He who blots out your transgressions for my own sake, I will not remember your sins" (Is 43:25). "As far as the east is from the west, so far does he remove our transgressions from us" (Ps 103:17; cf. Jer 31:34; 2 Cor 5:17-19).

Forgiveness in a marriage covenant involves forgetting the wrongs a mate has committed and choosing not to recount them later. If we continue to remember and to bring up past grievances every time a conflict breaks out, then we have not truly forgiven our mates because genuine forgiveness means blotting out past wrongs from memory (Acts 3:19). Such forgiveness is possible when we personally have experienced the blessing of God's forgiveness in our lives. When the love of Christ has flooded our hearts, we will have the motivating power to forgive.

Genuine forgiveness makes us free to love, to trust, and to grow with our mates. It enables us to break the cycle of retaliatory attacks. If we have been wounded by the words or actions of our mates, we refuse to retaliate, instead returning words or actions in kindness. Such an attitude can calm tensions and create a pleasant atmosphere conducive to a rational discussion of the problem.

A couple willing to forgive each other will also help each other to repent of wrong doings. In the Christian life, we are led to repentance by the convicting power of the Holy Spirit which reveals to us our sinfulness and God's forgiving grace. When we experience His forgiving grace in our lives, we feel sorry for our past sins, and we sincerely want to walk in newness of life. The same is true in the marital relationship. If my wife forgives me, I will feel sorry for my wrong doings, and I will seek not to betray her love and trust again. Forgiveness gives us a chance to begin again and develop a stronger relationship based on the power of forgiving love which can conquer conflicts and reconcile us to God and to one another.

CONCLUSION

Some conflicts are inevitable in every marriage because no two persons have exactly the same personality, attitude, and values. A successful Christian marriage is not necessarily one in which there are no conflicts, but rather one in which partners have learned to handle their conflicts constructively, turning them into opportunities for improving communication and building a stronger marriage covenant. We have found that seven basic rules can help in turning conflicts into constructive opportunities.

First, we must be totally committed to preserving our marriage covenant. It is only within the context of a loving and steadfast commitment that marital conflicts can be successfully resolved.

Second, we must be honest and fair in handling marital conflicts, avoiding hitting below the belt or lying to win the argument. Our concern should be to find the best solution to the problem, without any thought of "winning " or "loosing."

Third, we must learn to keep our anger under control, avoiding outbursts of anger, insulting language, and cutting remarks. If the conflict gets out of control, the more spiritually mature partner will seek to still the storm by refusing to retaliate for the hurt received.

Fourth, we must choose an appropriate time to discuss a problem, avoiding raising issues *just before* anything that would not provide adequate time to deal with them satisfactorily.

Fifth, we must learn to stick to the issue at hand, and not use the occasion to bring up past grievances. This includes avoiding sweeping generalizations and accusations.

Sixth, we must learn to listen carefully to the words of our mates and to speak tactfully. Such an approach will make it possible to uncover hidden feelings which may be the cause of the conflict.

Seventh, we must be willing to forgive and to forget the wrongs of our mates, not because we are morally upright, but because we have experienced God's forgiving grace in our lives. By learning to forgive and to forget, we become free to love, to trust, and to grow into a stronger covenant relationship.

NOTES TO CHAPTER IV

1. Cecil Osborne, *The Art of Understanding Your Mate* (Grand Rapids, 1970), p. 36.

2. James H. Jauncey, *Magic in Marriage* (Grand Rapids, 1966), p. 42.

3. Dwight Harvey Small, *Design for Christian Marriage* (Westwood, New Jersey, 1959), p. 89.

4. Tim and Beverley LaHaye, *The Act of Marriage* (Grand Rapids, 1976), p. 22.

5. See, for example, Robert O. Blood and Donald M. Wolfe, *Husband and Wife* (New York, 1960), p. 245; Marcia Lasswell and Thomas E. Lasswell, *Marriage and the Family* (Lexington, Massachussetts, 1982), p. 503.

6. Lloyd Saxton, *The Individual Marriage and the Family* (Belmont, California, 1980), p. 547.

7. W. Clark Ellzey, "Money, Marriage and Romance," in *The Marriage Affair,* ed. J. Allan Petersen (Wheaton, Illinois, 1971), p. 353.

8. Tim LaHaye, *How to Be Happy Though Married* (Wheaton, Illinois, 1978), p. 29.

9. Stephen A. Grunlan, *Marriage and the Family. A Christian Perspective* (Grand Rapids, 1984), p. 209.

10. George R. Bach and Peter Wyden, *The Intimate Enemy: How to Fight Fair in Love and Marriage* (New York, 1968), p. 70.

11. Stephen A. Grunlan (n. 9), p. 208.

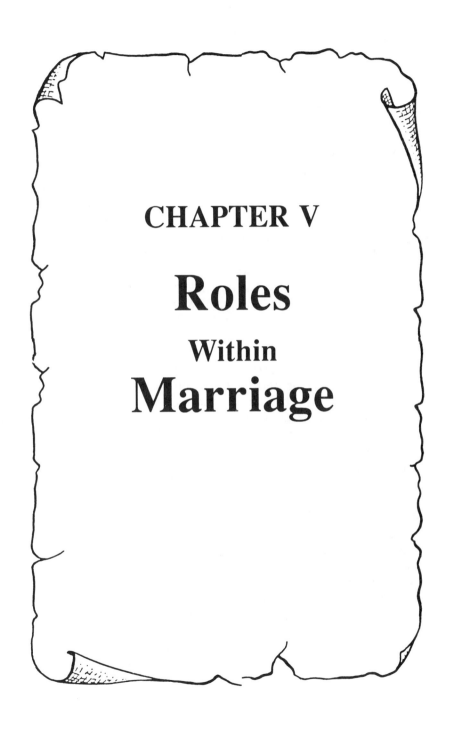

CHAPTER V

Roles
Within
Marriage

ROLES WITHIN MARRIAGE

The stability of the marriage covenant depends largely upon the way the husband and the wife fulfill their respective roles. Marriage counselors often point to "role conflicts" as a major cause for the breaking up of marriages. "Those of us who do marriage counseling," writes Paul Stevens, "realize that many marriages are struggling desperately at just this point. Some men insist that the Bible makes them responsible to God for the family. They are boss. Some women believe this is true and try for years to submit to a weak man or a tyrant. But there comes a day, almost inevitably, when the woman revolts. She may revolt by having a nervous breakdown, by getting a plane ticket and flying away, or by leaving him for another man."[1]

In a similar vein Robert C. Williamson writes: "In some cases the inability or failure to carry out a given role or a number of roles proves disastrous to the marriage. Differences in role perception are illustrated when the husband prefers the patriarchal pattern, and the wife looks forward to the equalitarian one. Divorce may be the only outcome for these role discrepancies."[2]

At the root of much of the role conflict within marital relationship are the different interpretations and applications of the Biblical teaching on husband-headship and wife-submission. The very mention of the terms "headship/submission" is anathema for many who during the last three decades have made the quantum leap from "Adam's rib to women's lib." Anyone who dares to drop the phrase "submission of the wife" into a conversation with a "woman's libber" risks the danger of being "categorized as some ignorant weirdo who believes in slave chambers of torture and one who promotes chaining women in a washroom. The very idea! I mean, what thinking person today can possibly imagine squashing a woman under the heels of a man . . . or shoving her in a corner, reducing her activities to changing diapers, doing dishes, checking off a grocery list, and mopping floors?"[3]

The widely publicized misrepresentation and rejection of the Biblical view of roles within marriage has been largely influenced by the Women's Liberation Movement which received renewed impetus in 1966 with the founding of the National Organization for Women (NOW). The radical groups in the movement promote the liberation of the wife from her submissive role through the abolition of marriage itself. Sheilia Cronan, a leader in the Women's Liberation Movement, unequivocally states: "Since marriage constitutes slavery for women, it is clear that the Women's Movement must concentrate on attacking this institution. Freedom for women cannot be won without the abolition of marriage."[4]

The more moderate groups take issue with the radicals who reject marriage altogether, promoting instead "role interchangeability" within marriage and full political, economic and civil equality of women in society. It must be said that many American women do not support the cry for equality of the Women's Liberation Movement. They realize that being the "weaker sex" entails privileges denied to men, thus making women "the favored sex."

Elsieliese Thorpe expresses this view, saying: "If they [the Women's Liberation Movement] don't stop their commotion, their rumbling of discontent and pleas for equality, we might end up getting what they are asking for. And who wants equality when we women are doing so much better now? Biologically, legally, temperamentally, and just about every other way that matters, we women are the favored sex."[5]

In some ways Thorpe's prediction is being fulfilled today as more and more women are treated as men in the working place by being asked to perform heavy manual tasks such as loading and unloading baggage at airports or by being expected to be back at work a few days or at the most a few weeks after the birth of their babies. Even worse, more and more women find themselves deserted by men who have been freed of their marital obligations by the feminist movement.

In her article "The Failure of Feminism" published in *Newsweek*, Kay Ebeling laments: "Today I see feminism as the Great Experiment That Failed, and women in my generation, its perpetrators, are the casualties. Many of us, including myself, are saddled with raising children alone. The resulting poverty makes us experts at

corn meal recipes and ways to find free recreation on weekends
. . . Feminism freed men, not women. Now men are spared the
nuisance of a wife and family support. After childbirth, if his wife's
waist does not return to 20 inches, the husband can go out and find
a more petite woman. It's far more difficult for the wife, now tied
with a baby, to find a new man."[6]

In the face of the "role confusion" existing in our society, it is
not difficult to realize why Christian couples are also confused
about their roles and often seek greater self-fulfillment by assuming different roles. To resist the societal trend bent on eliminating
or reversing roles within marriage, it is imperative for Christian
spouses and young people planning for marriage to study what God
has to say in Scripture regarding the proper roles for the husband
and the wife. The Biblical view of marital roles, as we shall see,
derives not from ancient patriarchal culture but from divine revelation. The acceptance of such a view provides the only solid
foundation for a marriage covenant.

Objectives of the Chapter. This chapter examines the meaning, implications, and applications of the Biblical principle of
husband-headship and wife-submission. The chapter is divided
into two parts. The first part considers the major New Testament
passages concerning the roles of husband and wife. An attempt will
be made to interpret the Biblical meaning of "headship" and
"submission." The second part examines the practical implications
and applications of the Biblical principle of headship/submission.
Specifically, we shall consider what it means from a practical
standpoint for the husband to practice headship and for the wife to
practice submission.

PART I:
THE INTERPRETATION OF THE HEADSHIP/
SUBMISSION TEXTS

The major New Testament passages concerning the roles of
husband and wife are Ephesians 5:18-33, Colossians 3:18, and 1
Peter 3:1-7. These passages are known as the "household codes"
(in German, *Haustafeln*), since they summarize the duties of the

various members of the household: the husband, the wife, the children, masters, and slaves. A strenuous effort has been made in recent times to reinterpret these and other passages in accordance with the "partnership paradigm" promoted by the Women's Liberation Movement. Three major interpretations are espoused by three different groups of scholars whom I shall designate as: (1) Liberal Feminists, (2) Evangelical Feminists, and (3) Biblical Feminists.

1. Three Interpretations

"**Liberal Feminists.**" Most liberal feminists concede that Scripture teaches the principle of husband-headship and wife-submission, but they argue that such a principle need not be taken seriously because it is time-bound, culturally conditioned, adrocentric (male-centered), rabbinic in origin, anti-feminist in nature, and hopelessly conditioned by a patriarchal mentality. Thus they *reject* the Biblical teaching on headship and submission.[7] Their final authority is their own critical, socio-cultural interpretation of Scripture which ultimately makes them victims of their own culturally conditioned interpretation. No attempt will be made to examine the arguments of Liberal Feminists since their rejection of the authority and applicability of Scripture offers no basis for any fruitful dialogue.

"**Evangelical Feminists.**" For the most part, Evangelical Feminists respect the authority of Scriptures, but they *reinterpret* those passages which speak of male-headship and female-submission in accordance with the partnership position. Husbands and wives are to be mutually submissive to one another and share responsibility in the home in a 50-50 arrangement.[8] Their arguments will be examined below.

"**Biblical Feminists.**" Whereas Liberal Feminists *reject* the Biblical teaching on headship and submission and the Evangelical Feminists *reinterpret* it, the Biblical Feminists *reaffirm* it. They maintain that the Bible clearly teaches that God has established functional role distinctions between husbands and wives—distinctions which do not imply superiority or inferiority but complementarity.[9]

This chapter is written from a Biblical Feminist's perspective. I will endeavor to examine the "household code" texts in order to establish the Biblical meaning and contemporary application of the husband-headship and wife-submission.

2. Head as "Source"

What did Paul mean when he wrote that "the head of a woman is her husband" (1 Cor 11:3) and that "the husband is the head of the wife" (Eph 5:23)? Historically these texts have been understood to mean that husbands have "authority over" their wives. Recently this interpretation has been challenged, especially by liberal and evangelical feminists who contend that the word "head" in such passages means "source" or "origin" rather than designating "authority over."[10] The implication of this interpretation is that Paul was not teaching that man "has authority over" (= head over) his wife, but rather that he is her "source" and consequently he must be especially concerned for her.

This interpretation is used by feminists to reject any form of wives' submission to their husbands and to argue for sexual equality and role-interchangeability. For example, Scanzoni and Hardesty write: "If we think of the term 'head' in the sense of *arche* (beginning, origin, source), we are again reminded of the *interdependence* of the sexes, each drawing life from the other."[11] This interdependence supposedly allows both spouses to fill the roles of father, mother, breadwinner, housekeeper in the home and the roles of pastor, elder or priest in the church.[12]

Modern Authors. The first to propound that "head" (*kephale*) in 1 Corinthians 11:3 should be understood as "origin" or "source" seems to have been Stephen Bedale in an article published in 1954.[13] Since then, numerous writers have expressed the same view.[14] Among them, the most influencial have been Berkeley and Alvera Mickelsen. In several articles, they have argued that Paul used the term "head" not in the sense of "authority or hierarchy" but rather in the sense of "source, base, derivation" in 1 Corinthians 11:3 and of "one who brings to completion" in Ephesians 5:23.[15] The implication of this interpretation is that the "head texts" do not preclude wives from serving as "head-leader" in the home and women from serving as "head-pastor, elder" in the church.

Arguments for "Source." Briefly stated, the various arguments advanced for interpreting "head" as "source" or "origin" rather than as "ruler or authority" fall into four categories:[16]

(1) Linguistic. In classical and contemporary Greek, "head" (*kephale*) does not normally mean "ruler" or "authority over."[17] The Mickelsens support this claim by appealing to the Liddell-Scott lexicon where the meaning of "authority over" is not listed. Instead, this lexicon cites two examples (Herodotus 4, 91 and *Orphic Fragments* 21a) where "head" is used with the meaning of "source."[18] Thus, it is argued that the meaning of "head" as the ruling part of the organism "would be unintelligible to St. Paul or his readers."[19]

(2) Cultural. The ancient world did not view the head as the seat of thinking and the executive part of the body. "In St. Paul's day, according to popular psychology, both Greek and Hebrew, a man reasoned and purposed, not 'with his head,' but 'in his heart.'"[20] Consequently, the metaphor of "source" is supposedly present in the "head texts" (1 Cor 11:3; Eph 5:23).

(3) Septuagint. The Septuagint (the Greek translation of the Old Testament) supposedly shows that "head" (*kephale*) can mean "source." The main support for this conclusion is that when the Hebrew word *ro'sh* ("head") means "ruler" or "chief," it was translated by either *kephale* ("head") or *arche* ("beginning" or "ruler"). Since *arche* sometimes means "source," then *kephale* in Paul's writings may mean "source" as well.[21]

(4) Parallelism. The word "head" (*kephale*) is supposedly used by Paul in Colossians 2:19 and Ephesians 4:15 with the meaning of "source of life." Christians are exhorted in Colossians 2:19 to hold fast "to the Head, *from whom* the whole body, nourished and knit together through its joints and ligaments, grows with a growth that is from God." The Mickelsens argue that in this passage Christ is the "head" in the sense that He is "the source of life," and not of "superior rank."[22] They believe that the same meaning applies to 1 Corinthians 11:3, since in verses 8 and 12 of the same chapter Paul says that "woman was made *from* man."

Analysis of the Linguistic Argument. The above arguments have been examined and compellingly refuted by Wayne Grudem. He discredits the linguistic argument that "head" in Greek (*kephale*) normally means "source" rather than "ruler," by quoting thirty-two examples in which the term is used to mean "authority over" or "ruler" in Greek writings outside the New Testament (seventeen are from Greek translations of the Old Testament and fifteen are from other literature).[23]

The absence in the Liddell-Scott lexicon of "authority over" as a meaning for "head" is not conclusive evidence for the non-existence of such a meaning. The reason is, as Grudem rightly explains: "Liddell-Scott is the standard lexicon for all Greek literature from about 700 B.C. to about A.D. 600 with emphasis on classical Greek authors in the seven centuries prior to the New Testament. Liddell-Scott is the tool one would use when studying Plato or Aristotle, for example; but it is not the standard lexicon that scholars use for the study of the New Testament. (The standard lexicon for that is Bauer-Arndt-Gingrich-Danker)."[24]

Analysis of the Cultural Argument. While it is true that in the ancient world "the heart" rather than "the head" was generally viewed as the seat of thinking (Prov 14:33; 22:17, in Hebrew and KJV; Luke 5:22), there is also significant evidence that the "head" was regarded as the thinking and ruling part of the body. Plutarch (A.D. 46-120), a prominent Greek author contemporary to the New Testament period, explains why the words "soul" (*psyche*) and "head" (*kephale*) can be used to refer to the whole person: "We affectionately call a person 'soul' or 'head' from his ruling parts."[25]

Similarly the Jewish philosopher Philo (c. 30 B.C.—c. A.D. 45) writes: "As the head in the living body is the ruling place, so Ptolemy became head among kings."[26] Examples such as these discredit the claim that the metaphor of the head as the ruling part of the organism would have been "unintelligible to St. Paul or his readers."

Analysis of the Septuagint Argument. The argument that "head" in the Septuagint sometimes means "source" is a gratuitous assumption, devoid of any textual support. The reader will search in vain for examples in the articles by Stephen Bedale and by the Mickelsens showing that "head" (*kephale*) was ever used with the meaning of "source" in the Septuagint. The fact that *kephale* is sometimes used in the Septuagint interchangeably with *arche,* which can mean "source," or "beginning," does not per se demonstrate that *kephale* generally means "source."[27]

Wayne Grudem explains this inconsistency by using a fitting example from the English language: "A parallel to Bedale's argument in English would be if I were to argue (1) that 'jump' and 'spring' could both be used to translate some foreign word when it referred to a 'leap in the air,' and (2) that therefore there is a virtual equation of 'jump' and 'spring' in English." I would then go on to argue that 'jump' also can mean 'a fountain of water,' or 'a coil of metal,' or 'a pleasant season of the year when flowers begin to bloom.'"[28]

Analysis of the Parallelism Argument. The metaphor of Christ as "the Head" of the church, which is compared to the word "body" in Colossians 2:19 and Ephesians 4:15, does allow for "Head" to mean "source," but it certainly does not exclude the meaning of "authority over." The context of Colossians 2:19 indicates that Paul encourages his readers to abandon the worship of angels and serve only Christ as the true "Head." In this context of allegiance to Christ instead of to angels, the reference to Christ as the "Head" best implies "authority over" the church. Moreover, even if it meant "the source" of the church, it would still imply "authority over" the church by virtue of the very fact that the church derives her origin and sustenance from Christ.

Similarly, the context (vv. 8, 10-12) of Ephesians 4:15 shows that Christ is "the Head" of the church in the sense that He is the sovereign Lord who rules the church and nourishes her growth. The fact that Christ as "the Head" is the source of growth of the church presupposes that He is also the leader of the church.

This brief analysis of the four arguments used to interpret "head" in 1 Corinthians 11:3 and Ephesians 5:23 as meaning that husbands are "the source" rather than "the leaders" of their wives, suffices to show that this interpretation lacks textual, contextual and historical support.

3. Head as "Authority Over"

Several lines of evidence indicate that "head" is used in 1 Corinthians 11:3 and Ephesians 5:23 as meaning "authority over." This means that when Paul writes that "the head of a woman is her husband" (1 Cor 11:3) and "the husband is the head of the wife" (Eph 5:23), he means that the husband functions in a position of authority with respect to his wife. Such a position, as we shall see, entails not domination but a leadership of sacrificial love. This conclusion rests on the following five major considerations:

(1) **New Testament Lexicons.** All the standard lexicons and dictionaries for the New Testament do list the meaning of "authority over," or "ruler," or "superior rank" for "head" (*kephale*). The Bauer-Arndt-Gingrich lexicon gives the following definition under the word *kephale*: "in the case of living beings, to denote superior rank."[29] Thirteen examples are then listed of such usage, including 1 Corinthians 11:3 and Ephesians 5:23.

The same meaning is given by Heinrich Schlier in the *Theological Dictionary of the New Testament*. Referring to the use of *kephale* in the Septuagint, he writes: "*kephale* is used for the head or ruler of a society."[30] Again, with reference to 1 Corinthians 11:3, Schlier says: "*kephale* implies one who stands over another in the sense of being the ground of his being."[31] Similar definitions are given by *The New International Dictionary of New Testament Theology* and by the older New Testament lexicons by Thayer and Cremer.

(2) **Textual Evidences.** Ample textual evidences from ancient Greek literature attest to the use of "head" (*kephale*) with the meaning of "authority over." Wayne Grudem conducted a painstaking survey of 2,336 examples, by utilizing a computerized database of the Thesaurus Linguae Graecae at the University of California-Irvine. This listing included the major classical Greek

authors, in addition to the Septuagint, Philo, Josephus, the Apostolic Fathers, the New Testament and others.

The results of the survey are very significant. In the vast majority of instances *kephale* refers to an actual physical head of a man or animal (87%).[32] Of the 302 instances where *kephale* is used metaphorically, 49 times it is used to denote a "ruler" or a "person of superior authority or rank." "The other interesting conclusion from this study is that no instances were discovered in which *kephale* had the meaning 'source, origin.'"[33] These data openly contradict the Mickelsens' statement that "a more common meaning [of "head"] was source, or origin, as we use it in the 'head of the Mississippi river.'"[34]

(3) **Patristic Testimonies.** The early Christian writers who referred to 1 Corinthians 11:3 and Ephesians 5:23 understood the word "head" used in these texts to mean "authority, superior rank." The testimony of such writers as Clement and Tertullian, who lived about a century away from the time of the New Testament, deserves consideration. Ruth A. Tucker, though an Evangelical Feminist herself, concludes her survey of the patristic usage of "head," saying: "It [*kephale*] was generally interpreted by the church fathers and by Calvin to mean authority, superior rank or pre-eminence. These findings bring into question some of the Mickelsens' assumptions—particularly that the 'superior rank' meaning of *kephale* is not 'one of the ordinary Greek meanings' but rather a 'meaning associated with the English word *head*.' . . . it seems clear that the fathers used this so-called English meaning long before they could have in any way been influenced by the English language."[35]

(4) **Contextual Evidences.** The context of both 1 Corinthians 11:3 and Ephesians 5:23 excludes "source" as a possible meaning of "head." In 1 Corinthians 11:3, Paul presents three sets of parallels: Christ/man, man/woman, God/Christ: "But I want you to understand that the head of every man is Christ, the head of a woman is her husband, and the head of Christ is God." As James Hurley convincingly shows, if "head" is taken to mean "source," "there is no way to construct a satisfactory set of parallels."[36]

Adam could be the source of Eve in the sense that she was physically taken out of him, but Christ cannot be the source of Adam in the sense that Adam was physically taken out of Him. Nor can God be the source of Christ in the sense that Christ was physically created from a piece taken out of God. The latter is not only incompatible with other Pauline teachings but was also specifically rejected at the time of the Arian controversy.

On the other hand, if "head" means "authority or head over," a consistent set of parallels can be established. The husband is the head over his wife in the sense that she is "subject" to him (Eph 5:22). Christ is head over every man in the sense that every man is subject to Christ after whom he must model his behavior (Eph 5:25). God is head over Christ in the sense that the incarnate Son of God was obedient to God's authority (headship), even to the point of death (Phil 2:8).

The meaning of "source or origin" is excluded also by the context of Ephesians 5:23, where Paul calls upon wives to be *subject* to their husbands "for the husband is the head of the wife as Christ is the head of the church, his body, and is himself its Savior" (Eph 5:22-23). In this context, the language of headship and submission precludes the notion of "origin or source" for three major reasons.

First, the idea of subjection to an authority ("head") is implied by the very verb "be subject" *(hypotasso)*—a verb which implies a relation to authority (cf. Eph 1:22). Second, while Adam was in a sense the source of Eve, husbands in the New Testament were not the physical source of their wives. Third, even if the husband were the actual source of his wife, that would make his authority more rather than less complete, contrary to what some wish to argue.

(5) Unnecessary Opposition. The attempt to interpret the meaning of "head" as "source" to the exclusion of "authority, head over" creates an unnecessary opposition between the two meanings. This fact is recognized even by Stephen Bedale himself, who is often quoted by those who argue against the meaning of "authority" in Paul's use of "head" in Ephesians 5:23 and 1 Corinthians 11:3. Having stated that Paul saw man as *kephale* ("head") of the woman in the sense of being her *arche* ("source, beginning"), Bedale goes on to say: "In St. Paul's view, the female in consequence is 'subordinate' (cf. Eph 5:23). But this principle of submission ... rests upon the order of creation. ... That is to say, *while the word kephale (and arche also, for that matter) unquestionably carries with it the idea of "authority*," such authority in social relationships derives from relative priority (causal rather than merely temporal) in the order of being."[37]

It is obvious that Bedale offers no support to those who quote his article to prove that the idea of authority is not inherent in Paul's use of *kephale* ("head"). Even if it could be proven that Paul uses "head" with the meaning of "source," such a conclusion would still carry with it the idea of man's "authority, leadership" role in marriage and in the church.

4. Mutual Submission?

The foregoing considerations have shown that "head" is used by Paul in Ephesians 5:23 and in 1 Corinthians 11:3 with the meaning of "authority over." Before examining the nature of the husband's headship role and of the wife's submissive role, we need to consider the meaning of the opening statement of the "household code" found in Ephesians 5:21-33, which reads: "Be subject to one another out of reverence for Christ" (Eph 5:21).

This statement is seen by many Evangelical Feminists as the key that interprets the whole passage in terms of mutual submission. In other words, Paul is supposedly calling upon husbands and wives to be mutually submissive by serving one another in love. This interpretation obviously excludes the notion of the husband's headship over the wife. Though the idea of mutual submission is not foreign to the intent of the passage, in my view it does not represent the main teaching of the passage. Verse 21 can best be understood as a general heading for the whole section which deals with the role relations of wives/husbands, children/parents, slaves/masters (Eph 5:21—6:9). I have four basic objections to the mutual submission interpretation of the passage:

Structure of the Passage. First, the whole passage (Eph 5:21-6:9) consists of a series of three exhortations in which wives, children and slaves are urged to submit to or obey respectively husbands, parents and masters. These exhortations negate the notion of mutual submission, especially in the case of children/ parents and slaves/masters. They can best be understood as explanations of what is meant by being subject to one another.

Exhortation to Subordinate. Second, the exhortation to be submissive or to obey is given to the subordinate partner, not to both. The corresponding exhortations to husbands/parents/masters are not for them to be submissive but to respect and love their subordinates. Thus both the structure and context of the passage recognize a distinction of roles. This view is also strengthened by the absence of the corresponding exhortation for masters and husbands in the parallel passage of 1 Peter 2:18-3:2.

Meaning of Verb. Third, the New Testament use of the verb *hypotasso*, translated "to make subject" in the active and "to be subject" in the passive, consistently expresses the idea of exercising or yielding to authority.[38] "Each of the more than forty New Testament uses of the verb carries an overtone of authority and subjection or submission to it."[39] The meaning of the verb "to be subject" then, contains the idea of an order where one person submits himself or herself to the leadership of another.

Meaning of "to one another." Fourth, the phrase "to one another," which is the basis for the idea of mutual submission, does not always require identical reciprocity. An example of this is found in James 5:16 where the same phrase occurs: "confess your sins *to one another*." This instruction is given in the context of a sick person confessing his or her sins to an elder as part of the healing process. In this context, there is no indication of a reciprocal confession of sin, that is, of the elder also confessing his sins to the sick person. In the same way the exhortation "Be subject to one another" does not necessarily require the idea of identical reciprocity. In the light of the above structural, contextual, and verbal considerations, the phrase "Be subject to one another" simply refers to the general principle of mutual respect for and submission to one another's authority.

5. The Nature of the Wife's Submission

The admonition to "Be subject to one another" is followed immediately by Paul's exhortation to wives: "Wives, be subject to your husbands, as to the Lord. For the husband is the head of the wife as Christ is the head of the church, his body and is himself its Savior" (Eph 5:22-23). In what sense are wives to be subject or submissive to their husbands? There are different kinds of submission and for different motivations. There is the calculating kind of submission designed to achieve the fulfillment of secret desires through the practice of "feminine wiles." There is the submission of conciliation which is accepted for the sake of peace. There is the submission of resignation to bitter necessity. There is the submission to the superior wisdom of another person.

Submission for the Sake of Christ. Paul rejects the worldly patterns of submission, substituting for them a new definition: "as to the Lord." This does not mean that a wife's submission to her husband must have the same unconditional ultimacy of her commitment to Christ. This would be an idolatrous form of submission. The phrase suggests two possible meanings. First, the *manner* of a wife's submission to her husband should be similar in quality to her devotion to the Lord. This meaning is supported by the parallel text, Colossians 3:18, which states: "Wives, be subject to your husbands, as is fitting in the Lord."

Second, the *reason* for a wife's submission is "because the Lord wants it." This meaning is suggested by the preceding and following verses. In the preceding verse (v. 21) the reason given for being submissive is "out of reverence for Christ." "Reverence" is a soft translation of the Greek *phobos* which means "fear." The KJV retains the literal meaning: "in the fear of God."

In Scripture, the "fear of the Lord" is the response which produces obedience to His commandments. Thus, submission "in the fear of Christ" means to accept the authority of another (in this case, the husband) out of obedience to Christ who has delegated that authority. This interpretation is supported by the following verse (v. 23) which says, "For the husband is the head of the wife," that is to say, because the Lord has appointed the husband to function as the head. The recognition of this fact leads Paul to conclude his exhortation by urging wives again to fear their husbands: "Let the wife see that she respects [literally "fears"—*phobetai*] her husband" (Eph 5:33).

Theological, not Cultural Reasons. The main conclusion relevant here is that a wife's submission to her husband rests not on cultural but on theological reasons. *Wives are asked to submit not for the sake of social conventions or the superior wisdom of their husbands, but for the sake of Christ.* Paul grounds his injunction not on a particular culture, but on the unique relationship of loving mutuality and willing submissiveness existing between Christ and the church.

Christ has appointed the husband to function as the "head," so that when the wife subordinates herself to him, she is obeying Christ. This does not mean that a wife is to relate to her husband as if he were Christ. Paul's exhortation is "Wives, be subject to your husbands, *as* to the Lord," and *not* "*because* they are the Lord." Husbands are human beings, but are appointed by the Lord to act as "heads" in the marital relationship. Thus, Paul takes what could be a natural submission and places it within a spiritual order, an order that Christ stands behind.

The wife's submission to her husband is not based on the husband's superiority or the wife's inferiority but, as we have seen, on the husband's headship role established by God at creation (1 Cor 11:8-9). This order has been established because it affords greater harmony and effectiveness in the marital relationship. The authority to which a wife bows is not so much that of her husband as that of the creational order to which both of them are subject.

Voluntary Submission. A wife's submission to her husband is not imposed, but consciously chosen. It is a free, willing and loving submission. It is not subservience, but loving assistance. The voluntary nature of her submission is indicated by two facts: first, by the command to the husband to love his wife rather than to make her obey; second, by the model of the submission of the church to Christ which Paul gives as an example for the wife's submission to her husband. This means that as the church willingly chooses to obey Christ in response to His creative and redeeming love, so the wife willingly chooses to obey the husband as a response to his caring and self-sacrificing love. This form of active obedience is not self-demeaning, but self-fulfilling and upbuilding.

The purpose of this submission is not to suppress the individuality of the wife, but to ensure a deeper and more solid oneness between husband and wife as they function together in the household. Elisabeth Elliot perceptively points out that "To say that submission is synonymous with the stunting of growth, with dullness and colorlessness, spiritlessness, passivity, immaturity, servility, or even the 'suicide of personality,' as one feminist who calls herself an evangelical has suggested, is totally to miscontrue the biblical doctrine of authority."[40]

In the Christian faith, authentic self-realization for men and women is found in the willing submission to the divinely-established roles grounded in creation and clarified by Christ's redemption. This liberating dynamic is exemplified in the life of the Trinity and expressed in the Scriptures.

6. The Nature of the Husband's Headship

The exhortation "Wives, be subject to your husbands" is followed by Paul's admonition to husbands: "Husbands, love your wives, as Christ loved the church and gave himself up for her" (Eph 5:25). It is noteworthy that Paul speaks of the headship role of the husband only when exhorting wives and not when addressing the husbands themselves. In other words, the wives are reminded that "the husband is the head of the wife" (Eph 5:23), but that husbands are *not* exhorted to exercise their headship role by keeping their wives in submission. Instead, Paul chose to confront husbands with the headship model of Christ's sacrificial love (Eph 5:25-27).

Paul's approach reveals his sensitivity to human abuse of power. He was aware of some men's over-concern with asserting their authority. Consequently, he chose to emphasize not the husband's right to be the head over the wife, but rather his obligation to exercise his headship through care for his wife. Paul acknowledges the headship role of the husband in the marital relationship as an indisputable principle: "the husband is the head of the wife" (Eph 5:23). There was no need to restate this principle when addressing the husbands. What husbands needed to hear was what it means to be the head over their wives.

Headship Clarified. Paul clarifies the meaning of headship by calling upon husbands to imitate the sacrificial leadership of Christ Himself: "Husbands, love your wives, as Christ loved the church and gave himself for her, that he might sanctify her, having cleansed her by the washing of water with the word, that he might present the church to himself in splendor, without spot or wrinkle or any such thing, that she might be holy and without blemish "(Eph 5:25-27).

Paul here goes into great detail to explain how Christ exercises His headship role over the church, namely, through the sacrificial giving of Himself for her redemption and restoration. In the same way, the husband's authority is to be expressed in self-giving love for the well-being of his wife. The husband who follows Christ's leadership will exercise his headship, not by forcing his wife into a mold that stifles her initiative, her gifts, her personhood, but rather by encouraging her to develop her mental and spiritual potential.

Paul further clarifies the meaning of headship by shifting back to the head/body analogy (vv. 28-30). The husband should care for his wife as he does for his own body. This means that a husband must be dedicated to his wife's welfare by providing for all her needs. This kind of loving and sacrificial leadership eliminates all the evils associated with hierarchical marriage and enables the two to "become one flesh" (Eph 5:31).

Biblical headship is for the sake of building others and not for one's own benefit. Headship means that the husband assumes a responsibility for the family in a way that is different from that of the wife. The husband serves as the provider and the wife as the home-builder. The two are not superior or inferior but complementary. Each supplements the special gifts and responsibilities of the other.

Headship and Submission. The model of Christ's sacrificial love for the church provides a most eloquent example of how headship and submission can be compatible in marital relationships. Christ's headship over the church is not diminished by his self-sacrificing love for her. By the same token, the church's submission to Christ does not diminish the possibilities for her fullest development, but rather enhances them.

The comparison between Christ's relationship with the church and the relationship of a husband and wife points to the ultimacy of the authority structure in marriage. The marriage relation, however, must always mirror the relation of Christ to the church. "It was not the design of God" writes Ellen White, "that the husband should have control, as head of the house, when he himself does not submit to Christ. He must be under the rule of Christ that he may represent the relation of Christ to the church."[41]

Neither headship nor submission must crush or distort the possibilities for self-growth or personal fulfillment. Effective leadership in any organization must encourage the fullest development of the abilities of those under authority. This requires that a leader be aware of the concerns of those under him and that the subordinates respect the wishes of the leader. As Christians we need to maintain the delicate balance between the exercise of authority (headship) and the response to authority (submission).

7. Reasons for the Rejection of Husband-Headship

A Gross Misunderstanding. Why are some feminists so offended by the Biblical principle of husband-headship that they even call for the abolition of marriage? "Marriage," states a feminist declaration, "has existed for the benefit of men and has been a legally sanctioned method of control over women . . . the end of the institution of marriage is a necessary condition for the liberation of women."

At the root of the rejection of husband-headship, is a gross misunderstanding of its Biblical meaning. In the Bible, husband-headship relates to function, not to value. If male headship in the home and in the church meant that man was innately more valuable than woman, then something would be terribly unjust in the Bible. But male headship in the Bible does not mean that women are inferior or of lesser value than men.

The value of a human being is not determined by office or function. The head of an academic department is not of greater worth than a regular teacher in the department. Human worth in

Scripture is determined not by our office or function but by our status before God by virtue of creation and redemption. By virtue of creation, both men and women are equal before God because both have been created in the image of God (Gen 1:27). Similarly, by virtue of redemption, both men and women are equal before God because, as we read in Galatians 3:28, we "are all one in Christ Jesus."

Difference Between Value and Function. The divine order of headship has nothing to do with men being of greater worth than women, for they are not. The issue is the different and yet complementary functions God has assigned to men and women. Weldon M. Hardenbrook perceptively observes that "The failure to differentiate between value and function lies behind much of the power struggle that ravages families across America. Men who actually think they are *more* valuable because God asks them to be head of the family unit are deceived. And women who feel reduced in personhood because they are not in charge are equally deceived."[42]

The Trinity provides a perfect model of how equality in worth can coexist with submission in functions. God the Father is the Head in the Trinity (1 Cor 11:3), but His headship does not lessen the value of the Son, because both are equally God. Some argue that the Son's functional submission to the Father was temporary, limited only to the time of His incarnation and/or of the completion of His redemptive mission. This argument is untrue, because 1 Corinthians 15:28 clearly tells us that at the consummation of His redemptive mission, Christ, who has been reigning until He subjects all things under His Father's feet, will Himself be subject to God: "When all things are subjected to him, then the Son himself will also be subjected to him who put all things under him, that God may be everything to everyone" (1 Cor 15:28).

The Son is not of less value because of His functional submission to the headship of the Father, since both fully share the divine nature. Similarly, a woman is of no less value because of her functional submission to her husband, since both men and women are "joint heirs of the grace of life" (1 Pet 3:7), having been equally created and restored in God's image (Gen 1:27).

Irresponsible Male Headship. A major reason that husband-headship is hotly contested today is that all too often men demand submission from their wives without in turn submitting themselves to the headship of Christ. With complacency, men will quote the Scripture which says "the head of the woman is man" (1 Cor 11:3, NIV) to assert their authority, forgetting the preceding statement which says: "the head of every man is Christ" (1 Cor 11:3). Before a man can serve as an effective head of his wife and children, he must himself submit to the headship of Christ. "Proper headship operates within a clearly defined chain-of-responsibility. If the chain is broken at any link, authority becomes impaired."[43]

One can hardly blame wives who resent being under the irresponsible headship of husbands who are not accountable to Christ. That is not only unfair but also unchristian. Biblical husband-headship, however, is patterned after the sacrificial headship of Christ over the church, manifested in the sacrificial giving of Himself for her redemption and restoration (Eph 5:25-30).

It was through His act of love and self-sacrifice that Christ became Lord and Master of the church. Similarly a man cannot rightfully claim to be the head of a home unless he is willing to give himself for the well-being of all the members of his family. As Christ is both the Head and Servant of the church, moving from one role to the other, so a man who lives under the headship of Christ must be willing to exercise both headship and servanthood in the home (Phil 2:8-9; Matt 20:26; 23:11; Mark 9:35; 10:43).

Conclusion. Ephesians 5 presents the headship of the husband and the submission of the wife as an order established by God to ensure unity and harmony in the home. Paul defines and defends headship and submission in marriage on a theological and not on a cultural basis. By utilizing the model of Christ and the church, Paul effectively clarifies the meaning of headship and submission in marriage. The purpose of this clarification, however, was not to do away with role distinctions in marriage, but rather to ensure their proper expression in accordance with God's intended purpose.

PART II:
THE APPLICATION OF THE PRINCIPLE OF
HEADSHIP AND SUBMISSION

1. Practicing Headship

To appreciate more fully the validity and value of the Biblical principles of headship and submission, we shall now reflect on the practical implications and applications of such principles in marital relationships.

Leadership in Love. We noticed earlier that Paul clarifies the meaning of headship by exhorting husbands not to exercise authority over their wives, but to love them "as Christ loved the church" (Eph 5:25). To put it differently, Paul exhorts husbands to exercise not a headship of power, control, competence or domination, but a leadership of love. The model is the headship of Christ over the church manifested in His willingness to sacrifice Himself for her sanctification ("that he might sanctify her"–v. 26), purification ("having cleansed her"–v. 26), and glorification ("that he might present the church to himself in splendor"–v. 27).

This is the way I am to be the head of my wife, by loving her with the sacrificial and unconditional love of Jesus. Jesus so loved the church that He gave up everything for her— equality with God, heaven's majesty and glory, the right to an earthly family, the understanding and appreciation of his fellows, a fair trial and a humane death. This is a headship of total sacrificial and unconditional love, without rights. As a husband, am I the kind of head who is willing to give up everything for the well-being of my wife and children?

Christ's love cleanses and improves the church. Through His Spirit, Christ works to "present the church to himself in splendor, without spot or wrinkle" (Eph 5:27). Jesus loves to make every believer as pure and perfect as He is. "Does my love for my wife wash away her inner wounds and hurts and bring out the best in her character? Do I make it easy or difficult for Jesus to make her radiant and blameless? Jesus does not repress and inhibit my character but enables it to flower and realise its full potential. Is my wife suppressed or enriched through my relationship with her?"[44]

Should God ask me or you one day, "Did you love your wife unconditionally as I loved you?" What are we going to say? Shall we look for excuses, saying, "Well, Lord, you know that I loved my wife in many areas. I provided for all her material needs and I supported many of her plans and initiatives. But it was difficult to love her completely because she was not always submissive. Sometimes she insisted on doing things her own way, disregarding my feelings or instructions. And remember God, she was not always trustworthy. Sometimes she left me and the kids at home and went out to have fun. How could I love her unconditionally?" The Lord will reply, "I never asked you about your wife's weaknesses. I asked you, Did you love your wife unconditionally as I love you?"

God knows our spouse's weaknesses as well as our own. Yet He calls us as husbands to exercise a headship of love by loving our wives no matter what their weaknesses might be. He calls us to exercise our headship by being first in forgiving our spouses' mistakes, first in nurturing and building our marital relationship, first in assuming responsibility for the physical, social, emotional, and spiritual needs of our wife and children. Exercising such a headship of love is not easy. In fact, it is impossible on our own. It can only be done by the enabling power of the Holy Spirit. That is why Paul introduces his discussion of the proper relationships between husband and wife, parents and children, and servants and masters by exhorting Christians to "be filled with the Spirit" (Eph 5:18). It is only by the enabling power of His Spirit that a husband *can* begin to love his wife as Christ loved the church and that a wife *can* submit herself to her husband as to the Lord.

Leadership in Service. The husband-headship of sacrificial love is manifested especially through his willingness to serve his wife and children. This does not mean that he is under the authority of his family members or that he takes orders from them. Rather, it means that he serves his family by giving them a loving, intelligent and sensitive *service of leadership*.

Headship in Scripture presupposes a leadership of service. Christ is the head of the church because He came not to be served by the church, but to serve her (Matt 20:28). There is a radical difference between God's view and the world's view of leadership. "You know," Jesus explained, "that those who are supposed to rule over the Gentiles lord it over them, and their great men exercise authority over them. But it shall not be so among you; but whoever would be great among you must be your servant, and whoever would be first among you must be slave of all" (Mark 10:42-44).

A husband fulfills the headship of service by leading, encouraging, protecting, providing, and caring for his wife and children. As the wife has a unique role in procreation, so the husband has a unique role in provision and protection. "The Lord," writes Ellen White, "has constituted the husband the head of his wife to be her protector; he is the house-band of the family, binding the members together, even as Christ is the head of the church and the Savior of the mystical body."[45] Peter emphasizes this point, saying: "Husbands, in the same way be considerate as you live with your wives, and treat them with respect as the weaker partner and as heirs with you of the gracious gift of life, so that nothing will hinder your prayers" (1 Pet 3:7, NIV).

The wife is "the weaker partner," not morally, spiritually or intellectually, but physically. The considerate husband will protect her from such heavy tasks as moving furniture, repairing automobiles, transplanting trees, building fences, doing masonry. Sometimes the husband must protect his wife's health by taking over some of her burdens. Especially if the wife works outside the home or if she is not well, the considerate husband will alleviate his wife's burdens by assuming responsibility for some of them.

Speaking of the husband, Ellen White writes, "If he wishes to keep her fresh and gladsome, so that she will be as sunshine in the home, let him help her bear her burdens. His kindness and loving courtesy will be to her a precious encouragement, and the happiness he imparts will bring joy and peace to his own heart."[46] She continues, noting that if a mother is deprived of the care and protection of her husband, "if she is allowed to exhaust her strength through overwork or through anxiety and gloom, her children will be robbed of the vital-force and of the mental elasticity and cheerful buoyancy they should inherit."[47]

Leadership as Management. An important aspect of the headship of the husband is to provide a caring and competent management to the family. This involves establishing and maintaining directions, setting priorities and delegating responsibilities. In his book *Christian Living in the Home*, Jay Adams writes: "The husband as the head of the home is its manager. He is the head; the head does not do the work of the body. The husband is not to answer every question or think every thought for his wife—exactly not that. Rather, he is to recognize that God gave him a wife to be a helper. A good manager will look at his helper and say, 'She has certain abilities. If I am going to manage my household well, I must see that every last one of those gifts is developed and put to use as fully as possible.' He will not want to squash her personality; rather, he will seek to bring it to the fullest flower."[48]

In a well-ordered family a husband exercises his headship by delegating and not by abdicating responsibilities. This involves taking into consideration the ideas, the talents and convictions of his wife and children. Wives are expected to "rule their household" (1 Tim 5:14) by properly managing their homes. The wise woman of Proverbs 31 is emotionally and physically able to work creatively and sacrificially.

"Part of the conflict and confusion which we see in homes today," write Larry and Nordis Christensen, "stems from a too simplistic exercise of headship. To be head of the house means more than a man occupying the captain's quarters and barking out orders. It means learning to shoulder the responsibility for giving informed and intelligent direction to the family.

A husband won't have all the good ideas. His wife and children, as well as people from outside the immediate family, may have important things to say about what the family ought to be doing. It is the husband's responsibility to weigh every suggestion, determine what should be done, and see that it happens."[49]

The husband bears a heavy responsibility for the outcome of his decisions. If the family does not gather for worship or does not attend church, God holds the father responsible. If the children are disobedient and rebellious, the father is primarily to blame. It was Eli and not his wife who came under God's condemnation for raising two evil sons (1 Sam 3:13).

A family without the competent and dedicated leadership of a father is like a corporation without a capable president. In both instances the organization disintegrates very quickly. One of the greatest needs of America today is for husbands and fathers who provide their families not only financial support but also moral and spiritual leadership.

Leadership as Provider. An important part of the husband's leadership of service is his responsibility to provide his wife and children with food, clothing, shelter and educational opportunities. This is a sacred obligation placed upon the husband by God. "If anyone does not provide for his relatives, and especially for his own immediate family, he has denied the faith and is worse than an unbeliever" (1 Tim 5:8, NIV).

Providing only a living, however, is not enough. A common misconception husbands have goes something like this: "I work hard to provide my wife and children for all their needs. What more could they ask of me?" Or, "My wife has no reason to complain because she has much more than most women have."

Providing a living for our wives and children is not a valid substitute for sharing our personal lives with them. Our wives marry *us*, not our paychecks. What many wives miss most is not the paycheck, but the personal attention, presence, and fellowship of their husbands. They wait to be noticed, appreciated, and given time. It is the feeling of being neglected that often will tempt a wife to look for another man willing to give her time and attention.

Peter's counsel to husbands is clear: "Be considerate as you live with your wives" (1 Pet 3:7). The Greek verb translated "live" (*sunoikountes*), literally means "being at home with." Just "being at home with" the wife instead of going out with friends, however, is not enough. A husband may be home and yet ignore his wife by being totally absorbed in reading the newspaper or watching a game on television. As the head of his home, a husband must learn to exercise leadership in self-sharing. He must learn to set aside a block of time each day to give undivided attention to his wife and children. The benefits that will accrue from such a practice are beyond estimation.

Leadership in Discipline and Instruction. As the head of the home, the husband must take responsibility for the moral and spiritual development of his family. In the Old Testament, God instructs fathers to be diligent in teaching His commandments to their children: "These words which I command you this day shall be upon your heart; and you shall teach them diligently to your children, and shall talk of them when you sit in your house, and when you walk by the way, and when you lie down, and when you rise" (Deut 4:7). A similar exhortation is given to fathers in the New Testament: "Fathers, do not provoke your children to anger, but bring them up in the discipline and instruction of the Lord" (Eph 6:4).

The two areas in which a husband must take "first responsibility" is "discipline and instruction." The enforcement of proper discipline is fundamental to the character development of a child. All too often husbands abdicate their responsibility as the moral and spiritual leaders of the home, expecting their wives to fulfill these functions. The result is that more and more wives have to serve as the moral and spiritual heads of the home. When this happens, the children suffer and the marital relationship is strained. The children suffer because they are deprived of the important role model of father as the authority figure and leader of the home. The marital relationship is strained because the wife may resent her husband's inability to function as the moral and spiritual head of the family, and the husband may react to his failure by seeking fulfillment outside the home.

Despite all the anti-male-headship propaganda of the women's libbers, "it is precisely the *absence* of male authority," as Larry and Nordis Christiansen point out, "which plagues American families."[50] We are fast becoming a matriarchal society where women are primarily responsible for teaching and disciplining children, for supporting the family, for maintaining the house, for leading out in worship, and for participating in church and civic affairs.

"The problem," as aptly stated by the Christiansens, "is mass abdication on the part of husbands. The need in American families today is not some kind of manufactured 'equality' between husband and wife. The equality is already there—God-given, waiting to be discovered. The need is for *headship*. Let men accept the responsibility of being head of the family, and wives will find under their authority a freedom, a liberation, such as no constitutional amendment could ever guarantee."[51]

Leadership as Lawmaker and Priest. A Christian father must not betray his sacred trust to be the lawmaker and priest of the home. Ellen White emphasizes this important function, saying: "All members of the family center in the father. He is the lawmaker, illustrating in his own manly bearing the sterner virtues: energy, integrity, honesty, patience, courage, diligence, and practical usefulness. The father is in one sense the priest of the household, laying upon the altar of God the morning and evening sacrifice. . . He is a laborer together with God, carrying out the gracious designs of God and establishing in his children upright principles, enabling them to form pure and virtuous characters, because he has preoccupied the soul with that which will enable his children to render obedience not only to their earthly parent but also to their heavenly Father."[52]

As husbands we are ultimately responsible for the moral and spiritual development of our families. Children naturally look to their father for moral direction. The larger size, greater strength, and deeper voice of the father bespeak to them of authority and leadership. This is why mothers need the involvement of their husbands in enforcing discipline. Fathers serve as a basis upon which parental authority is constructed.

As fathers we need to be involved in the discipline of our children, watching for power struggles between our wives and children. We must take responsibility for any of our children's behavioral problems that cause emotional stress to our wives. We must take time to communicate with our children in order to find out their moral and spiritual needs. We must serve as the priests of the home by leading the family in a daily worship experience and renewed commitment to Christ. Family worship is the symbolic center of a family's spiritual commitment. By bringing the family together for worship, the husband teaches his family members to look up to God for wisdom and strength and to make God first and supreme in their lives.

Conclusion. Practicing headship, as we have seen, means not to lord it over the family by barking out orders to the wife and children but rather to shoulder the responsibility of providing them with a caring and intelligent leadership. This includes a *leadership* *in loving,* shown by loving our wives with the unconditional and sacrificial love of Jesus; *a leadership in service* manifested in our willingness to give intelligent and sensitive service to our wives and children; *a leadership in management* of the home shown by our setting priorities and delegating authority; *a leadership in providing* our wives and children not only with food, clothing , and shelter, but also with our personal attention, presence and fellowship; *a leadership in discipline and instruction,* shown by our taking first responsibility in enforcing proper discipline and in providing instruction to the children; *a leadership as lawmaker and priest* manifested in taking responsibility for the moral and spiritual development of our family members. In a word, practicing headship means being willing to serve our family by providing for the physical, emotional, social, intellectual and spiritual needs of our wives and children. This is the kind of headship exemplified by Christ, the model of the husband's headship.

2. Practicing Submission

Few Biblical injunctions can stir up as much emotion and controversy as the command for the wife to submit to her husband (Eph 5:22, 24; Col 3:18, 1 Pet 3:1). Both liberal and evangelical feminists are shocked and offended by this command. They view this command as a basic denial of women's rights to equality with men. To correct this alleged evil, the women's liberation movement is promoting marriages where roleless partners match their career goals. The very titles "husband" or "wife" are obsolete in such marriages. Each spouse has a right to terminate the relationship when it is no longer beneficial to his or her self-fulfillment.

The traditional roles of wife, mother, and homemaker are being deliberately and systematically dismantled, especially through the influence of the Women's Liberation Movement on the public media. James Dobson offers a most graphic description of this process, saying: "The image of women now being depicted by the media is a ridiculous combination of wide-eyed fantasy and feminist propaganda. Today's woman is always shown as gorgeous, of course, but she is more-much more. She roars around the countryside in a racy sports car, while her male companion sits on the other side of the front seat anxiously biting his nails. She exudes self-confidence from the very tips of her fingers, and for good reasons: she could dismantle any man alive with her karate chops and flying kicks to the teeth. She is deadly accurate with a pistol and she plays tennis (or football) like a pro. She speaks in perfectly organized sentences, as though her spontaneous remarks were planned and written by a team of tiny English professors sitting in the back of her pretty head. She is a sexual gourmet, to be sure, but she wouldn't be caught dead in a wedding ceremony. She has the grand good fortune of being perpetually young and she never becomes ill, nor does she ever make a mistake or appear foolish. In short, she is virtually omniscient, except for a curious inability to do anything traditionally feminine, such as cook, sew, or raise children. Truly, today's screen heroine is a remarkable specimen, standing proud and uncompromising, with wide stance and hands on her hips. Oh, yeah! This baby has come a long way, no doubt about that."[53]

Have Women Been Really Liberated? A fundamental problem with the Women's Liberation Movement is that it assumes to liberate women by doing away with the divine plan for successful marital relationships. The plan consists, as we have seen, of a relationship based on loving leadership and loving submission. Women's libbers reject this divine plan, promoting instead a contractual inter-relationship where each partner is free to come or go, to live in or live out.

In their struggle for women's rights, women's libbers, including some evangelical Christians, have made the mistake of absolutizing their own freedom. They have failed to realize that real freedom is to be found, not by becoming centers of absolute will, but by living according to the order of relationships established by God.

The result of the Women's Liberation Movement has been not a greater liberation for women, but a rise in women's frustration, juvenile delinquency, and divorce rate. Elizabeth Achtemeier offers the following perceptive description of the results of feminist ideologies: "Some modern so-called 'liberated' women have absolutized themselves by being so concerned about their own rights that they have trampled over the rights of their husbands and children. There is nothing more tragic these days than those homes in which the marital relationship is being destroyed by feminist ideologies. The wife has suddenly realized that she is an 'incomplete' or 'unfulfilled' person. So she has precipitously rushed out and found a job, or is spending hours in women's meetings, or has abandoned all those little courtesies, amenities, and mutual services which make the life between a husband and wife possible. She has become an absolute center of self-assertion, with no regard for the welfare and feelings of her husband. Marriage is not possible under such circumstances, and it is not surprising that many of the militant feminists are also divorced."[54]

Finding Life by Losing it. Militant feminists have forgotten Christ's counsel that we find our lives by losing them (Mark 8:35); we find a "better relationship" not by fighting for our rights but by assuming our God-given responsibilities. Biblical faith is concerned not with rights but with responsibilities. A woman who insists on fighting for her rights may eventually end up losing protection, sympathy, love, security, and even her husband.

From a Biblical perspective, we have no rights. All that we have—life, love, forgiveness, freedom, companionship, and salvation—are precious gifts offered to us by our gracious Savior so that we may use them to bless others. This applies to God's command, "Husbands, love your wives" and "Wives, be subject to your husbands" (Eph 5:21, 25). Theyse commands were given not to secure our rights, but to ensure a harmonious, happy relationship.

"When God said love and submit," writes Don Meredith, "there was *only good* intended! Without love and submission, God cannot meet our 'aloneness' needs. Without love and submission, Christians are divided and the cause of Christ is seemingly thwarted. If I do not submit myself to you in humility, then I am a threat, a discouragement, a source of rejection and judgment in your life. Unless I love you unconditionally, it will be hard for you to submit to me. There are no *agape* relationships without *both* love and submission."[55]

The Model of Submission. Christ is the perfect model of both loving headship and loving submission. Both of these roles function in Christ not as limitations but as opportunities for greater service and blessings. In his letter to the Philippians, Paul exhorts us to follow the example of Christ's submissive attitude to find oneness with God and others: "Your attitude should be the same as that of Christ Jesus: who, being in very nature God, did not consider equality with God something to be grasped, but made himself nothing, taking the very nature of a servant, being made in human likeness. And being found in appearance as a man, he humbled himself and became obedient to death—even death on the cross! Therefore God exalted him to the highest place and gave him the name that is above every name, that at the name of Jesus every knee should bow, in heaven and on earth and under the earth, and every tongue confess that Jesus Christ is Lord, to the glory of God the Father" (Phil 2:5-11, NIV).

Christ's submissive mental attitude enabled Him not to question his Father's headship or to grasp for equal authority, even though He shared the same divinity of the Father. He did not question the right of His Father to function as His head, nor did He attempt to redefine the notion of headship and submission through a "careful exegesis." Instead, he submitted Himself to the Father by being obedient to the point of death on the cross. The result of Christ's obedience is that the Father exalted Him to the highest honor. Christ's example teaches us that in God's order, submission is the way to glorification. The submission of Christ to the headship of His Father provides us a model to understand the nature and manner of a wife's submission to her husband.

Submission as Loving Response. The headship of a husband consists, as noted earlier, in providing a sacrificial and loving leadership to his family members. Such a leadership provides the basis for a loving and joyful submission on the part of the wife. The common abuse by men of their headship as a "club" over their wives has led many women to see God's command to submit as irrational and discriminatory. Some women will submit to their husbands half-heartedly, that is, as a necessary divine requirement rather than as a loving response. They hope that God will reward their unwilling submission. Such legalistic submission is joyless, frustrating, and often results in the dissolution of the marriage.

Legalistic submission fails to see that headship and submission were given by God not to deprive us of something but to ensure a happy and harmonious marital relationship. Without loving leadership and loving submission, no successful relationship can be maintained. The fundamental cause of legalistic headship or submission is self-centered, unyielding wills clashing with God's commands. When by God's grace the battle of the wills is dissolved, then we are able to accept and experience God's command to love and submit, not as a source of strife, but of joy, order, blessing, and security. The conflict over roles in marriage is caused not by a mistake in God's job description of husbands and wives, but by sin, manifested in self-centered, unyielding dispositions.

God's plan for husbands to be loving, sacrificial heads and for wives to be loving, respectful helpmates is designed to promote not competition and conflicts, but completion and harmony. The two roles can be compared to the lock and the key. If the lock wants to be the key or the key wants to be the lock because either or both of them are unhappy with their assigned roles, both of them become useless. It is only when the lock and the key function as designed that they work properly. In the same way, it is only when husband and wife function as loving head and responsive helpmate, that their marital union will work properly in accordance with God's design. Each spouse is unfulfilled alone, but together they make a whole.

Submission as Respect. The submission of a wife to her husband is manifested especially through her respect for him. Paul summarizes his exhortation to husbands and wives, saying: "Let each one of you love his wife as himself, and let the wife see that she respects her husband" (Eph 5:33). Respect is something that must be gained through proper conduct. When a Christian husband exercises a loving, sacrificial headship, his wife finds him worthy of trust, honor, and respect.

Respect is an essential quality of love. If love is to grow through the years, it must be based on mutual respect. In his epistle to Titus, Paul encourages older women to teach younger wives "to love their husbands" (Titus 2:4). The fact that Paul exhorts wives "to respect" their husbands in Ephesians and "to love" them in Titus shows that in the apostle's mind, love and respect go hand in hand.

A wife can show respect toward her husband in different ways: by accepting and affirming his moral and spiritual leadership in the

home; by deferring to him certain decisions, questions, or problems; by admiring and praising him for his achievements; by
putting him first when planning activities; by supporting his
financial plans. When a man knows that his wife respects, supports,
and admires him, no sacrifice will be too great for him.

Submission as Acceptance. The submissive wife accepts her
husband the way he is, without conditioning her love to changes in
his behavior. We learn to accept and love our husbands or our wives
unconditionally by realizing how God accepts us: "God shows his
love for us in that while we were yet sinners Christ died for us"
(Rom 5:8).

At times a wife may feel that it is impossible for her to accept
her husband the way he is. Humanly speaking this may well be true,
but as she accepts and experiences God's unconditional love, she
is empowered to accept and love her husband unconditionally.

In her book, *You Can Be the Wife of a Happy Husband,* Darien
Cooper says: "When you accept your husband the way he is, you
will give him the freedom to be the man he wants to be. He will have
freedom to come and go as he pleases and to make his own
decisions. In other words, true love is letting go! Your husband will
love you freely as he did when he chose to marry you unless you
stifle that love with your possessiveness."[56]

As a plant needs good soil, water, and sun to grow healthy, so
a man needs the unconditional love and acceptance of his wife to
live a healthy, happy, and satisfying life. When a husband feels that
he is constantly on trial, that he has to constantly prove himself
worthy to his wife, he becomes discouraged and tempted to look for
another woman who will accept him the way he is.

It is the work of the Holy Spirit to convict a person of his or her
wrongdoings (John 16:8-11). When we take upon ourselves the job
of convicting our spouses of their mistakes, we get in God's way
and hinder the work of His Spirit. This does not mean that a wife
should ignore her husband's wrongdoing. To do so would be
morally irresponsible. The submissive wife can and must express
her concerns and views freely. In fact, a mature husband will want
her to do so. But once a wife has told her husband in what way she

thinks he is wrong, she should not continue to nag him on that matter. Instead, she should place her trust in God's ability to convict and change her husband.

"It might be comforting to realize," rightly observes Darien Cooper, "that negative traits are distorted positive traits. If negative traits can be modified or channeled in the right direction, they can become strengths. Stubbornness can become perseverance. Cowardice can be turned to gentleness. Tactlessness can be turned to frankness. If you trust Jesus Christ to take care of your husband's problems and fix your mind on his assets, you can help him turn bad traits into good ones."[57]

Submission as Putting Husband First. As believers, we submit ourselves to Christ by placing Him first in our lives. Our submission to Christ is presented in Ephesians 5:24 as the model of the wife's submission to her husband. When Jesus is first in a woman's life, He will enable her to place her husband first in her thoughts and actions. A man who has the assurance of being first in his wife's life will be able to face challenges with greater courage and self-confidence.

Placing one's husband first means avoiding certain negative attitudes and actions. One of these is criticism of his character or performance, especially in front of others. This can hurt him even more than a slap on the face. True "love does not delight in evil but rejoices with truth. It always protects, always trusts, always hopes, always perseveres" (1 Cor 13:6-7).

Another negative attitude to avoid is selfishness. A submissive wife will consider her husband's likes or dislikes when purchasing clothes, planning a meal, accepting or rejecting an invitation to a program or social function. Darien Cooper asks wives: "Do you plan your activities so you can stop and visit with him if he should need to talk when he gets home from work? Remember, he can easily tell if he does not have your complete attention when he talks to you. The uninterested look on your face, glancing at the clock or out of the window, or yawning will give you away. Your interest must be sincere."[58]

A submissive wife will also avoid jealousy and possessiveness. She will not deny her husband some legitimate pleasures that could draw him away from her. A wife who resents the time consuming career or activities of her husband may be loving herself more than her husband.

Putting one's husband first means also centering all one's activities around the husband. Good things such as children, homemaking, in-laws, appearance, church or civic functions can easily get out of balance, controlling the time and interest of a wife. It is therefore essential for a wife to learn to balance her activities in such a way that they are the spokes circling the hub, which is the husband, and not vice versa. If the spokes are well-proportioned and balanced, the wheel, that is, marital life, will roll smoothly. On the contrary, if the spokes are out of adjustment and unbalanced, the wheel will wobble and eventually will smash in pieces.

Putting the husband first also includes supporting his financial plans. This may require making the dollar stretch by being thrifty, as described in Proverbs 31:13-14: "She seeks wool and flax, and works with willing hands. She is like the ships of the merchant, she brings her food from afar. She rises while it is yet night and provides food for her household and tasks for her maidens."

Submission as Role-Acceptance. Headship and submission are roles established by God to ensure order, peace, and harmony in the home. The submissive wife accepts her role as homemaker and mother, finding joy in fulfilling such roles creatively, efficiently, and lovingly.

Radical feminists belittle the role of homemaker and mother, promoting instead the male's roles. For them, the only life worth living is a man's life. To be successful, a woman must strive to achieve the attributes, goals, and performances of a man. In their striving to be like men, women are in danger of losing their feminine qualities which make them attractive to men. Women who become hard and aggressive in competing with men often discover to their sorrow that they are treated as if they were men. Competition damages something which is basic and precious to a right relationship between men and women, both in marriage and in the larger social structure.

Our families, churches, and societies need women who are willing to accept their vital role as wives, homemakers, and mothers. God has equipped women with unique biological and spiritual resources needed for the survival and growth of the home. Biologically, God has endowed the woman with the marvelous capacity to conceive and nourish human life in her womb. Spiritually, God has endowed every woman who becomes a mother with the unique power to mold her children's characters for time and eternity.

A woman who willingly and joyfully accepts her role of wife, mother, and homemaker can experience greater reward and fulfillment than any academic or business career can provide. No greater joy and satisfaction can come to a woman than to have her children rising up and calling her "blessed" and her husband praising her, saying: "Many women have done excellently, but you surpass them all" (Prov 31:28-29).

Submission as Acceptance of the Husband's Leadership. God's order for the home is for the husband to serve as a loving leader and for the wife to accept his leadership (1 Cor. 11:3; Eph. 5:23). This order has been divinely established to ensure harmony, happiness, and protection. A home with two heads or with the wife as the head is an abnormality because it distorts the distinctive male-female roles.

"As homes have become more wife-dominated," writes Darien Cooper, "there has been a rise in juvenile delinquency, rebellion, homosexuality, the divorce rate, and the number of frustrated women because the home was designed by God to run efficiently with the man as the leader. Ignoring this principle of his leadership or devising substitutes creates untold problems."[59]

The wife who accepts and responds to her husband's leadership finds protection and satisfaction in the role God designed for her. She enjoys freedom from pressures and problems she is not supposed to carry. A major concern of my wife when I am away from home is that she may have to deal with some unexpected problems that I usually handle: a burned out water pump, a stalled furnace, malfunctioning air-conditioning, leaking faucets or roofs, flat tires, disciplining children. When I am home, it is reassuring for her to know that I am around to take care of such unexpected problems. This gives her peace of mind and freedom to pursue her various activities which do not conflict with her role of wife and mother. By accepting my leadership in the home, my wife is relieved of many worries while I am challenged to develop my God-given strengths and abilities.

Submission Is Not Slavery. A Christian woman, who by God's enabling grace submits to her husband, is not in danger of becoming a slave. On the contrary, she may discover that her submissive attitude inspires her husband to be more thoughtful and kind toward her. Usually, a submissive wife enjoys a happier relationship with her husband than does a dominating wife. She will certainly enjoy a closer walk with God when she knows that she obeys God's command by being submissive to her husband than when she disobeys God by dominating her husband.

Domineering wives have caused great misery to themselves and to their partners. A woman who is aggressive and dominates her husband in the early years of marriage may discover to her disappointment that later in life, she will loathe the man she has trained to be submissive to her, because she has no one to lean upon.

Submission does not mean that a woman cannot voice her opinion. Rather, it means that she will speak "the truth in love" (Eph 4:15) and comply with her husband's decisions to the best of her abilities. "Always remember," writes Tim LaHaye, "you reap far more than you sow. If you sow submission in obedience to God, you will reap blessings in abundance; if you sow rebellion in disobedience to the will of God, you will reap abundant misery."[60]

CONCLUSION

The rejection of the Biblical view of role distinction within marriages is a major cause of marriage break ups today. Scripture clearly presents the headship of the husband and the submission of the wife as an order established by God to ensure unity and harmony in the home. Practicing headship does not mean lording over the wife or family members but rather providing a caring leadership which ensures the physical, emotional, social, intellectual, and spiritual needs of our wives and children. Similarly, practicing submission does not mean serving the husband as a slave but rather willingly and joyfully to accept the husband's loving leadership.

The fact that God has given a different roles for husbands and wives to fulfill does not mean that one is inferior to the other. Each role is equal in importance though different in function. The role of a husband complements that of a wife as a key complements a lock. Either is incomplete without the other. Respecting the husband/wife role distinctions is essential to ensuring the stability of the marriage covenant.

NOTES TO CHAPTER V

1. R. Paul Stevens, *Married for Good* (Downers Grove, Illinois, 1986), p. 113.

2. Robert C. Williamson, *Marriage and Family Relations* (New York, 1966), p.322.

3. Charles R. Swindoll, *Strike the Original Match* (Portland, Oregon, 1980), p. 42.

4. Quoted in Margaret M. Poloma and T. Neal Garland, "The Married Professional Woman: A Study in Tolerance of Domestication," *Journal of Marriage and the Family* (August 1971), p. 533.

5. Elsieliese Thorpe, "But Women Are the Favored Sex," *Reader's Digest* (May 1972), p. 82.

6. Kay Ebeling, "The Failure of Feminism," *Newsweek* (November 19, 1990), p. 9.

7. Among the writers representing this position are Rosemary Radford Ruether, Elizabeth Schüssler Fiorenza, Adela Yabro Collins, Mary Daly, Josephine Ford, Albertus Magnus McGrath, Phyllis Trible and George Tavard.

8. Some of the representatives of the Evangelical Feminist approach are Gilbert Bilezikian, Mary J. Evans, Letha Scanzoni and Nancy Hardesty, Paul K. Jewett, Patricia Gundry, Virginia Mollenkott, Ruth A. Tucker, Richard N. Longenecker, Berkeley and Alvera Mickelsen, David M. Scholer and Aida Besancon Spencer.

9. Among the large number of writers supporting the Biblical feminist position, the following may be selected as representative: Stephen Clark, Susan T. Foh, James B. Hurley, George W. Knight III, Wayne Grudem, Douglas J. Moo, and Charles Caldwell Ryrie.

10. See Philip Barton Payne, "Response to Berkeley and Alvera Mickelsen Chapter 'What Does *Kephale* mean in the New Testament?'" in *Women, Authority and the Bible*, ed. Alvera Mickelsen (Downers Grove, Illinois, 1986), pp.118-132; Richard and Joyce Boldrey, *Chauvinist or Feminist? Paul's View of Women* (Grand Rapids, Michigan, 1976), p. 34; Margaret Howe, *Women and Church Leadership* (Grand Rapids, Michigan, 1982), p. 60; F. F. Bruce, *1 and 2 Corinthians* (London, 1971), p. 248; Letha Scanzoni and Nancy Hardesty, *All We're Meant to Be: A Biblical Approach to Women's Liberation* (Waco, Texas, 1975), pp. 30-31, 100.

11. Letha Scanzoni and Nancy Hardesty (n. 10), p. 100.

12. Ibid., p. 110.

13. Stephen Bedale, "The Meaning of *Kephale* in the Pauline Epistles," *Journal of Theological Studies* 5 (1954): 211-215.

14. See above n. 10.

15. Berkeley and Alvera Mickelsen, "What Does *Kephale* Mean in the New Testament?" in *Women, Authority and the Bible* (n. 4), pp. 106-109; also by the same authors, "Does Male Dominance Tarnish Our Translations?" *Christianity Today* (October 5, 1979): 23-29; "The 'Head' of the Epistles," *Christianity Today* (February 20, 1981): 20-23.

16. For a compelling refutation of the various arguments advanced for interpreting "head" as "source" or "origin" rather than as "ruler" or "authority," see Wayne Grudem, "Does *Kephale* ('head') Mean 'Source' or 'Authority Over' in Greek Literature? A Survey of 2,336 Examples," appendix 1, in George W. Knight III, *The Role Relationship of Men and Women* (Chicago, 1985), pp. 49-80.

17. Berkeley and Alvera Mickelsen, "Does Male Dominance Tarnish Our Translations?" *Christianity Today* (October 5, 1979): 23, 25; Stephen Bedale (n. 13), p. 211.

18. H. G. Liddell and Robert Scott, eds., *A Greek-English Lexicon*, 9th ed., with Supplement (Oxford, 1968), vol. 1, p. 944.

19. Stephen Bedale (n. 13), p. 212.

20. Ibid.

21. Stephen Bedale (n. 13), p. 213.

22. Berkeley and Alvera Mickelsen, "What Does *Kephale* Mean in the New Testament?" (n. 15), pp. 105-106.

23. For the listing and quotation of each passage, see Wayne Grudem (n. 16), pp. 72-76.

24. Wayne Grudem (n. 16), p. 62.

25. Plutarch, *Table-Talk* 692, D, 11.

26. Philo, *Life of Moses* 2, 30. For other examples see Wayne Grudem (n. 16), pp. 73-74.

27. Stephen Bedale speaks of a "virtual equation of *kephale* with *arche*" without giving one text to prove it (n. 13), p. 213.

28. Wayne Grudem (n. 16), p. 56.

29. Walter Bauer, *A Greek-English Lexicon of the New Testament*, trans. and eds. William F. Arndt and F. Wilber Gingrich (Chicago, 1979), s. v. "*kephale*," p. 430.

30. Heinrich Schlier, *"Kephale," Theological Dictionary of the New Testament*, ed. Gerhard Kittel (Grand Rapids, Michigan, 1974), vol. 3, p. 675.

31. Ibid., p. 679.

32. Wayne Grudem (n. 16), p. 67.

33. Ibid., p. 68. Grudem questions the meaning of "source" in the two instances given by Liddell-Scott (Herodotus 4, 91 and *Orphic Fragments* 21a). See his reasoning on pp. 57-61.

34. Berkeley and Alvera Mickelsen, "Does Male Dominance Tarnish Our Translations?" (n. 17), p. 23.

35. Ruth A. Tucker, "Response to Berkeley and Alvera Mickelsen's article 'What Does *Kephale* Mean in the New Testament?'" in *Women, Authority and the Bible*, ed. Alvera Mickelsen (Downers Grove, Illinois, 1986), p. 117.

36. James B. Hurley, *Man and Woman in Biblical Perspective* (Grand Rapids, Michigan, 1981), p. 166.

37. Stephen Bedale (n. 13), p. 214 (emphasis supplied).

38. For a general discussion of the use of the term, see Gerhard Delling, *"Hypotassso," Theological Dictionary of the New Testament*, eds., Gerhard Kittel and Hergard Friedrich (Grand Rapids, Michigan, 1974), vol. 8, pp. 41-46.

39. James B. Hurley (n. 36), p. 142.

40. Elisabeth Elliot, "Why I Oppose the Ordination of Women," *Christianity Today* 19 (June 6, 1975): 14.

41. Ellen G. White, *The Adventist Home* (Nashville, 1952), p. 117.

42. Weldon M. Hardenbrook, *What Every Man Should Know About Fatherhood* (Arcadia, California, 1987), p. 13.

43. Larry and Nordis Christiansen, *The Christian Couple* (Minneapolis, 1977), p. 142.

44. David Phypers, *Christian Marriage in Crisis* (Whitstable, Kent, England, 1985), p. 23.

45. Ellen G. White, *The Adventist Home*, p. 215.

46. Ibid., p. 218.

47. Ibid.

48. Jay Adams, *Christian Living in the Home* (Grand Rapids,1972), p. 77.

49. Larry and Nordis Christiansen (n. 43), p. 151.

50. Ibid., p. 158.

51. Ibid., p. 159.

52. Ellen G. White, *The Adventist Home,* p. 212.

53. James C. Dobson, *Straight Talk to Men and Their Wives* (Dallas, 1984), p. 153.

54. Elizabeth Achtemeier, *The Committed Marriage* (Philadelphia, 1976), pp. 97-98.

55. Don Meredith, *Becoming One* (Nashville, no date), p. 120.

56. Darien B. Cooper, *You Can Be the Wife of a Happy Husband* (Wheaton, Illinois, 1978), p. 29.

57. Ibid., p. 35.

58. Ibid., p. 48.

59. Ibid., p. 58.

60. Tim LaHaye, *How to Be Happy Though Married* (Wheaton, Illinois, 1968), p. 109.

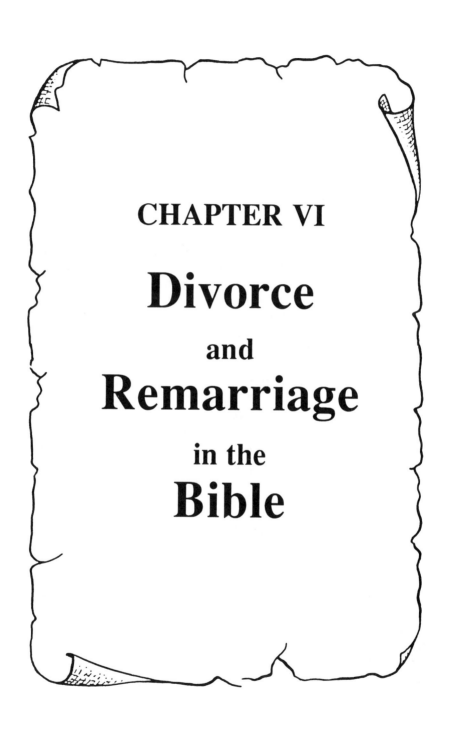

CHAPTER VI

Divorce

and

Remarriage

in the

Bible

DIVORCE AND REMARRIAGE IN THE BIBLE

Divorce is no longer a disease contracted only by Hollywood movie stars. People from all walks of life, including Christians, are affected by divorce. There is hardly a Christian family that, directly or indirectly, does not know the pain of divorce.

An important factor contributing to the alarming escalation of divorce among Christians is the growing acceptance of the societal view of marriage as a social contract, governed by civil laws, rather than as a sacred covenant, witnessed and guaranteed by God Himself. Instead of promising each other faithfulness "till death do us part," many couples are adopting the modern version of the marriage vow, by pledging to remain together "as long as we both shall love."

Recent "no fault" divorce laws make the dissolution of marriage so easy that some lawyers advertise divorce services for less than $100.00: "All legal fees and services included in one low price." What a sad commentary on the cheapness of marriage today! What God has united, many will put asunder for less than the price of a good pair of shoes.

We live today in a time of cultural transition when old values are being challenged both within and without the church. "They have been pulled up by the roots, thrown up into the air, and are now beginning to come down like tossed salad."[1] The result is that many Christians today are confused and do not know what to believe, especially in the area of divorce and remarriage. Many are asking, "Are there Biblical grounds for divorce and remarriage? Is a person who remarries guilty of continuous adultery? Why do some denominations prohibit their ministers from marrying divorced persons and yet allow them to receive divorced people into their membership after they have been married by ministers of other denominations? Isn't it better to suffer the pain of divorce than the tragedy of a marriage without love?"

Pastors, teachers, and Christian writers ofter contribute to the prevailing confusion about divorce and remarriage with their conflicting interpretation of key Bible passages. Some teach, like the ancient Pharisees, that the Bible allows divorce and remarriage for "every cause," while others maintain that the Bible prohibits divorce and remarriage under any circumstances. A reason for such conflicting interpretations is that many interpret the Bible more in the light of their experience in dealing with divorce than in the light of their study of what the Bible actually teaches on this subject.

The time of cultural transition and confusion in which we live offers unprecedented opportunities to seek truly Biblical answers to the questions Christians are asking. We must not allow the extremes of radicalism or liberalism to impede progress in understanding and applying what the Bible teaches on the important subject of divorce and remarriage affecting so many lives. Encouragement for such an effort comes to us from the growing number of conservative Christians who are seeking truly Biblical answers to their questions. My aim in this chapter is to meet the expectations of these Christians by examining the Scriptures in order to come to a more definite and concrete understanding of its teaching on divorce and remarriage. The reader must decide whether or not I have succeeded in "rightly handling the word of truth" (2 Tim 2:15).

Objectives of Chapter. The objective of this chapter is to ascertain what the Old and New Testaments teach regarding divorce and remarriage. We shall pursue this investigation by examining all the relevant passages. In the following chapter we shall consider how we can apply the Biblical teachings to concrete situations today.

DIVORCE AND REMARRIAGE IN THE BIBLE

No one knows how divorce began. The Biblical record shows that, unlike marriage, divorce was not instituted by God. There is no indication in the Bible suggesting that God introduced and institutionalized divorce after the Fall as part of His order for human society. Divorce is "man-made," not divinely ordained. It represents human rejection of God's original plan for the indissolu-bility of the marriage bond.

In His comments on divorce, Jesus explained that divorce represents a change in God's order because "from the beginning it was not so" (Matt 19:8). He further observed that it was because of the "hardness" of human hearts that Moses "allowed" divorce (Matt 19:8). To allow a practice is not the same as instituting it. When divorce first appears in the Bible, the practice was already in existence. What God did through Moses was to regulate divorce in order to prevent its abuse. This does not mean that God winked at divorce. Rather, it means that God acknowledged its existence and regulated it to prevent a bad situation from becoming worse.

The fact that God did not lay down a specific law in the Pentateuch prohibiting divorce reveals His realistic approach to human failure. It shows God's willingness to work redemptively on behalf of those who fail to live up to His ideal for them. Before considering the implications of God's attitude toward divorce in the Old Testament for us today, we want to examine the most explicit Old Testament passages concerning divorce.

1. The Teaching of Moses

In the pre-Mosaic period, divorce was common among the heathen nations. A man could divorce his spouse for any reason simply by telling her before witnesses, "You are no longer my wife." The divorced wife would have no recourse but to leave her home with only the few belongings she could carry on her back. This is one reason why women wore all their rings, jewelry, and coins on their bodies, since these provided a financial resource in the case of divorce.[2]

The practice of easy divorce became common among the Hebrews, encouraged by the absence of regulations restricting it. "Men were divorcing their wives for a 'weekend fling' and then taking them back again when the dirty laundry had piled up and the house needed cleaning."[3] It was this situation that occasioned the legislation found in Deuteronomy 24:1-4. The chief concern of the law is to discourage hasty divorce by preventing remarriage after divorce. The law contains three elements: (1) the grounds for divorce (Deut 24:1a), (2) the process of divorce (Deut 24:1b), and (3) the result of divorce (Deut 24:2-4).

The Grounds for Divorce. "When a man takes a wife and marries her, if then she finds no favor in his eyes because he has found some indecency in her, and he writes her a bill of divorce..." (Deut 24:1a). Note that the law does not prescribe or encourage divorce. It simply assumes the course of action a husband would take if he found "some indecency in her."

The precise meaning of the phrase "some indecency" (literally, "the nakedness of a thing") is uncertain. Rabbinical interpretation of this phrase was sharply divided. The school of Shammai interpreted it as unchastity, while the school of Hillel as anything displeasing to her husband. Neither of these two views is supported by the evidence. Shammai's view is discredited by the fact that in the Old Testament, divorce was not granted for adultery (Lev 20:10; Deut 20:22-24) or for morally defiling one's wife before marriage (Deut 22:28). This suggests that the "indecency" of Deuteronomy 24:1 must refer to something other than adultery or sexual uncleanness.

Hillel's looser interpretation is also devoid of Biblical support. The Hebrew word *erwath* (generally translated, "indecency" or "uncleanness") is often used to refer to shameful exposure of the human body (Gen 9:22, 23; Ex 20:26; Lam 1:8; Ezek 16:36, 37). In Deuteronomy 23:13-14, the word is used to describe the failure to cover human excrement. We would conclude, then, that according to Deuteronomy 24:1, divorce was allowed for some kind of shameful act or indecency other than illicit sexual intercourse.

The Process of Divorce. The procedure required of a man intending to divorce his wife was for him to write out a bill of divorce and give it to her: "he writes her a bill of divorce and puts it in her hand and sends her out of his house" (Deut 24:16). The wording of the bill of divorce was probably similar to the one generally used by the Jews of the Diaspora which reads: "On the _____ day of the week, the _____ day of the month _____, in the year _____ from the creation of the world, in the city of _____, I, _____, the son of _____, do willingly consent, being under no restraint, to release, to set free, and to put aside thee, my wife, _____, daughter of _____, who has been my wife from before. Thus I do set free, release thee, and put thee aside, in order that thou may have permission and the authority over thyself and to go and marry any man that thou may desire. No person may hinder thee from this day onward, and thou art permitted to every man. This shall be for thee from me a bill of dismissal, a letter of release, and a document of freedom, in accordance with the laws of Moses and Israel.

_____ the son of _____, witness

_____ the son of _____, witness."[4]

The bill of divorce served several purposes. It deterred a hasty action on the part of the husband by restraining frivolous and rash dismissal. It testified to the woman's freedom from marital obligations from the husband who sent her away. It protected the woman's reputation, particularly if she married another man.

The process of divorce that Moses required was not a license to repudiate the wife at will, but rather "a stringent requisition that whoever did so should secure his wife from injury by certifying that she was not chargeable with unchaste conduct, but divorced upon some minor pretext."[5]

It is important to note that Moses *did not require* a man to divorce his wife if he found "some indecency" in her. He simply permitted it due to the hardness of the Israelites' hearts (Matt 19:8; Mark 10:5), who had rejected God's original plan for marriage (Mark 10:9; Gen 2:24). What Moses required was that a divorce document be written to *discourage hasty divorces* and to mitigate the hardship of divorce. Even when the divorce document was given, the way for reconciliation was still open as long as the woman did not form a second marriage.

The Result of Divorce. The primary purpose of the divorce procedure was to close the way forever for the man to remarry his former wife once she had remarried: "And if she goes and becomes another man's wife, and the latter husband dislikes her and writes her a bill of divorce and puts it in her hand and sends her out of his house, or if the latter husband dies, who took her to be his wife, then her former husband, who sent her away, may not take her again to be his wife, after she has been defiled; for that is an abomination before the Lord, and you shall not bring guilt upon the land which the Lord your God gives you for an inheritance" (Deut 24:2-4).

The main point of this legislation is to prohibit a man from remarrying his former wife if she had married another man. Even if her second husband divorced her or died, she could not return to her first husband. To do so would be an "abomination before the Lord" (Deut 24:4) on the same level as fornication. If a husband could easily remarry the same woman, divorce would become a "legal" form of committing adultery. Later prophetic writings confirm this principle set forth by Moses. For example, the prophet Jeremiah says: "If a man divorces his wife and she goes from him and becomes another man's wife, will he return to her? Would not that land be greatly polluted?" (Jer 3:1).

Another possible reason for the Deuteronomic ban on the remarriage of divorcees to each other after one of them had married someone else is that such a marriage would constitute an incestuous relationship. From Leviticus 18, we learn that prior to the Israelite conquest, the land of Canaan had been "defiled" by "incest" among the Canaanites (Lev 18:25-26). On the basis of this connection, Heth and Wenham argue that Deuteronomy prohibits the remarriage of a divorced couple after one of them had married someone else, because such a remarriage constituted incest. A blood relationship was formed by the first marriage which made them not only husband and wife but kin relatives as well. Consequently, if they divorced and remarried each other again, that remarriage was akin to the marriage between a brother and sister.[6] If this interpretation is correct, then Deuteronomy 24 supports Genesis 1 and 2 by showing that divorce cannot break the bond established by marriage.

It is significant to note that what the Mosaic legislation strongly condemns is not the remarriage of a divorced woman, but her remarriage to her first husband after the termination of her second marriage. This suggests that remarriage per se in the Old Testament was not stigmatized as adulterous nor was a remarried woman regarded as an adulteress. The Pentateuch did not require that a divorced woman and her second husband be put to death, as was the case with adultery. This consideration should lead us to exercise caution before stigmatizing remarriage as adulterous.

Conclusion. Divorce was not instituted by Moses, nor was it approved as an intrinsic right of the husband. Deuteronomy 24:1-4 indicates that Moses sought to curb the evil of divorce by requiring the husband to give a bill of divorcement to his wife to protect her after her marriage to another man. The Mosaic concession does not alter God's original plan for marriage to be a sacred, permanent covenant. It simply provides protection for the divorced wife when sinful hearts violate God's original plan for marriage.

2. The Teaching of Malachi

Many of the Jews who returned from the Babylonian exile married unbelieving heathen women living in the land of Judah. Such marriages were strictly forbidden by the Mosaic law because they would inevitably lead to the worship of heathen gods (Deut 7:1-4; Judg 3:5-6; 1 Kings 11:1-8). The problem was met head-on first by Ezra (Ezra 10:2-3) and then by Nehemiah (Neh 13:23-24) during their tenure as governors. They ordered the offenders to separate from their foreign wives (Ezra 10:10-11; Neh 13:30).

It was at this time that God raised up the prophet Malachi to expose the causes of the spiritual decline and to lead the Jewish community into a restored fellowship with God. Malachi exposes not only the sin of hypocrisy (Mal 2:17), neglect of tithes (Mal 3:7-9) and mixed marriages (Mal 2:10-12), but also the sin of divorce: "And this again you do. You cover the Lord's altar with tears, with weeping and groaning because he no longer regards the offering or accepts it with favor at your hand. You ask, 'Why does he not?' Because the Lord was witness to the covenant between you and the wife of your youth, to whom you have been faithless, though she is your companion and your wife by covenant. Has not the one God made and sustained for us the spirit of life? And what does he desire? Godly offspring. So take heed to yourselves, and let none be faithless to the wife of his youth. 'For I hate divorce, says the Lord the God of Israel,' and covering one's garment with violence, says the Lord of hosts. So take heed to yourselves and do not be faithless'" (Mal 2:13-16).

In this passage, Malachi (whose name means "my messenger") clearly identifies and condemns the sin which had caused God to reject the offering and worship of His people, namely, the violation of the marriage covenant with the wife of one's youth in order to marry foreign idolatrous women. Here Malachi informs us that God sees marriage as a sacred covenant binding two persons in a permanent relationship before God (Gen 31:50; Prov 2:17). Since "the Lord was witness to the [marriage] covenant," breaking it by divorcing one's wife meant to be faithless not only to one's spouse but also to God.

Verse 15 is difficult to translate and interpret. If one follows the marginal reading of the Revised Standard Version ("Has he not made one?"), the text would refer to the original institution of marriage when God made and united two beings into one (Gen 2:24). In other words, God intended that marriage be the covenant union of one man to one woman in order for them to raise up godly offspring. Divorce, then, threatens not only the institution of marriage but also the security needed to raise a godly family.

In verse 16, Malachi concludes by expressing God's attitude toward divorce: "For I hate divorce, says the Lord the God of Israel, and covering one's garment with violence, says the Lord of hosts. So take heed to yourselves and do not be faithless." It is noteworthy that God hates *divorce* and not the *divorced*. As Christians, we should reflect Christ's caring and compassionate attitude toward those who have experienced the trauma of divorce. Christ dealt graciously with the Samaritan woman who had been married five times (John 4:6-26).

Divorce is likened to "covering one's garment with violence." This figurative expression may refer to the custom of spreading a garment of protection over a woman by a man who wanted to claim her as his wife (Ruth 3:9; Ez 16:8). Those Jews who had divorced their wives had acted treacherously, spreading over them a garment of violence rather than of protection. Malachi closes by repeating his plea for faithfulness to the marriage covenant: "So take heed to yourselves and do not be faithless" (Mal 2:16). Three times in four verses (13-16), Malachi speaks of the sin of divorce as faithlessness or, as rendered by the NASV, "treachery."

Conclusion. Malachi strongly emphasizes that divorce violates not only God's original plan for marriage but also the sacred marriage covenant to which the Lord Himself is a witness. Divorce is a grievous sin which God hates because it represents a betrayal of life's most intimate companion, a betrayal profoundly affecting the well-being of the family and community.

3. The Teaching of Jesus in Mark and Luke

The teaching of Jesus is fundamental to the study of the Biblical view of divorce and remarriage because Jesus clarifies the reason for the Old Testament concession (Deut 24:1) and reaffirms God's creational design for marriage to be a permanent, indissoluble covenant. The two major passages containing the teaching of Jesus on divorce and remarriage are found in Mark 10:1-12 and Matthew 19:1-12. Both passages report the same incident and are placed in the same geographical setting (Matt 19:1; Mark 10:1). Both passages record the same question asked by the Pharisees and the same response given by Christ (Matt 19:3-9; Mark 10:2-9).

In spite of the essential similarities, there is one crucial difference between the two passages, namely the exception found in Matthew 19:9 which teaches that divorce and remarriage "except for fornication" is adultery. Whereas Matthew includes twice what has come to be known as the "exception clause" (Matt 19:9; 5:32), Mark and Luke exclude it entirely. Before examining the possible reasons for the exclusion of the exception clause in Mark and Luke and for its inclusion twice in Matthew, it is helpful to consider the setting of the episode.

The Setting. Jesus had concluded His Galilean ministry and was journeying through Perea to Jerusalem for the Passover and His crucifixion when He was approached by the Pharisees with a theological *test* question: "And Pharisees came up to him and tested him by asking, 'Is it lawful to divorce one's wife for any reason?'" (Matt 19:3; cf. Mark 10:2).

The intent of the question was not to learn from Jesus but to get Him into trouble. They were determined to destroy Jesus (Matt 12:14; Mark 3:6) and His travelling through Perea, the territory under the jurisdiction of Herod Antipas, offered them a unique opportunity. After all, Herod Antipas had behaded John the Baptist for publicly condemning his incestuous marriage to Herodias, who was his niece and the wife of his half-brother Herod Philip (Matt 14:6-12). The Pharisees must have thought that if they could trick Jesus into condemning the illegitimate marriage of Herod Antipas by means of a "test" question on divorce, this would result in His arrest and execution.

The Pharisees' Question. The test question the Pharisees posed to Jesus centered on the significance of the phrase "some indecency" found in Deuteronomy 24:1. There was a major debate among the rabbis over the meaning of this phrase. The Mishna, which contains the oral traditions of Judaism, tells us how the conservative school of Shammai and the liberal school of Hillel interpreted the phrase: "The school of Shammai said: A man may not divorce his wife unless he has discovered something unchaste about her, for it is written, 'Because he has found some unseemly thing in her' (Deut 24:1). But the school of Hillel said: He may divorce her even if she spoiled a dish for him for it is written, 'Because he has found some unseemly thing in her.'"[7]

It is remarkable to see how the same Biblical text (Deut 24:1) was interpreted in two radically different ways. The Pharisees wanted to force Christ to choose between the two schools so that they could use His answer to accuse Him either of laxity or of narrow rigorism. Jesus, however, chose not to take sides. Instead, He answered by calling attention to God's original plan for marriage: "He answered, 'Have you not read that he who made them from the beginning made them male and female,' and said, 'For this reason a man shall leave his father and mother and be joined to his wife, and the two shall become one flesh?' So they are no longer two but one flesh. What therefore God has joined together, let not man put asunder" (Matt 19:4; cf. Mark 10:6-9).

Christ's answer is characteristic. He immediately calls attention to God's original plan for marriage, almost chiding them for failing to realize that divorce is totally alien to such a plan. God's original plan consists of a man and a woman being united in a marriage bond so strong that the two actually become one flesh

(Gen 2:26; Matt 19:6; Mark 10:8). The "one flesh" unity of the couple is reflected especially in their offspring who partake of the genetic characteristics of father and mother, and the two are absolutely inseparable. Jesus affirms that it is God Himself who actually joins a couple together in marriage and what God has joined together no human being has the right to separate.

Moses' Permission. It is significant that Christ answered the Pharisees' question as to whether it is lawful for a man to divorce his wife by affirming the permanence of the God-ordained marriage union. Such an answer, however, provoked another question on the part of the Pharisees: "Why then did Moses command one to give a certificate of divorce, and to put her away?" (Matt 19:7). By this question the Pharisees apparently intended to challenge the position Christ had just enunciated by assuming that Moses did command divorce. The argument of the Pharisees could be paraphrased as follows: if according to its original institution, marriage is a permanent union that cannot be dissolved by human authority, why then did Moses command divorce? Is not Your teaching contradicted by Moses' commandment?

Christ's answer is of fundamental importance because it clarifies the whole question of the Old Testament Mosaic provision. "He said to them, 'For your hardness of heart Moses allowed you to divorce your wives, but from the beginning it was not so'" (Matt 19:8; cf. Mark 10:5-6).

Two features of Christ's reply should be noticed. First, the phrase "for your hardness of hearts" implies that the Mosaic permission was occasioned by the insubordination and stubbornness of the Israelites. The latter did not invalidate the original institution of marriage as a permanent union. The bill of divorce was intended to regulate a perverse situation and not to abrogate the divine institution of marriage.

A second significant element of Jesus' reply is the distinction between the verb He used to describe Moses' provision and the verb used by the Pharisees. Jesus said that Moses "allowed" divorce while the Pharisees said that Moses "commanded" divorce.[8] The verb Jesus used implies sufferance or tolerance of divorce but not a sanction of its practice. In the Mosaic economy, divorce was permitted because of the hardheartedness of the Israelites, but from the beginning there was no such permission. This means that the Mosaic permission was a departure from the creation ordinance of marriage which no man has the right to put asunder.

Jesus utterly condemns divorce as contrary to the divine institution of marriage. Divorce is the sundering by man of a union God Himself has constituted. As John Murray puts it, "Divorce is the breaking of a seal which has been engraven by the hand of God."[9]

A Clarification for the Disciples. Christ's condemnation of divorce as a violation of God's original plan for marriage apparently perplexed the disciples. Presumably they were wondering what would be the moral consequences if a man divorced his wife. Later that day when Jesus had found lodging ("in the house"), the disciples began questioning Him on this subject. And Jesus said to them, "Whoever divorces his wife and marries another, commits adultery against her; and if she divorces her husband and marries another, she commits adultery" (Mark 10:11-12).

The unconditional form of Christ's statement in Mark 10:11-12 (and Luke 16:18) where no exceptions are allowed for divorce serves to emphasize the abrogation of the Mosaic permission for divorce (Deut 24:1-4). Jesus declares to His disciples in no uncertain terms that, contrary to the Mosaic concession, divorce and remarriage by either the husband or the wife is a sin of adultery clearly condemned by God's law. A man who divorces his wife and marries another woman is sinning not only against God but also against his former wife. He "commits adultery against her" because by marrying another woman, he is violating his covenant of commitment to his wife.

Mark applies the same rule to both the husband and the *wife*, a truth not expressed in Matthew's Gospel (cf. Matt 19:9). The reason is that Matthew was writing for Jews among whom it was most uncommon for a wife to divorce her husband. But what was most uncommon among the Jews was common in the Graeco-Roman world where, in matters of divorce, wives enjoyed equal rights with their husbands. Since Mark writes for a predominantly

Gentile readership, he records the application of Christ's teaching
to both the husband and the *wife*.

With a few simple words in Mark, Jesus overrides the Mosaic
concession and its rabbinic interpretations by pointing back to the
great marriage charter of Genesis. In view of the fact that in the
beginning when God established marriage, divorce was not permitted, for a husband or a wife to divorce his/her spouse means to act
against the will of the Creator for marriage.

Jesus envisions marriage not as a mere social or civil contract
that can be terminated through a legal proceeding but as a sacred
and lifelong covenant. Those who divorce and remarry are guilty
of adultery. Such a radical teaching, as Hugh Montefiore points
out, "was revolutionary to Jewish ways of thought. So far as we
know, Jesus was alone among Jewish teachers when He asserted
that marriage was intended by God to be lasting and permanent."[10]

The Contribution of Luke 16:18. In Luke, the teaching of
Jesus on divorce is placed in a different context, namely, in the
context of the proclamation of the Gospel of the kingdom of God
which began with John the Baptist: "The law and the prophets were
until John; since then the good news of the kingdom of God is
preached, and every one enters it violently" (Luke 16:16). The
subject matter that was expanded by the religious leaders until the
beginning of John the Baptist's ministry was the Law and the
Prophets. But with the appearance of John, the proclamation of the
good news of the kingdom of God began.

Some of the Pharisees mistakenly concluded that John and
Jesus taught the termination of the Law and the Prophets. Jesus,
however, emphasizes in Luke 16:17 that the inauguration of the
kingdom of God does not set aside God's law: "But it is easier for
heaven and earth to pass away, than for one dot of the law to become
void."

In the following verse Jesus drives home His point using
divorce as an illustration. The Pharisees thought they were upholding
the letter of the law by arguing about what constituted legitimate
grounds for a divorce. Jesus reveals the permanence and true spirit
of God's law by condemning divorce and remarriage as a sin of
adultery: "Every one who divorces his wife and marries another

commits adultery, and he who marries a woman divorced from her husband commits adultery" (Luke 16:18). In this statement, Jesus condemns as adultery not only the act of divorcing one's wife but also the act of marrying a divorced woman. The reason for the latter is that divorce does not destroy the indelible bond formed when a man and a woman enter into a marriage covenant.

The teaching of Jesus in Mark 10:11-12 and Luke 16:18 makes no allowance for divorce and remarriage by either the husband or the wife. Marriage for Jesus is not a mere civil contract that can be terminated but a divinely established covenant relationship that must not be put asunder. God is not interested in divorce but in the permanence of our marital relationship. If we divorce and remarry, we commit adultery.

4. The Teaching of Jesus in Matthew

The Contribution of Matthew. Matthew makes three significant contributions about Jesus' teachings on divorce which are not found in Mark or Luke. Before looking at them, we must understand why Matthew provides some of the Lord's teaching on divorce not found in Mark 10. The apparent reason is the different readership. Mark wrote for Gentile readers while Matthew for Jewish readers. Under the inspiration of the Holy Spirit, each writer recorded those elements of the teaching of Jesus that would apply to their audiences. This is indicated by the fact that Matthew frequently quotes Old Testament scriptures while Mark cites them only in a few instances, obviously because the Gentiles had little appreciation for the sacred Scriptures. Mark takes pains to explain certain Jewish tradition and terms (cf. Mark 7:2, 11, 34; 5:41; 9:43; 14:12, 36) unfamiliar to Gentile readers.

We noted earlier that only Mark mentions the possibility of a woman divorcing her husband (Mark 10:12) because that was common in the Graeco-Roman world. Matthew omits that part of Jesus' teaching because Jewish law made no allowance for a woman to divorce her husband. It is evident, then, that each gospel writer selectively recorded those elements of Jesus' teaching that would apply to his Christian community. Since Matthew is writing to Jewish-Christian readers he mentions three significant aspects of

Jesus' teaching on divorce and remarriage which are omitted by Mark and Luke.

The first significant Matthean contribution regarding Jesus' teaching on divorce and remarriage is found in the context of the Sermon on the Mount. Here Jesus encourages living in conformity to the spirit of the law rather than to its letter. Contrary to the Pharisees who allowed divorce by appealing to the letter of the Mosaic concession (Matt 5:31; cf. Deut 24:1-4), Jesus disallows divorce but for one exception (Matt 5:32) by revealing the true intent of God's law.

The second significant Matthean contribution is the response of the disciples to Jesus' teaching: "If such is the case of a man with his wife, it is not expedient to marry" (Matt 19:10). Apparently, the disciples had been following either the rabbinical view of Shammai which allowed divorce only on the ground of adultery or of Hillel which permitted divorce for any reason. When they understood that Jesus in essence made no allowance for divorce, they responded in astonishment, "If one cannot get out of marriage, then it is better not to marry in the first place." Jesus then declared that not all can accept a celibate life (Matt 19:11-12). This brief dialogue between Jesus and the disciples recorded by Matthew reveals, indirectly and yet forcefully, that Jesus taught the permanence of the marriage relationship.

The Exception Clause. The third significant Matthean contribution is the exception clause of Matthew 5:32 and 19:9 which teaches that to divorce and to remarry, "except for unchastity [*porneia*]" is adultery: "But I say to you that every one who divorces his wife, except on the ground of unchastity, makes her an adulteress; and whoever marries a divorced woman commits adultery" (Matt 5:32). "And I say to you: whoever divorces his wife, except for unchastity, and marries another, commits adultery" (Matt 19:9).

The exception clause found in these two texts has been the object of countless studies. A major reason is that many find in this clause the only legitimate grounds for divorce and remarriage. Scholarly opinion on the meaning of the exception clause is divided, reflecting the lack of unanimity among scholars about the precise meaning of the key word of the clause, namely *porneia*. The word is generally translated as "fornication" (KJV), "unchastity" (RSV), and "marital unfaithfulness" (NIV).

The Greek word *porneia*, from which we derive the word "pornography," comes from the root word *pernemi*—"to sell." The original idea was to offer one's body for a price. The word was used especially of slaves and meant "a harlot for hire."[11] Historically, *porneia* has been used with wider and narrower meanings. The wider meaning includes unlawful extra-marital intercourse such as prostitution, fornication, and adultery. The narrower meaning can refer to sexual aberrations such as homosexuality (cf. Rom 1:29), incest (cf. 1 Cor 5:1), and unlawful marriages within the forbidden degrees of relationship (Acts 15:20, 29). The question then is, what is the exact meaning of *porneia* in the exception clause (Matt 5:32; 19:9)? Is Jesus using the term in its wider or narrower meaning? Scholarly opinion differs on this matter as indicated by the five major interpretations of the exception clause.

Adultery or Sexual Misconduct. The traditional and most popular interpretation of the exception clause takes *porneia* in its wider meaning of sexual misconduct. Thus, Jesus allows divorce when one party has been guilty of marital unfaithfulness. This view is reflected in most translations where *porneia* is translated as "fornication" (KJV), "unchastity" (RSV), or "marital unfaithfulness" (NIV). Advocates of this view maintain that the exception clause allows for the divorce and remarriage of the innocent party, since divorce implies the dissolution of the marriage relationship. In this case, Jesus would be siding with the conservative school of Shammai which allowed divorce when the wife was convicted of serious sexual misconduct.

Problems with the Sexual Misconduct View. In spite of its popularity, this interpretation has several problems. In the first place, it contradicts the immediate context where Jesus rejects the Mosaic provision of divorce as being against God's creational plan for the permanence of the marriage union: "What therefore God has joined together, let not man put asunder" (Matt 19:6). The present negative imperative of the verb (*chorizeto*) "let not put asunder" enjoins the cessation of a practice in progress, namely, the severing of marriage unions permanently established by God.

In the light of Christ's refusal to accept the Mosaic provision for divorce, it is hard to imagine that He would make allowance for the dissolution of marriage in the case of sexual misconduct. If the latter were true, Jesus would be contradicting what He had just affirmed regarding the permanence of the marriage union. His teaching would represent not a rejection of the Mosaic concession but merely an interpretation essentially similar to that of the Shammaites. But the Pharisees certainly understood Jesus' teaching to be in conflict with Moses ("Why then did Moses command one to give a certificate of divorce, and to put her away?"—Matt 19:7). The clear conflict between Jesus' teaching on the permanence of the marriage union and the Mosaic concession, logically rules out the wider meaning of *porneia* as sexual misconduct.

Would Christ teach that our righteousness must exceed that of the Scribes and Pharisees and then side with one party of the Pharisees by saying that a man should not divorce his wife except for the cause of unfaithfulness? If that were true, where would the superiority of Christ's teaching be? And why would the disciples be astonished at His teaching? They could well have expected Christ to side more with the conservative view of Shammai than with the liberal view of Hillel. In the light of considerations such as these, *porneia* must have a narrower meaning that does not contradict the astonishingly radical and revolutionary teaching of Matthew 19:3-9.

A second problem with interpretating *porneia* as sexual misconduct is posed by the teaching of Jesus in Mark 10:1-12 and Luke 16:18 where divorce and remarriage are condemned as adultery without any exceptions. While today we can bring together the teaching of Jesus on divorce as found in all the three Synoptic Gospels, the Gentile readers of Mark's or Luke's Gospels, who did not have access to Matthew's Gospel which circulated primarily among the Jewish-Christians, had no way of knowing that Jesus made allowance for divorce and remarriage in the case of marital unfaithfulness.

A third problem with interpreting the exception clause as sexual misconduct is that it contradicts Paul's "no divorce" teaching in 1 Corinthians 7:10-11. In this passage, Paul claims to give Christ's own command by enjoining the wife not to separate from her husband and the husband not to divorce his wife. The total prohibition of divorce by Paul reflects the teaching of Jesus found in Mark and Luke.

A fourth problem with the interpretation of *porneia* as sexual misconduct (adultery) is that this term is not the normal word for adultery, though it may include it. The normal Greek term for adultery is *moicheia*, a term used by Jesus in all the divorce texts to describe the outcome of divorce and remarriage, namely, "commits adultery." If Jesus intended to permit divorce specifically in the case of adultery, He would probably have used the explicit term *moicheia*. The fact that He used another term suggests that *porneia* may refer to something other than adultery.

This conclusion is supported by the fact that there is no provision in the Pentateuch for divorce in the case of adultery. The penalty for proven adultery was death (Lev 20:10; Deut 22:22, 23-27) and not divorce. The same was true in the case of a woman who had engaged in sex before marriage (Deut 22:13-21). She was stoned to death and not divorced. There are no indications in the Pentateuch that divorce was ever allowed for sexual misconduct.

A fifth problem with interpreting the exception clause as sexual misconduct is that it fails to take into account the astonishment of the disciples at the saying of Jesus. As Edward Schillebeeckx points out, "If Matthew 19:9 is taken to mean that Jesus was siding with the followers of the school of Shammai, who permitted divorce on grounds of adultery, then the astonishment expressed in the apostles' answers would be incomprehensible—'then it is not expedient to marry' (19:10). Their astonishment is only explicable if Christ in fact rejected all possibility of the dissolution of marriage. His rejection is reinforced by the statement: 'Not all men can receive this precept, but only those to whom it is given'" (19:11).[12] In the light of the foregoing considerations, we are bound to conclude that it is most unlikely that by the exception of *porneia*, Jesus meant to allow for divorce and remarriage on the grounds of adultery or sexual misconduct. Respect for the astonishing and radical teaching of Matthew 19:3-9 requires that *porneia* be interpreted in a narrower sense.

Unfaithfulness During the Betrothal Period. A second interpretation of the exception clause is that Jesus allowed for divorce and remarriage in the case of sexual immorality during the betrothal period.[13] Unlike modern engagement, the Jewish betrothal was a legal contract that was as binding as marriage (Deut 20:7; 22:24). If the betrothed proved unfaithful prior to the consummation of the marriage, legal action could be taken and divorce could be obtained. Following this custom, when Joseph discovered that Mary was expecting a child while betrothed to him, he planned to divorce her quietly rather than exposing her to public disgrace (Matt 1:18, 19).

According to this view, the exception of *porneia* allows divorce only in the case of unfaithfulness during the betrothal period. By her infidelity, the betrothed girl had broken her agreement to marry, and consequently, the man could be released from his obligation to marry the girl since marriage had not yet been consummated. The exception clause would then apply only to the ancient Jewish betrothal practice and not to modern marriages.

The betrothal interpretation of the exception clause does take into account the Jewish orientation of Matthew's Gospel and finds support in the example of Joseph and Mary (Matt 1:19). The most obvious objection to this interpretation, however, is that the debate between Jesus and the Pharisees centered on *marriage* and not on betrothal. It seems unlikely that Jesus would reply to the Pharisees' question regarding the Mosaic provision for divorce by referring to unfaithfulness during the betrothal period, a situation which is foreign to the Mosaic provision and to the subject under discussion. Moreover, this interpretation does not account adequately for the absence of the exception clause in Mark and Luke, for the betrothal practice was common among the Greeks and the Romans to whom the exception would also apply. Another point to be noted is that the word *porneia* is never used elsewhere in the New Testament to describe the sin of illicit relations during the betrothal period.

Refusal of Jesus to Comment. A third interpretation attempts to explain Matthew's exception clause by concentrating on the sentence as a whole. Some scholars argue that *porneia* is to be equated with "something indecent" of Deuteronomy 24:1 and then suggest that Jesus refused to comment on the meaning of the Deuteronomic phrase. According to this view, the exception clause should be translated as "setting aside the matter of *porneia*."[14]

This view is attractive because it concentrates on the overall meaning of the passage, rather than on a single word. It upholds the fundamental truth affirmed by Jesus that from the beginning God established marriage as an indissoluble, life-long relationship. It also harmonizes the difference between Matthew and Mark/Luke in Jesus' teaching on divorce. Writing to Jewish readers, Matthew refers to their legitimate concern about *porneia* without suggesting that Jesus has made it a ground for divorce. In spite of its attractiveness, this view lacks grammatical support because the Greek words do not allow such a translation.

Inclusive Meaning of Exception Clause. A fourth interpretation gives the exception clause an *inclusive* rather than exclusive meaning. A number of modern exegetes have argued that the Greek words translated as "except for unchastity" (RSV), do not have any limiting meaning in this context. In this case, the passage of Matthew 19:9 would read: "Whoever divorces his wife, even if she has committed adultery, and marries another, commits adultery."[15]

According to this interpretation, Matthew wanted to impress upon his Jewish readers that not even adultery constituted a valid ground for divorce. This interpretation may be grammatically possible, but it seems rather unusual because it is based on a rather uncommon inclusive usage of the word *parektos*, usually translated "except for." This inclusive interpretation is based upon what Bruce Vawter calls "linguistic acrobatics," which turns "except" into "even including."[16] It must be granted, however, that this interpretation does harmonize with the immediate context where Jesus rejects the Mosaic provision for divorce by pointing back to God's original plan for marriage as a permanent covenant.

Marriages Unlawful According to Mosaic Law. A fifth view is based on a narrower interpretation of *porneia* as referring to marriages which conflicted with the conditions laid down by Leviticus (Lev 18:6-18).[17] In His call to practical holiness, God prohibited His people from marrying near relatives. Such marriages are condemned presumably because they are the result of sexual passion rather than of genuine love.

According to this interpretation, Jesus allows for divorce only where a marriage should not have taken place in the first place, namely, within the degrees of prohibited relationships. Consequently, in Matthew, Jesus does not envisage any exception to the absolute ban on divorce but only allows for the dissolution of a marriage which was validly contracted according to Graeco-Roman laws but which was in conflict with the Mosaic law of prohibited relationships.

It may be objected that the Mosaic prohibition against incestuous marriages precludes any provision on the part of Christ for a legitimate divorce. This objection, however, as Carl Laney points out, "does not hold up under close scrutiny, for the Israelites were commanded not to marry foreign women (Deut 7:3-4), but when the command was violated in Ezra 9-10, the unlawful marriages were dissolved. The prohibition would not preclude the possibility of violation and the need to deal with an illegal incestuous situation."[18]

This view appears to me as the most satisfactory and enjoys considerable scholarly support. Among the scholars who advocate this view, mention can be made of J. Bonsirven, H. Cazelles, M. Berrouard, J. Kahmann, W. K. Lowther Clark, and more recently Charles Ryrie and the noted New Testament scholar, F. F. Bruce.[19] Commenting on the use of *porneia* in Acts 15:20, 29, Bruce notes: "But fornication could bear a more technical sense of marital union within the prohibited degrees of consanguinity or affinity laid down by the Hebrew 'law of holiness' (Lev 18:6-18). There are one or two other places in the New Testament where fornication may have this technical sense—e.g. the concession 'except on the ground of fornication' added in the Matthean version of Jesus' prohibition of divorce for his followers (Matt 5:32; 19:9)."[20] Four major arguments support this view of the exception clause.

(1) *New Testament Use of Porneia.* One of the possible lexical meanings of *porneia* is "incest" or "incestuous marriage."[21] We find this meaning in 1 Corinthians 5:1 where Paul demands the expulsion of a Christian who has married his stepmother, a clear violation of Leviticus 18:8. The same meaning of *porneia* appears in Acts 15:20, 29 where the Jerusalem Council recommends that Gentile converts should abstain from idol sacrifices, blood, meat of strangled animals, and *porneia*. It is significant to note, as Carl Laney points out, "the order suggested first by James (Acts 15:20) and then given by the Council (Acts 15:29):

James

Idol Sacrifices	Lev. 17:8-9
Porneia	Lev. 18:6-18
Things Strangled	Lev. 17:13-14
Blood	Lev. 17:10-12

The Council

Idol Sacrifices	Lev. 17:8-9
Blood	Lev. 17:10-12
Things Strangled	Lev. 17:13-14
Porneia	Lev. 18:6-18

It is quite apparent that James was thinking of the Leviticus 17-18 restrictions but suggested them in the wrong order (Acts 15:20). Then, when the Council formulated its decision, the restrictions were recorded in their correct order according to Leviticus 17-18 (Acts 15:29)."[22]

In the light of the correlation existing between the four recommendations of the Jerusalem Council and the regulations of Leviticus 17-18 which appears to be the source of the Council's recommendations, it seems plausible to conclude that *porneia* refers not to sexual immorality in general, but to the forbidden marriage relationships of Leviticus 18:6-18 in particular.

There was no need for the Jerusalem Council to require Gentile converts to abstain from sexual immorality in general for they were required to abstain from it anyway. Since the recommendations of the Council were designed to reduce tensions between Jewish and Gentile Christians, the requirement to abstain from *porneia* must be, like the others, based on levitical laws still respected by Jewish Christians. "It is clear from Acts 15," note

Bernard Leeming and R. A. Dyson, "that there was, early in Christian history, considerable discussion about the matter [of *porneia*] among Hebrew converts, and the Council of Jerusalem may well have legislated before Matthew's Gospel was written, with full knowledge that Christ had spoken in this sense."[23]

The Jews who became Christians continued to obey the Mosaic laws of prohibited relationships, but Gentile converts did not feel bound to such laws as indicated by the case of a Corinthian Christian who had married his step-mother (1 Cor 5:1). This inevitably led to a conflict which the Jerusalem Council solved by exempting the Gentiles from the law of circumcision while expecting them to obey the laws relating to idol sacrifice, blood, things strangled, and illicit marriage to a near relative.

"Since," as Lowther Clark points out, "the first three articles of the compromise are concerned with practices which were abhorrent to the Jews but seemed innocent enough to the Gentiles, the fourth must be of a similar nature. The passage of 1 Corinthians gives us the clue. *Porneia* here means *marriage within the prohibited Levitical degrees*. In this matter, Gentile Christianity wholly adopted Jewish standards, and the decree became obsolete because there was no longer any difference of opinion. But for a decade or two, especially in places like Antioch, where Jew and Gentile met and where the agitation culminating in the decree arose, *marriage within the prohibited degrees* was a live issue, and *porneia* was the word by which it was known."[24] Applying this meaning of *porneia* to the exception clause, the Lord in Matthew allows one exception to the universal rule of no-divorce, namely, in the case of an illicit marriage to a near relative.

(2) *Jewish Context of Matthew's Gospel*. Matthew wrote his gospel principally for Jewish converts to Christianity. Jewish-Christians continued to follow the Mosaic marriage laws which prohibited marriage with a near relative (Lev 18:6-18). Gentile converts to Christianity kept the Graeco-Roman laws of marriage. This would explain why Matthew, in writing to a Jewish-Christian audience familiar with the prohibitions against marriage to a near relative, includes the exception clause ("except for *porneia*"). Mark and Luke omit the clause presumably because Gentile Christians were less likely than Jewish Christians to marry a near relative. Gentile people were not as tribally related as Jewish people.

Support for this interpretation of *porneia* in Matthew 5:32 and 19:9 is provided by first century Palestinian literature. Joseph Fitzmyer has shown that *porneia* is the Greek translation of the Hebrew *zenut* (cf. LXX Jer 3:2, 9) which is used in the Qumran material to refer to marriage within the forbidden degrees of relationship.[25] The same use is found in later Jewish literature.[26]

(3) *Historical Setting.* The narrower interpretation of the *porneia* exception as referring to incestuous marriages prohibited in Leviticus 18:6-18 is supported also by the historical setting of Christ's dispute with the Pharisees. Since the dispute occurred in Perea (Matt 19:1; Mark 10:1), the territory governed by Herod Antipas, it is quite likely that the Pharisees wanted to trick Jesus into making a statement against the incestuous marriage of Herod Antipas. John the Baptist was imprisoned and executed for condemning Herod Antipas for divorcing his wife in order to marry the wife of his brother Philip (Matt 14:4). Antipas had violated the Mosaic law which stated, "You shall not uncover the nakedness of your brother's wife; she is your brother's nakedness" (Lev 18:16; cf. 20:21).

The Pharisees presumably hoped that Jesus would follow John in openly condemning the incestuous marriage of Herod Antipas. Jesus, however, chose not to condemn Herod Antipas directly, but rather to state the principle that divorce is only permitted in the case of an unlawful marriage. Thus, the historical and geographical setting of the exception clause supports the interpretation of *porneia* as a reference to marriage within prohibited relationships (Lev 18:6-18).

(4) *Immediate Context.* The immediate context supports the narrower interpretation of the *porneia* exception as a reference to the prohibited relationships of Leviticus 18:6-18. In Matthew 19:4-8, Christ rejects the Mosaic provision for divorce as a mere concession to human rebellion running contrary to God's original plan for marriage. In this context, it would be inconsistent for Jesus to proceed to make a concession of his own for divorce in the case of sexual misconduct.

The whole purpose of Christ's argument which moved from Deuteronomy to Genesis, that is to say, from the Mosaic letter of the law which allowed divorce to the creational design of the law which excluded divorce, would be nullified if in the end He simply returned to Deuteronomy again. On the other hand, it would be consistent with what Christ had just declared for Him to say that God's plan for marriage allowed for divorce only in the case of an illegally contracted marriage to a near relative. In all other instances, marriage is a lifelong and binding covenant commitment.

The possibility of marrying a near relative was very real in the tribal Jewish society which consisted of large blood-related families. I was made forcefully aware of this fact while teaching in Ethiopia. Students belonging to the same tribe often referred to one another as brothers or sisters because to some degree they were all related to one another. The situation was not much different in tribal Jewish society where it was relatively easy to marry a near relative. This can explain why Jesus in Matthew—a gospel written for Jewish Christians—would make allowance for divorce in the case of an illegally contracted marriage to a near relative.

Another aspect of the immediate context, which indirectly supports the unlawful marriage view of *porneia*, is the reaction of the disciples: "If such is the case of a man with his wife, it is not expedient to marry" (Matt 19:10). Such a reaction is only explicable if Jesus rejected the possibility of divorce, except in the rare cases of marriage among near relatives where marriage should not have occurred in the first place.

Had Jesus permitted divorce for sexual misconduct, He would hardly have provoked such a reaction on the part of His disciples, since such a view was widely known and promoted by the rabbinical school of Shammai. The astonishment of the disciples indirectly proves that they understood Christ's standard for marriage to be immeasurably higher and more exacting than that of the stricter rabbinical school of interpretation.

Conclusion. Our study of the Jewish setting, historical and geographical background, and the immediate context of Matthew 19:1-12 suggests that by the exception clause ("except for *porneia*") Jesus permitted divorce only in the case of an unlawful marriage to a near relative. By means of the *porneia* exception, Christ did not intend to impose the Levitical norms for legitimate marriage, but simply to declare that when such norms were violated, there was a valid reason for the dissolution of marriage.

This view is consistent with the absolute value that Mark, Luke, and Paul place on the saying of Jesus. We are bound to conclude that by the exception phrase about *porneia*, Jesus did not intend to open the way for divorce and remarriage in the case of sexual misconduct. Rather, He wished to reaffirm the creational principle of the permanence of the marriage union by allowing for divorce only in the case of an unlawful marriage. In the light of this conclusion, Matthew 19:9 would read: "whoever divorces his wife, unless his union with her is illegitimate, and marries another, commits adultery."

The teaching of Jesus in the Gospels can be summarized in two points. First, divorce is forbidden because it violates God's intention that marriage be a permanent union of two persons. Second, remarriage after divorce is adultery because divorce does not dissolve the marriage union.

5. The Teaching of Paul in Romans 7:2-3

Next to Jesus no other person influenced early Christian thought and practice as much as Paul. His teachings on divorce and remarriage are most significant since they represent the earliest Christian interpretation and application of Christ's teaching to concrete situations. The two main passages where Paul speaks on marriage and divorce are Romans 7:2-3 and 1 Corinthians 7:10-16.

Paul opens the seventh chapter of Romans by setting forth the principle that death releases a person from the obligation to obey the law. His concern is to show that believers "have died to the law through the body of Christ" (Rom 7:4), who enables them to live not according to the flesh (by the sinful passions condemned by the law), but according to the Spirit (by a righteous life approved by the law—Rom 8:1-4).

To illustrate the principle that the jurisdiction of the law is limited to *living* persons, Paul uses the example of the marriage union: "Thus a married woman is bound by law to her husband as long as he lives; but if her husband dies, she is discharged from the law concerning the husband. Accordingly, she will be called an adulteress if she lives with another man while her husband is alive. But if her husband dies she is free from that law, and if she marries another man she is not an adulteress" (Rom 7:2-3).

In this passage, Paul asserts a basic principle respecting marriage, namely that a woman is bound by the marriage law to her husband as long as he lives, but when he dies, she is released from her marital bond. Death alone releases a spouse from the marriage bond. Paul then applies this principle figuratively to the release of the believer from slavery to the law of sin through his death with Christ (Rom 7:4-6).

Paul's illustration from the marriage relationship sheds light on his view of marriage as a permanent union severed only by death. A woman's obligation to conjugal fidelity continues throughout the whole life of her husband. Any suggestion of exception to such a basic law would be an ethical paradox.

Paul's emphasis upon the binding nature of the marriage law, however, does not exclude the possibility of a woman being released from this law if, for example, her unbelieving husband willfully deserts her. This possibility, as we shall see below, is mentioned in 1 Corinthians 7:15. Such an exceptional case does not invalidate the principle of the sacred and permanent nature of the marriage union. The reason is that the unbelieving spouse by his or her willful and determined desertion has violated the sacredness of the marriage covenant and thus *de facto* destroyed the marriage union. This situation, however, is not contemplated in Romans 7:2-3 where Paul uses the marriage law simply to illustrate the principle that death releases a person from the obligation to obey the law. The illustration sheds light on Paul's view of marriage as a lifetime union, but does not necessarily imply that *only* death dissolves the marriage bond.

6. The Teaching of Paul in 1 Corinthians 7:10-16

Paul's treatment of the divorce question in 1 Corinthians 7:10-16 is most significant because it reveals how the teaching of Jesus on divorce was understood and applied to certain concrete marital situations in the apostolic church. He begins the chapter by setting forth some general principles about marriage. To avoid the temptation to sexual immorality, "each man should have his own wife and each woman her own husband" (1 Cor 7:2). Both husband and wife should fulfill their respective conjugal duties (1 Cor 7:3-5). The unmarried and the widows who have the gift of celibacy should remain single as himself (1 Cor 7:7-8). Next Paul discusses three different divorce situations: (1) the divorce of two believers (vv. 10-11), (2) the divorce of a believer and an unbeliever where the unbeliever does not want to divorce, and (3) the divorce of a believer and an unbeliever where the unbeliever wants to divorce.

Divorce of Two Believers. Paul first speaks to married believers who might consider divorce as a means to resolve their marital conflicts: "To the married I give charge, not I but the Lord, that the wife should not separate from her husband (but if she does, let her remain single or else be reconciled to her husband)—and that the husband should not divorce his wife" (1 Cor 7:10-11). Appealing to the teaching of Christ (cf. Mark 10:9, 11, 12; Luke 16:18; Matt 19:3-9), Paul declares in absolute terms that a Christian couple should not seek divorce. Twice he affirms the no-divorce principle: ". . . the wife should not separate from her husband . . . and the husband should not divorce his wife" (1 Cor 7:10-11). The basis of Paul's prohibition is Christ's teaching that husband and wife are one flesh and what God has joined together no man should put asunder.

Paul recognizes, however, that human nature is perverse and that even a Christian husband or wife can make marriage intolerable for the other partner. A spouse who is out of fellowship with God can become intolerant, abusive, unfaithful, domineering, inconsiderate. Undoubtedly, Paul had run into situations of this kind and recognizes that sometimes separation may be inevitable. However, if separation becomes a necessity, Paul leaves Christian partners with two options: (1) to remain permanently unmarried, or (2) to be reconciled to one's partner.

It is important to note that Paul appeals to the teaching of Jesus ("not I but the Lord") in ruling against the possibility of divorce for a Christian couple. On this point, F. F. Bruce comments: "For a Christian husband or wife, divorce is excluded by the law of Christ: here Paul has no need to express a judgment of his own, for the Lord's ruling on this matter was explicit."[27]

To appreciate the revolutionary nature of such teaching, it is important to remember that divorce and remarriage were allowed in both the Jewish and Roman society. Yet Paul affirms the no-divorce principle for Christians as a word of the Lord which will be accepted without challenge. This goes to show that within twenty-five years of the crucifixion itself, the Apostolic Church believed and taught that Christ had proclaimed the permanence of the marriage union. This belief played an important role in the Christian mission to revolutionize the values of the existing society.

In Paul's day, there was no provision for a wife to be legally separated from her husband without being divorced. Fortunately today, the law provides for legal separation as an alternative to divorce. Legal separation offers to a Christian the protection of the law while leaving the door open for reconciliation. Such a door must be left open because Christians believe that no marital conflict is impossible for God to solve.

Since there was no legal separation in Paul's day, the apostle recommends a legal separation–type of divorce. This is indicated by his use of the verb *koridzo* ("to separate") rather than the normal verb for divorce *apoluo* used by Jesus. By recommending a legal separation–type of divorce, Paul respects the spirit of Christ's teaching while at the same time providing protection for the believing wife until a reconciliation with her husband can be realized.

Divorce of a Believer Married to an Unbeliever Who Does Not Want a Divorce. The second situation that Paul addresses is that of a believing spouse married to an unbeliever: "To the rest I say, not the Lord, that if any brother has a wife who is an unbeliever, and she consent to live with him, he should not divorce her. If any woman has a husband who is an unbeliever, and he consents to live with her, she should not divorce him" (1 Cor 7:12-13).

Since the Lord had not given instruction concerning marriage between believers and unbelievers, Paul exercises his own apos-tolic authority and inspiration ("I say, not the Lord") in enjoining again the principle of *no separation*. The personal nature of Paul's instruction does not weaken its binding authority because he speaks as one who had received mercy of the Lord to be faithful (1 Cor 7:25) and one who had the Spirit of God (1 Cor 7:40). Cognizant of this divine mandate, Paul openly declares without fear of presumption: "This is my rule in all the churches" (1 Cor 7:17).

The instruction of Paul is clear: if the unbeliever does not want a divorce, the believer should not seek for it. The reason given for preserving the marriage union is the sanctifying influence of the believing partner upon the unbelieving spouse and children: "For the unbelieving husband is consecrated through his wife, and the unbelieving wife is consecrated through her husband. Otherwise, your children would be unclean, but as it is they are holy" (1 Cor 7:14-15).

The reason given by Paul for maintaining the marriage union is pertinent to the fears entertained by Corinthian converts regarding a possible defilement contracted by being married to an unbeliever. Paul puts such fears to rest by revealing the sanctifying power of the Christian faith. The faith of the believing spouse becomes a channel of saving grace to the unbelieving partner. The presence of a believer in the home sets it apart ("sanctifies") and gives to it a Christian influence that can bring the unbelieving partner and children to Christ. As Paul puts it in verse 16: "Wife, how do you know whether you will save your husband? Husband, how do you know whether you will save your wife?"

Divorce of a Believer Married to an Unbeliever Who Wants a Divorce. The third situation that Paul addresses is that of an unbelieving partner who wants a divorce. His instruction in this case is: "But if the unbelieving partner desires to separate, let it be so; in such a case the brother or sister is not bound. For God has called us to peace" (1 Cor 7:15). Paul is not commanding the unbelieving partner to separate. The permissive imperative "let it be so" (*korizestho*) presupposes that the unbelieving spouse has already willfully initiated or accomplished the separation. Consequently, Paul advises to let the separation take its course and become an accomplished fact. The believer need not pursue the deserting spouse and is free from all marital obligations. The Greek verb *ou dedoulotai*, literally "no longer enslaved," implies that cohabitation with such a person is slavery for the believing partner. Since Christ has called us to peace, the believer may withdraw from slavery in such a case.

This introduces us to one of the most debated questions in the interpretation of a New Testament passage. The question centers on the exact meaning of the verb "is not bound" or "is not enslaved" (*ou dedoulotai*). Does it mean that the believing party is free in the sense of being permitted to remarry after the separation, or in the sense of being free to separate but not remarry? In other words, is Paul granting to the believing spouse only the right to separate from bed and board or the right to separate and marry another? Does desertion give to the innocent partner the right of divorce with the liberty to remarry?

Some maintain that Paul grants to the deserted believer only the freedom to separate but not to remarry. They appeal to the fact that "Paul says nothing in verse 15 about a second marriage for the deserted spouse."[28] They interpret the silence of Paul as indicating that he offers to a deserted believer the same two alternatives given to separated believers, namely, reconciliation or lifelong single life (1 Cor 7:11).

This view ignores the striking difference between the conditional separation of believing spouses mentioned in verses 10 and 11 and the unconditional separation caused by the desertion of an unbelieving spouse envisaged in verse 15. In the former case, Paul strictly enjoins the spouse who has separated to remain unmarried or be reconciled. In the latter case, Paul recognizes the finality of the separation caused by the deserting party by saying, "Let it be so." In other words, "let the case be closed and the separation take place."

"In verse 15," as John Murray points out, "we find a terseness and severity of terms which, viewed from the standpoint of the separation envisioned, are indicative of decisiveness and finality—'let him (or her) depart,' that is, 'let him (or her) be gone.'"[29] Because the separation is final, it is unconditional. That is to say, there is no injunction to remain unmarried or be reconciled. Instead, there is the affirmation that the deserted spouse "is not bound" (1 Cor 7:15).

The phrase "not bound" (*ou dedoulotai*) presupposes the dissolution of the marriage bond and consequently the freedom of the deserted spouse to remarry. This conclusion is supported by Paul's affirmation in verse 39 of the same chapter that a husband's death releases the wife from the marriage bond and frees her to marry again: "A wife is bound to her husband as long as he lives. If the husband dies, she is free to be married to whom she wishes, only in the Lord" (1 Cor 7:39).

The dissolution of the marriage bond by a willful and obstinate desertion is somewhat similar to the dissolution of the marriage bond by death. In both instances, the marriage relationship is terminated by the permanent departure of a spouse. Whether such a departure is caused by death or by the obstinate desertion of an unbelieving partner, the outcome is the same. The surviving spouse is released from the marriage bond and is free to remarry.

Some argue that if Paul taught that the desertion by an unbelieving partner dissolved the marriage bond, then he would be setting up a double standard of ethics: one which excludes the dissolution where two believers are involved and one which includes dissolution where an unbelieving partner deserts the believing spouse. This apparent contradiction can be resolved by recognizing the substantial difference that exists between the two cases. In the first case, the initiative in the separation is taken by a Christian who knows that marriage is a sacred, lifelong covenant that can and must be preserved. In the second case, the initiative in the separation is taken by a non-Christian partner who does not accept the Christian view of marriage as a sacred, lifelong covenant.

To a believer, marriage has a deeper and more radical meaning than to an unbeliever. A believer marries "in the Lord" (1 Cor 7:39), that is, according to the will of God who joins together two partners into a sacred, lifelong covenant, enabling them to become "one flesh." An unbeliever marries "in the pagan society" which views marriage as a civil or social contract that can be terminated through a legal proceeding. Since a believing spouse cannot impose his/her Christian view of marriage upon the unbelieving partner, if the latter is obstinately determined to desert his/her believing spouse, then the marriage union is dissolved.

The difference that Paul makes between the marriage of two believers which cannot be dissolved and the mixed marriage of a believer to an unbeliever which can be dissolved when the latter deserts the believing partner, offers perhaps the strongest biblical evidence for the sacred, permanent nature of the Christian marriage. This does not mean that a mixed marriage is automatically less sacred than a Christian marriage, since Paul explains that a believing partner exercises a sanctifying influence upon the marriage relationship (1 Cor 7:14). What it does mean is that marriage has a special character for two believing partners. Their common faith and commitment to God unite them in a real, objective, and lifelong marriage bond. Such a permanent commitment is possible because their faith in Christ offers them the means for fulfilling God's original design of marriage: the two shall be one flesh.

Conclusion. Paul's teaching on the question of divorce in 1 Corinthians 7:12-16 not only closely reflects Jesus' teachings concerning the permanence of marriage, but also reveals its full depths. It does this by showing how the Christian faith causes the marriage covenant to become a sacred and lifelong relationship. There is for Paul an intimate connection between the permanence of the marriage bond and the Christian faith.

A Christian couple who marries "in the Lord" accepts the responsibility by divine grace to honor their covenant commitment both to God and to one another. It is the sacred and permanent nature of the Christian covenant commitment to God that makes a Christian marriage sacred and permanent. On account of this fact, a Christian couple experiencing marital problems may separate with the hope of reconciliation but may not divorce and remarry. This condition does not apply to a mixed marriage where the unbelieving partner deserts his believing spouse, because by the very act of desertion the unbeliever rejects the Christian view of marriage as a sacred and permanent union.

Summing up, like Jesus the apostle Paul affirms the principle that Christian marriage is a union binding and permanent for life. If a separation should occur, Paul presents only two alternatives to believing partners: be reconciled to one another or remain single.

7. The Teaching of Paul on Divorce and Church Leadership

Paul's view of Christian marriage as a lifelong union which admits no divorce and remarriage is indirectly supported by the marriage qualifications he sets forth for church leaders: "Now a bishop must be above reproach, the husband of one wife" (1 Tim 3:2; cf. Titus 1:6). "Let deacons be the husband of one wife, and let them manage their children and their households well" (1 Tim 3:12).

The basic qualifications given by Paul for the church offices of elder (or overseer) and deacon were designed to enable Timothy in Ephesus and Titus on Crete to appoint church leaders qualified to serve in such offices. The first qualification for the office of elder is that the man must be "above reproach." His blameless lifestyle is to serve as a role model to the congregation and is to offer no reason for criticism in the community. The first important aspect of his role modeling is his marital status, which Paul defines as "husband of one wife" (1 Tim 3:2; Titus 1:6). This qualification occurs both in 1 Timothy and Titus immediately after the demand for blamelessness, thus indicating the prominence Paul gives to the marital status of a church leader.

The Greek words translated "husband of one wife" can be rendered literally as "one-wife-man." This short phrase has been the subject of considerable discussion. Did Paul mean that a church leader should be married only to one woman at a time or only once during his lifetime? Did Paul intend to exclude from church leadership *polygamists*, that is, men married to several wives or *digamists*, that is, men married twice or more legally?

Exclusion of Polygamists. Some, including John Calvin, have understood the phrase "husband of one wife" to exclude polygamists from church leadership.[30] This interpretation is discredited by two main considerations. First, there was no need for this qualification since no Christian, whether church leader or not, was allowed to practice polygamy. Second, in New Testament times polygamy was generally outlawed in the empire and thus the church hardly needed such a stricture from Paul.[31]

Exclusion of Digamists. The more plausible meaning of the phrase "husband of one wife" appears to be "married only once." This is in fact the rendering of the New Revised Standard Version. According to this view, divorce and remarriage would disqualify a man from the office of elder and deacon. Paul would be stressing the importance of appointing to church leadership only men whose marital status was beyond suspicion by having been married only once. Several considerations favor this interpretation.

The priests in the Old Testament were enjoined to uphold a higher marriage standard by marrying only a virgin, and not "a widow, or one divorced, or a woman who has been defiled, or a harlot" (Lev 21:14; cf. 21:7). This Old Testament precedent supports the New Testament higher marriage standards for elders and deacons. Elsewhere I have shown that even the requirement for church leaders to be "abstinent" (1 Tim 3:2) finds its precedent in the Old Testament strict prohibition against the use of alcoholic beverages by the priests (Lev 10:9).[32]

The Greek construction of the phrase *mias gunaikos andra* ("one-wife-man") without the definite article emphasizes the moral character of the individual as being totally committed to one woman. Such a total commitment is best exemplified by faithfulness to one's spouse "till death do us part." In an age when the marriage bond was lightly regarded and commonly dishonored, Paul emphasized that a church leader must be an example of marital fidelity. Such a fidelity would exclude the possibility of divorce and remarriage.

This may be inferred also from the requirement that a woman enrolled in the official order of widows was to have been "the wife of one husband" (1 Tim 5:9). In Greek, the phrase corresponds to "the husband of one wife." Since the widows enrolled in the ministry of the church were to have been married only once, it seems safe to assume that the same qualification applied to the office of elder. The linguistic similarity between the two phrases ("husband of one wife" and "wife of one husband") strongly suggests that in both instances the person was to have been married only once.

Historical Support. This view was commonly held in early Christianity. Tertullian, for example, writing at the beginning of the third century, says: "Among us the prescript is more fully and more carefully laid down, that they who are chosen into the sacerdotal order must be men of one marriage; which rule is so rigidly observed that I remember some removed from their office for digamy."[33]

Tertullian then argues that the same rule should apply to the laity because in a sense all Christians are priests. While his extension to the laity of the "one marriage" principle may have been influenced by his Montanistic views, his reference to the rigid application of such a principle to the clergy provides historical support for the "married only once" interpretation of the phrase "husband of one wife" (1 Tim 3:2; Titus 1:6).

Another example can be found in the fourth century collection of ecclesiastical laws, known as *The Apostolic Canons*. The seventeenth canon establishes that "He who has been twice married after his baptism, or has a concubine, cannot be made a bishop, or presbyter, or deacon."[34] The same rule appears in the related work, known as *The Constitutions of the Holy Apostles*, which states: "We have already said, that a bishop, a presbyter, and a deacon, when they are constituted, must be but once married, whether their wives be alive or whether they be dead."[35] Historical testimonies such as these strongly support the "married only once" interpretation of the Pauline requirement "husband of one wife."

Objections. Some object to this interpretation becausethey feel it reflects a low view of marriage. The prohibition of a second marriage after the death of one's spouse would seem to make marriage almost a necessary evil that can be allowed only once. Such a view of marriage is contradicted by the Scripture which presents marriage as a divinely established, honorable institution. Furthermore, this objection ignores the fact that the restriction against a second marriage applies not to Christians in general but to elders and deacons in particular. Their leadership responsibilities place some restrictions on their personal liberty in the area of marriage. While a lay member is permitted to remarry after the death of his or her spouse (1 Cor 7:39; 1 Tim 5:14), a church leader is advised not to remarry.

The reason for the "married only once" requirement could be that a second marriage after the death of one's spouse would entail additional family responsibilities, especially if children are born to the second marriage. These additional obligations could certainly limit a church leader's opportunities for ministering to the needs of the congregation. A man who prefers to establish a second family through a second marriage at the expense of greater opportunities for serving Christ may lack the total commitment to Christ required of a church leader.

Another objection to the "married only once" interpretation is that it allegedly makes the *past marital history* more important than *one's present character.* "It is possible," writes Stanley A. Ellisen, "to have a good marital history of a single marriage and have a 'cat-calling' character of wandering affections at the same time. On the other hand, it is also possible to have a sorrowful marital history of a broken marriage while having a personal character that is above reproach."[36]

No one will dispute the truth that the present moral character of a man is more important than his past sorrowful marital history. The problem with this reasoning is that it creates an alternative that is not applicable to a church leader. We have seen that the qualifications for church leadership require both a good *past* marital history *and* a *present* blameless moral character. The reason for this high standard is that a church leader serves as a living model of Christian principles and practices, both to church members and to those outsidethe church.

In summary, both the Old and New Testaments uphold the principle of high marriage standards for church leaders (Lev 21:7, 14-15; 1 Tim 3:2, 12; Titus 1:6). In the New Testament church the elders and deacons must stand before the congregation as role models of blameless lifestyle, especially by being the "husband of one wife," that is to say, married only once and totally devoted to one's wife. This excludes the possibility for church leaders to divorce, remarry or to lust after other women. The standard is admittedly high, but God could hardly allow a lesser standard for those who have been called to give spiritual leadership to His church. To allow a man who has been divorced and remarried to serve as the spiritual leader of a congregation means to tempt its members to follow his bad example by divorcing their spouses and remarrying, if the occasion arises.

The foregoing discussion of the marriage qualifications for church leaders has served to corroborate the principle that Christian marriage is a permanent, lifelong union, which admits no divorce and remarriage. This principle is to be upheld especially by church leaders because their lifestyle and teaching serve as a role model for many to follow.

CONCLUSION

In this chapter we have found that both the Old and New Testaments clearly and consistently condemn divorce as a violation of God's original plan for marriage as a lifelong union that enables a man and a woman to become "one flesh." Respect for this fundamental principle demands that a Christian couple experiencing marital conflicts should not seek to resolve them through divorce. If a marriage relationship becomes intolerable, a Christian couple can consider a legal separation. The purpose of the separation should be to provide an opportunity for the couple to work toward a possible reconciliation. It is only when reconciliation is no longer possible that divorce and remarriage are permissible.

NOTES TO CHAPTER VI

1. Jay E. Adams, *Marriage, Divorce and Remarriage* (Phillipsburgh, New Jersey, 1980), p. xiii.

2. See Fred H. Wight, *Manners and Customs of the Bible Lands* (Chicago: Moody Press, 1953), p. 125.

3. J. Carl Laney, *The Divorce Myth* (Minneapolis, 1981), p. 29.

4. *Encyclopedia Judaica*, 1971 ed., s.v. "Divorce."

5. Joseph Addison Alexander, *The Gospel According to Matthew Explained* (London, 1884), p. 145.

6. William A. Heth and Gordon J. Wenham, *Jesus and Divorce* (London, 1984), pp. 106-110.

7. Talmudic Tract *Gittin* 9:10.

8. There is an apparent discrepancy in the form of the Pharisees' question and of the Lord's reply between Matthew 19:7, 8 on the one hand, and Mark 10:3-5 on the other. In Matthew 19:7 the Pharisees ask: "Why then did Moses *command* one to give a certificate of divorce, and to put her away?" In His reply Jesus says: "For your hardness of heart Moses *allowed* you to divorce your wives." But in Mark 10:3-5 the verbs appear in the reverse order. Jesus asks, "What did Moses *command* you?" and the Pharisees reply, "Moses

allowed a man to write a certificate of divorce and put her away." To which Jesus replies, "For your hardness of heart he wrote you this *commandment*" (Mark 10:5).

The apparent discrepancy between Matthew and Mark can be resolved by considering several points. First, by saying "What did Moses *command* you?" (Mark10:3), Christ was possibly referring not merely to Deuteronomy 24:1-14 but primarily to the whole Mosaic revelation, including Genesis 2:24. In such a case Christ would have meant, "What are the teachings of Moses on this matter?"

Second, even if Jesus alluded only to Deuteronomy 24:1-4, it does not necessarily follow that Jesus meant that Moses required men to put away their wives. He could have simply meant, "What was the Mosaic legislation on this matter?" The Mosaic legislation did not require divorce, but it did require certain strict procedures if a divorce was given. In that sense it would be a prescription or a command. (Emphasis supplied.)

9. John Murray, *Divorce* (Phillipsburgh, New Jersey, 1961), p. 33.

10. Hugh Montefiore, "Jesus on Divorce and Remarriage," in *Marriage, Divorce and the Church: The Report of the Archbishop's Commission on the Christian Doctrine of Marriage* (London, 1971), p. 37.

11. Friedrich Hauck and Siegfried Schulz, "*Porne, Pornos, Porneia, Porneuo, Ekporneuo,*" *Theological Dictionary of the New Testament*, eds. Gerhard Kittel and Gerhard Friedrich, (Grand Rapids, 1968), vol. 6, p. 580.

12. Edward Schillebeeckx, *Marriage, Human Reality and Saving Mystery* (London, 1965), p. 153.

13. For a defense of this view, see Mark Geldard, "Jesus' Teaching on Divorce: Thoughts on the Meaning of *Porneia* in Matthew 5:32 and 19:9," *The Churchman* 92, 2 (1978): 134-143.

14. See, for example, William A. Heth and Gordon J. Wenham, *Jesus and Divorce* (London, 1984), p. 181.

15. For an analysis of this view, see Bernard Leeming and R. A. Dyson, "Except it Be for Fornication," *Scripture* 8 (1956): 75-81.

16. Bruce Vawter, "The Divorce Clauses in Matthew 5:32 and 19:9," *Catholic Biblical Quarterly* 16 (1954): 155-167.

17. See Joseph A. Fitzmyer, "The Matthean Divorce Texts and Some New Palestinian Evidence," *Theological Studies* 37 (1976): 213-221.

18. J. Carl Laney (n. 3), p. 72.

19. For bibliographic references see Edward Schillebeeckx (n. 12), p. 147, and Carl Laney (n. 3), pp. 71, 72.

20. F. F. Bruce, *Paul: Apostle of the Heart Set Free* (Grand Rapids, 1977), p. 185.

21. Edward Robinson, ed., *Greek and English Lexicon of the New Testament,* new and revised ed., s.v. *Porneia,* p. 609.

22. J. Carl Laney (n. 3), p. 73.

23. Bernard Leeming and R. A. Dyson, "Except it Be for Fornication," *Scripture* 8 (1956): 82.

24. W. K. Lowther Clarke, "The Exceptive Clause in Matthew," *Theology* 15 (1927): 167.

25. Joseph A. Fitzmyer (n.17), pp. 213-221.

26. *Testament of Judah* 13:6; *Testament of Reuben* 1:6.

27. F. F. Bruce (n. 20), p. 267.

28. See, for example, J. Carl Laney (n. 3), p. 87.

29. John Murray (n. 9), p. 74.

30. John Calvin, *Commentaries on the Epistles to Timothy, Titus and Philemon,* trans. William Pringle (Grand Rapids, 1948), p. 77.

31. See Will Durant, *The Story of Civilization: Caesar and Christ* (New York, 1944), p. 396.

32. See Samuele Bacchiocchi, *Wine in the Bible* (Berrien Springs, MI., 1989), pp. 206-210.

33. Tertullian, *On Exhortation to Chastity* 7, *The Ante-Nicene Fathers* (Grand Rapids, 1972), vol. IV, p. 54.

34. *The Ecclesiastical Canons of the Holy Apostles* 17, *The Ante-Nicene Fathers* (Grand Rapids, 1970), vol. VII, p. 501.

35. *The Constitutions of the Holy Apostles* 6, 17, *The Ante-Nicene Fathers* (Grand Rapids, 1970), vol. VII, p. 457.

36. Stanley A. Ellisen, *Divorce and Remarriage in the Church* (Grand

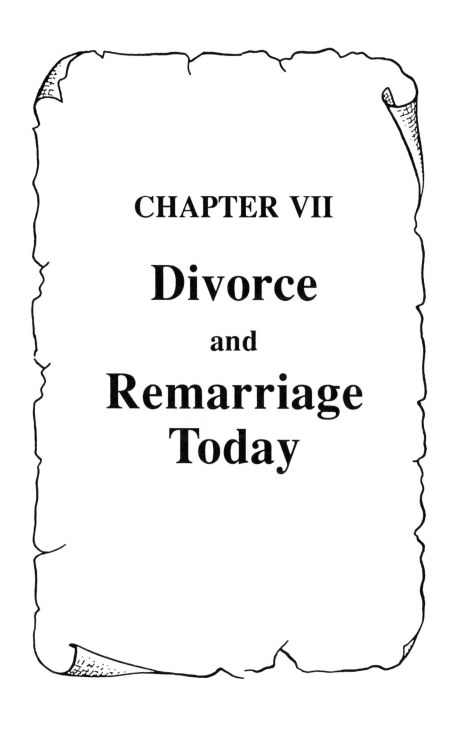

CHAPTER VII

Divorce

and

Remarriage
Today

DIVORCE AND REMARRIAGE TODAY

Often, it is easier to take a machine apart than it is to put it back together into working order. Even skilled technicians sometimes have problems in reassembling certain machines. The same can be true in the study and application of Biblical teachings on divorce and remarriage. To examine the various Old and New Testaments texts relating to divorce and remarriage is in a way an easier task than applying the teaching of such texts to concrete situations. Yet in the final analysis, what really counts is the way Biblical principles are applied to actual marital situations today.

Our task in this chapter is twofold. First, we shall endeavor to summarize the fundamental principles that have emerged from our study of the Biblical teachings on divorce and remarriage in the previous chapter. Second, we shall discuss how the church, in faithful obedience to the Word of God, can uphold and apply its teachings on divorce and remarriage today. We shall endeavor to be both specific and practical while recognizing the complexity of the subject.

PRINCIPLES AND THEIR APPLICATION

1. Divorce Violates God's Intent for Marriage

Prohibition of Divorce and Remarriage. The first fundamental principle stressed in both the Old and New Testaments is that divorce represents a violation of God's original intent for marriage. The Biblical vision of marriage as a sacred, lifelong covenant is rooted in the creation account of the institution of marriage (Gen 2:18-24). Here, marriage is seen as an institution established by God to enable a man and a woman to become "one flesh" (Gen 2:24). It is because God designed marriage to be a thorough merging of two personalities into one life that separation is disapproved.

The condemnation of divorce expressed by Malachi (2:13-16) in the Old Testament and by Jesus (Matt 5:39; 19:3-9; Mark 10:3-12) and Paul (1 Cor 7:10-14) in the New Testament is based on the Creator's vision of the institution of marriage as an indissoluble union.

Difficult Application. The application of the Biblical prohibition of divorce and remarriage is a most difficult task. A major reason is the fact that, in our secular society, marriage is seldom viewed as a sacred, divine institution designed to merge two personalities into an indissoluble union. For the most part, marriage has been "desacralized." It is no longer a permanent, sacred covenant, witnessed and guaranteed by God Himself, but rather a social contract that can be easily terminated. The goal of marriage in our society is not to achieve a spiritual union but to enjoy mutual satisfaction. If one or both partners no longer feel satisfied by the performance of their spouses, they feel free to terminate their relationship and to establish new ones.

The growing acceptance of the secular view of marriage by Christian churches is influencing Christians, including some church leaders, to believe that divorce is a guiltless and at times proper procedure. This perception contributes to the rising divorce rate among Christians. This means that if Christian churches want to substantially reduce the divorce rate among their members, they must propagate through all their resources the Biblical view of marriage as a sacred, permanent covenant. The acceptance of this view will lead to the rejection of divorce as a violation of God's intent for marriage.

It is interesting to note in this regard that Roman Catholics have one of the lowest divorce rates in America. The 1985 study of S. Kenneth Chi and Sharon K. Houseknecht, two sociologists from Ohio State University, indicates that among Catholics there are just 8 divorced persons for every 100 non-divorced persons.[37] This divorce rate is three times lower than the national average. The reason, as the sociologists point out, is that Catholics have greater reverence for marriage and the family. Their deeply rooted theological conviction that marriage is an indissoluble, sacramental union, contributes to a high view of marriage, thus discouraging the possibility of divorce.

If Christian churches wish to alter the permissive attitude of people toward divorce and remarriage, they need to reject divorce by aggressively promoting the Biblical view of marriage as a sacred, lifelong covenant. Such a program would involve actively engaging all of the preaching, teaching, and counseling resources that Christian churches possess.

Preaching Efforts. Preaching on the Biblical vision of the indissolubility of marriage and on the Biblical disapproval of divorce and remarriage can be risky business today. Chances are that most pastors would not survive very long in most parishes if they boldly proclaimed what the Bible teaches on marriage, divorce, and remarriage. Considering that in many congregations half or more members are divorced and remarried, it can be suicidal for any pastor to dare to preach against divorce and remarriage. This may explain why we seldom hear sermons on this subject. By being silent, however, pastors become part of the problem rather than part of its solution.

The solution must be found in encouraging pastors to seek divine grace, wisdom, and courage in preaching the truth in love. This involves, for example, following the example of Jesus in choosing not to attack those who are divorced and remarried but to help everyone understand what God wants our marriages to be. It involves helping married people to learn how to resolve their differences openly, honestly, and constructively without making recourse to divorce. It involves teaching how to build up the marriage covenant by being willing every day to make a total, exclusive, continuing, and growing commitment to one's marriage partner. To the same extent that pastors succeed in helping their members recover and experience the Biblical vision of marriage as a sacred, lifelong covenant, they will be successful in stemming the tide of divorce in their congregations and eventually in the society at large.

Educational Endeavors. This task, however, cannot be left to preaching alone. Another important avenue is teaching. Christian churches can effectively propagate the Biblical vision of marriage through their various educational programs and publications. There is a great need for literature articulating not the cultural, but the Biblical view of marriage, divorce, and remarriage.

Much of the literature available in libraries and bookstores treats this subject purely from a sociological perspective. Marriage is seen as a societal institution governed by the laws of the land rather than by the higher moral law of God. The "no fault" divorce law makes it possible to put asunder what God has united for less than the price of a good suit. To counteract this societal trend, it is imperative to teach in our church schools, Sabbath, or Sunday schools the Biblical view of marriage as a sacred, lifelong covenant, witnessed and guaranteed by God Himself. It is essential to strengthen the conviction that God, who has joined our lives together in holy matrimony, wants us to stay together and will help us to stay together in love and peace.

An important part of the educational program is pre- and post-marital counseling. Christian counselors need to help couples contemplating marriage to understand the serious nature of their marriage commitments. They need to help couples find out whether or not they are suited for one another and are willing to commit themselves to maintaining their marital union, no matter what. If the counselor discovers that partners are not suited for each other or that their commitment is superficial at best, then he or she must advise them to reconsider their marriage plans or at least postpone them temporarily until some of the existing problems have been resolved.

Counseling should continue into the first two or three years of marriage. This is the time when problems arise and the harsh realities become known. More marriages are made or broken during the first few years than at any other period. Counseling during this crucial period can help partners resolve their conflicts and thus facilitate the adjustment process that will gradually lead to the merging of their two lives into "one." Preparing couples for good marriages and helping them to maintain their unions through the storms of the first few years of marriage will go a long way toward rendering divorce obsolete and unnecessary.

2. A Christian Couple Should Not Seek Divorce

A second important principle that has emerged in the course of our study is that a Christian couple experiencing marital conflicts should not seek to resolve them through divorce. We have found this principle best expressed in 1 Corinthians 7:10-11 where Paul emphatically affirms twice the "no divorce" principle: ". . . the wife should not separate from her husband . . . and the husband should not divorce his wife." The basis of Paul's ruling is the teaching of Jesus in the Synoptic Gospels to which he appeals ("not I but the Lord"—1 Cor 7:10).

It is important to note that while today Christians debate whether or not it is right for a divorced person to remarry, both Christ and Paul dealt with the issue of whether or not it is right for married people to divorce. Their answer is abundantly clear: "Absolutely not!" A believer should not seek divorce because the marriage union is sacred and lifelong. To destroy such a union through divorce and remarriage is to commit adultery.

No Application by Jesus. Jesus made no attempt to apply the "no divorce" principle to concrete marital situations. His concern was to counteract the prevailing trend of easy dissolving of marriages simply because Moses seemed to have allowed it. This He did by reaffirming God's creational intent for marriage to be a sacred, lifelong union. While Jesus condemned as "adultery" any attempt to destroy the marriage union through divorce and remarriage, He offered no advice on what Christian couples should do when their marriage relationships becomes intolerable.

Christ's concern was to reveal God's creative intent for marriage and to challenge people to live according to such a divine ideal. This does not mean that Christ was insensitive to those who had already come short of God's expectations by divorcing and remarrying. On the contrary, He drew close to publicans and sinners because He had come "to seek and save the lost" (Luke 19:10). When He met the Samaritan woman at Jacob's well, He did not sit in judgment over her abysmal record of five past marriages and a current illicit relationship. Instead, He ministered to her spiritual needs by helping her understand the spiritual nature and worship of God (John 4:16-26).

The purpose of Christ's ministry was to reveal, on the one hand, God's absolute creative will and, on the other hand, God's absolute redemptive love. He revealed God's *absolute will* in terms of general principles rather than in terms of specific applications of such principles. He taught, for example, that nursing anger is the equivalent of murder (Matt 5:22), that lusting is the equivalent of adultery (Matt 5:28), and that divorcing and remarrying is also the equivalent of adultery (Matt 19:9). In none of these instances, however, did Christ explain how to deal with those who had committed such sins. Instead, He chose to reveal God's *absolute acceptance* of sinners. The prodigal son is accepted back and fully pardoned for his sins (Luke 15:11-32). The lost sheep is sought and found (Luke 15:1-10). The penitent tax collector is justified by God while the self-righteous Pharisee is not (Luke 18:11-14).

The same dual perspective applies to marriage and divorce. We have found that, on the one hand, Jesus condemned divorce as a violation of God's original plan for marriage to be a permanent union of a man and a woman. Yet, on the other hand, He showed divine forgiveness and acceptance of those who had thwarted God's intent for their marriage. He offered, however, no explicit directives on how the church should deal with those experiencing marital problems. Perhaps the Lord chose to do so to prevent our mechanical application of a few rules to complex marital situations. He left to His followers the responsibility of applying the principles He had revealed.

3. Conditional Separation is Permissible in Cases of Serious Marital Problems

Paul offers us an example of how he applied Christ's prohibition of divorce and remarriage by allowing for a conditional separation in cases of serious marital problems. This is the third important principle that has emerged in the course of our study. We have found that, on the one hand, Paul appealed to Christ's teaching in ruling that a Christian couple should not seek divorce, but, on the other hand, he recognized that marriage can become intolerable even when both partners are believing Christians. In this case, he interprets the "no divorce" ruling of Christ as allowing a conditional separation. The condition consists of remaining permanently unmarried or of being reconciled to one's partner (1 Cor 7:11).

We noted earlier that by recommending a legal separation-type of divorce, Paul respects the spirit of Christ's "no-divorce" ruling by providing an opportunity for the couple to separate while working toward a possible reconciliation. Paul's recommendation suggests that a Christian couple should never feel that it is God's will for them to terminate their marriage relationship. Even if they are so incompatible that it would have been better for them not to get married in the first place, it is always God's will for them to remain married once they are. Overcoming incompatibilities is part of the challenge of being transformed by God's enabling grace. The Lord provides us with resources that can turn incompatible differences into complementary strengths.

Divine Resources. In times of marital stress, it is important to remember that divine resources are available for helping us resolve our conflicts. Such resources include the guidance of the Word of God, prayer, and the transforming power of His Spirit. As we learn to utilize the resources God provides, we will discover that no problem is too big for God to handle. It is important to remember that God is interested in our homes, and that He will move heaven and earth, if necessary, to resolve our marital conflicts. But He needs our cooperation. The problem is that sometimes we fail to cooperate with God by neglecting or rejecting the divine resources He offers us. The inevitable result is marital breakups.

Reconciliation. When separation becomes necessary, God's one desire for the Christian couple is that they be reconciled (1 Cor 7:11). To facilitate the reconciliation process, a Christian couple who wishes to register their marital breakdown should file for legal separation rather than for divorce. By choosing this option, they leave the door open for reconciliation. Many difficult marriages could be saved if the church upheld the principle of "no-divorce," allowing instead only a separation in view of a possible reconciliation. If Christian couples experiencing marital problems were told by their churches that they could file for legal separation but they must leave the door open for reconciliation by not remarrying, chances are that most couples would earnestly seek to resolve their conflicts, rather than risk remaining single.

When separation has taken place, it is God's desire for the Christian couple to be reconciled (1 Cor 7:11). God desires reconciliation because He hates divorce (Mal 2:16). Reconciliation should begin with repentance on the part of both partners since breakups are rarely one-sided. As repentance is the first step in our reconciliation with God, so it is also the first step in our reconciliation with our marriage partners. The spirit of repentance should manifest itself in a forgiving and submissive attitude and in an earnest desire to seek the spiritual resources God has provided to bring about healing and reconciliation.

An Example. An example might help to illustrate the principle enunciated above. Mary and John were married for twenty-five years and had brought up two children together. When their two children were "out of their nest," without warning, Mary told John that their relationship had become boring and she wanted to start a new life on her own. She filed for divorce and soon afterward she moved away into an apartment by herself. John was devastated. It took him over a year to recover from the shock and to put the pieces of his life back together. Then he began asking, "What shall I do?" An unbeliever would advise him to forget about Mary and look for a good woman with whom to enjoy the rest of his life. But the advice of Scripture is different. John must continue to pray and work for a possible reconciliation with Mary as long as there exists the possibility of reconciliation.

4. Divorce and Remarriage are Permissible When Reconciliation is no Longer Possible

Reconciliation, however, is not always possible. Such would be the case if Mary had remarried or if she were living in a common-law situation. In such instances our study has shown that divorce and remarriage are permissible. When remarriage has taken place or when the other partner persists in maintaining an adulterous relationship, the former union is permanently dissolved in God's eyes.

We have found this truth emphasized in Deuteronomy 24:2-4 where God prohibits resuming a former union following a second marriage. Such an action is condemned as an "abomination" that pollutes the land (Jer 3:1). When remarriage has taken place, the former marriage is unalterably broken and reconciliation is no longer possible. In such a situation, the other partner is no longer bound. With repentance, he or she will seek divine guidance in determining whether or not to enter into a new marriage relationship.

The Right to Remarry. The question many divorced persons ask today is, "Do I have the right to remarry according to the Scriptures?" This is a crucial question because it involves the lives of an increasing number of church members who seek assurance from their pastor or church that they can enter into a new marriage relationship with a clear conscience. Such assurance must be rooted in the teachings of the Bible and not on personal feelings. If the Bible is normative for our beliefs and practices, it ought to provide guidance on this crucial issue affecting so many lives today. We believe it does.

Our study has shown that remarriage is wrong while the possibility exists of maintaining a marriage relationship or of working toward a reconciliation. We have found that only the permanent departure of a spouse dissolves a marriage bond (1 Cor 7:15). Such a departure can be caused by death (1 Cor 7:39; Rom 7:2) or by the permanent desertion by an unbelieving spouse (1 Cor 7:15). In either case, the surviving spouse is released from the marriage bond and is free to remarry.

The Unbelieving Partner in Paul's Time. Since we have found that the willful and permanent desertion by the unbelieving partner constitutes legitimate grounds for divorce and remarriage (1 Cor 7:15), it is important at this juncture to define "the unbelieving partner." It is evident that for Paul "the unbelieving partner" was a pagan who refused to accept the Christian faith. In view of the fact that in cities like Corinth most of the church members were converts from paganism, there must have been a considerable number of mixed marriages, where only one partner was a Christian. This situation caused serious marital problems when, for example, the pagan husband did not want to put up with a Christian wife who refused to engage in pagan practices condemned by the Christian faith.

This posed a serious problem. How can a Christian maintain a marriage with an unbelieving partner who wanted out of the marriage? Paul knew that Jesus forbade divorce. But applying this principle was difficult in a concrete situation of a mixed-marriage where an obstinate unbeliever wanted out of the relationship. In seeking for a practical solution, Paul, under the guidance of the Holy Spirit, upheld the "no-divorce" ruling of Jesus for believing partners while allowing for the dissolution of marriages in the case of desertion by an unbelieving partner. The reason given by Paul is that "God has called us to peace" (1 Cor 7:15). No peaceful marital relationship would be possible with a hostile unbelieving partner.

The Unbelieving Partner Today. How can we practice the "interpretative freedom" of Paul today in dealing with difficult marriage situations not contemplated in the Scriptures? In Paul's time, the major problem in the Corinthian church was that of mixed marriages in which the unbelieving partner made it impossible to maintain a peaceful relationship and willfully deserted his or her believing spouse. In our times, the situation can be quite different. Often the deserter is not an unbeliever, but a nominal Christian. In Paul's time, most of the church members in cities like Corinth were converts from paganism. Today, most of them come from a Christian background.

Being born, brought up and baptized in a Christian church, however, does not necessarily make a person a "believer." Biblically speaking, a "believer" is one who practices the principles of the Christian faith he or she professes to believe in. This means that spouses who are homosexual, sexually promiscuous, physically and verbally abusive, addicted to alcohol or drugs, treacherous, slanderous, or lovers of pleasure rather than lovers of God, can hardly be called "believing Christians," though baptized members of Christian churches. Such persons may hold a form of religion but by their lifestyle deny its power (2 Tim 3:5).

How should a Christian relate to a spouse who persists in his or her perverse lifestyle? Paul's admonition is straightforward, "Avoid such people" (2 Tim 3:5). This admonition applies both to social and marital relationships. Living with and loving a person who blatantly and obstinately violates the moral principles of Christianity means condoning such an immoral lifestyle.

This means that the rule Paul applied to desertion by an unbelieving partner from a pagan background can also be legitimately applied to desertion by a nominally "believing partner" from a Christian background. In both instances, the desertion is caused by unwillingness to accept or at least to respect the principles and practices of the believing partner. In both instances, "if the unbelieving partner desires to separate, let it be so; in such a case, the brother or sister is not bound" (1 Cor 7:15).

An Example. The following example may help to illustrate the principle under consideration. Julie met Robert in her junior year at a Christian college. He appealed to her as a responsible, mature, and intelligent Christian young man. They were married soon after graduation. For the first couple of years, they got along quite well, until gradually Robert started going out with the "boys." When he returned home late at night, he was usually drunk and became verbally abusive and physically violent. Julie soon discovered that Robert also had homosexual preferences, enjoying being with the "boys" more than being with her. When Julie urged Robert to repent of his evil ways and return to the Lord, he left her for good.

Julie was devastated by this whole experience. It took her over a year to recover and to put the pieces of her life back together. Then she began asking, "Do I have the right to remarry according to the Scripture?" In the light of our study, the answer is "yes," because Robert by his lifestyle proved to be an unbelieving partner who wanted out of the marriage. "In such a case," the Scripture says, "the brother or sister is not bound" (1 Cor 7:15).

Julie was released from her marriage bond because in spite of her best efforts, there was no longer a possibility of maintaining a peaceful marital relationship or of helping Robert to change his perverse lifestyle. We noted that Scripture enjoins "no-separation" as long as a peaceful marital relationship can be maintained and the Christian spouse can exercise a sanctifying influence on his/her unbelieving partner (1 Cor 7:12-14). But if a spouse persists in his or her wicked ways and/or endangers the life of family members, the admonition of Scripture is clear: "Avoid such people" (2 Tim 3:5). This admonition applies both to social and marital relationships. For the sake of peace and mental sanity, it becomes a necessity for a Christian spouse to break up a marital relationship with an abusive, violent, and perverse partner.

Desertion and Remarriage. A question that often comes up is, "When is desertion proper grounds for divorce and remarriage?" This question is most relevant because desertions are nearly as numerous as legal divorces. In some ways, desertions are more devastating than divorces, not only because of their suddenness but also because of the deserter's failure to make proper provisions for those left behind.

The Scripture gives no explicit guidelines on when desertion becomes proper grounds for divorce and remarriage. We have found that Paul simply states that the believing partner is no longer bound when his or her unbelieving spouse leaves (1 Cor 7:15). The marriage relationship is terminated by the willful, obstinate, and permanent desertion of a spouse. We can assume that if a desertion continues for a year or more, the deserter has given ample proof of his or her permanent desertion. Though some would argue for a shorter period of time, any uncertainty about the future would be better allayed if at least a year were allowed to test the permanence of the deserter's intentions. Such a period of desertion would give ample proof of the dissolution of the marriage.

4. The Church Can Help Prevent Marriage Breakups

A fourth important principle is that the church can play a vital role in preventing marriage breakups. Most of the marital breakups I have known in my itinerant ministry in many parts of the world were caused not by the abusive, violent, perverted behavior of the other partner as in the case of Julie and Robert, but rather by differences in personalities, values, and social or cultural interests. The inability to discuss openly and to resolve differences gradually weakens the marital commitment, thus tempting many to consider divorce as a solution to their marital problems.

Counseling. The church can play an important role in preventing marriage breakups in these common situations. First, through counseling. A pastor trained not only theologically but also in counseling skills can help a couple having marital conflicts to understand how to resolve their differences constructively, not by seeking divorce but by improving their communication skills. In chapter 4, we discussed seven basic Biblical principles on how to handle marital conflicts constructively. We have found that learning to apply such principles can help a Christian couple to turn conflicts into opportunities for building a stronger marriage covenant.

Teaching. Second, the church can help prevent marriage breakups by teaching that Christians should not consider divorce and remarriage as options for resolving their marital problems. If a Christian couple finds it intolerable to live together, they may choose to separate for a time or to file for legal separation. In such instances, the church must make it clear that the only two Scriptural options are (1) to remain single, or (2) to work toward a possible reconciliation. When confronted with the stark reality of choosing between remaining single or being reconciled, chances are that more couples will opt for the latter. Unfortunately, this Biblical teaching is seldom implemented. Most churches have come to accept, in practice if not in principle, divorce and remarriage as a guiltless and normal procedure. By so doing, they are facilitating rather than preventing marriage breakups.

Disciplinary Actions. Third, the church can help prevent marriage breakups by taking disciplinary action against spouses who choose to divorce and/or remarry on unbiblical grounds. Such action could involve placing the transgressors under censure for a time and not giving them leadership responsibilities. If during such a time there are no indications of repentance, the church should disfellowship these people in order to express her abhorrence of such evil. Addressing a case of sexual immorality in the church of Corinth, Paul explicitly enjoins, "Let him who has done this be removed from among you" (1 Cor 5:2). Such an action is necessary in order for the church to uphold its high standard and to sound a clear warning to anyone contemplating divorce.

When church members know that their church does not condone but resolutely condemns any unbiblical divorce and remarriage by punishing them with censure or even disfellowship, they will be less prone to consider divorce as a way out of their marital problems. What encourages Christians to divorce and remarry is the social acceptance of such practices both outside and inside their own church.

On numerous occasions, I have preached in congregations where over half the members, including the pastors, were divorced and remarried. Such situations can only encourage the perception that divorce and remarriage is a guiltless and normal procedure when so many of the members, including some of the church officers, have done it. To the extent that the church tolerates divorce and remarriage obtained on unbiblical grounds, she becomes morally responsible for failing to prevent marriage breakups.

5. The Church Must Minister to Divorced and Remarried Persons

A fifth important principle is that the church has a responsibility to minister to divorced and/or remarried persons. The church is called, on the one hand, to proclaim God's will for marriage to be a sacred and permanent covenant and, on the other hand, to extend God's forgiving grace to those who have sinned by divorcing and remarrying. The challenge is how to extend God's forgiving grace to sinners without condoning their sin. The tendency is to go to extremes either by totally condemning or by entirely condoning their sin.

Some churches taking the no-divorce position adopt an attitude of hostility and standoffishness toward divorced and/or remarried people. Their perception seems to be that such people have committed the unpardonable sin and that consequently there is not much the church can do for them.

Other churches adopt the opposite position of total tolerance. They welcome divorced and remarried persons, making them feel that there is nothing wrong with what they have done. They extend automatic membership to all, without looking for signs of repentance for past sins or for signs of commitment to a new life of discipleship.

To be faithful to her calling, the church must avoid both extremes. On the one hand, it must avoid the extreme of maximizing sin while minimizing God's forgiving grace. On the other hand, it must avoid the other extreme of maximizing God's forgiving grace while minimizing sin.

The church must proclaim that divorce, wrongly obtained, is *sin*—a heinous offense against God and one's partner. But it must also proclaim that such sin is not too big for God to forgive when genuinely repented of. The Good News of the Gospel is that Christ has saved us from all kinds of sins, including those involving divorce and remarriage. Too often, Christians seem more interested in passing judgment on divorced and remarried people than in extending to them God's grace and forgiveness.

Role of Pastor. The pastor can play an important role in altering the prejudices of church members against divorced and remarried people. Some of their prejudices may be rooted in a misunderstanding of Biblical teachings. For example, some believe that anyone who divorces and remarries on unbiblical grounds commits the unpardonable sin and consequently cannot be fully accepted into the fellowship of the body of Christ.

The pastor can correct such an attitude by helping his members understand that God forgives all sins, including those of divorce and remarriage. We read in 1 Corinthians 6:10-11 that some of the Corinthian church members, prior to their conversions, had been "adulterers, . . . sexual perverts, . . . thieves, . . . drunkards." Yet, Paul reassures them that they "were washed, . . . sanctified, . . . justified." If God forgives murder and sexual immorality of the basest sort, *the church must do so too.* Forgiveness involves not only cleansing but also acceptance and restoration to full fellowship among the members of Christ's church (2 Cor 2:7-8).

It is significant that in the geneology of Christ we find Rahab the harlot and David who committed adultery and murder. In fact, Christ descended from the sinful union of David and Bathsheba, a union that was eventually blessed by God because of David's repentance and forgiveness. We must not be more pious than God Himself by refusing to accept into full church fellowship those whom God has forgiven and accepted because of their sincere repentance.

The Example of Jesus. Throughout His ministry, Jesus showed more interest in healing broken relationships than in exposing sin in people's lives. The story of the woman taken in adultery (John 8:1-11) exemplifies Jesus' attitude of acceptance and forgiveness. His words reveal no condescension or self-righteousness. He accepts and forgives the woman without condoning her sins. He was the only one righteous enough to cast the first stone, but He would not. Jesus' attitude offers profound insights for the church's ministry to divorced and remarried persons.

In following the example of Jesus, the church must demonstrate more affirmation of than condemnation toward those who are already feeling their guilt deeply . Divorced persons are often weighed down with a deep sense of guilt because they have broken one of the most important commitments of their lives. The responsibility of the church is not to add to the burden of guilt but to extend God's forgiving grace to those in need. Pastors can play a vital role in showing God's forgiving grace through their teachings and attitudes. Sometimes what is caught by the congregation of the pastor's attitude toward divorced and remarried persons may be more influential than what is taught by the pastor in this area.

The Sin of Omission. It is possible that one of the reasons why some members or congregations have difficulty in accepting divorcees is because the members fail to realize the responsibility they share for marriages that end in divorce. The church is a corporate body in which we all share responsibility for one another's attitudes, actions, failures, and successes. If we as a church neglect the teaching of the Biblical view of the sacredness and permanence of marriage, if we fail to help engaged couples see the seriousness of the marriage covenant, and if we fail to attend to their spiritual needs shortly after marriage and during the period of separation, do we dare cast a stone?

In the final analysis, we all share a degree of responsibility in the marital breakups of our fellow believers, if not by commission, then at least by omission. When we fail to challenge the growing acceptance of divorce inside and outside the church, we become indirectly responsible for marital breakups. This does not mean that we should minimize the guilt of those who sin by divorcing or remarrying. It only means that we should accept our fair share of responsibility. When this happens, we will be more charitable and redemptive toward divorced and remarried persons.

Programs for Divorcees. Forgiveness and acceptance of the divorced can best be shown through concrete programs. Words help but often they are not enough. Divorced persons will test the credibility of the church's concern for them by evaluating the programs the church offers them. Generally, divorced persons have practical, emotional, and spiritual needs. They experience a great sense of guilt, loneliness, and devastation of their self-image. The church can help by developing programs to meet such needs.

The church can occasionally, or even regularly, offer a special church service for divorced members. This can be a semi-private service in which an opportunity is provided for expressing sorrow and repentance as well as for experiencing forgiveness and rejoicing. Besides special religious services, support groups for divorced persons may be needed. One such group could be made up of single parents from one or more local congregations. They can get together to discuss and share the problems divorce brings, such as loneliness, child discipline, lack of finances, and church expectations. Sometimes a professional person can be invited to talk on a subject and this can be followed by open discussion. Such group gatherings can provide fellowship, counseling, and practical help.

What I am proposing is not that the church become a social agency for divorced persons. Most churches do not even have the financial and professional resources to offer such services. Rather, I am proposing that the church must translate its message of forgiveness and acceptance of divorced persons into concrete programs. Actions speak louder than words. These programs must be seen as part of the mission of the church to reach out to those who are hurting.

The ultimate aim of the ministry of the church is to help divorced persons to experience repentance, forgiveness, cleansing, and reconciliation with God, the church, and themselves. When divorced persons experience this three-dimensional reconciliation, they will develop a new sense of self-esteem, so essential to their well-being. They will also come to view the church as Christ's agency for the reconciliation of the asundered.

CONCLUSION

Faithful to her calling, the church must hold high the banner of marital permanence. It must resist the prevailing secular view of marriage by aggressively promoting the Biblical view of marriage as a sacred, lifelong covenant. Such a program should actively engage all the preaching, teaching, and counseling resources of the church.

To be faithful to her calling, however, the church must not only proclaim God's will for marriage to be a sacred, lifelong covenant, but it must also extend God's forgiving grace to those who have sinned by divorcing and remarrying. It is part of the mission of the church to help divorced and remarried persons to experience repentance, forgiveness, cleansing, and reconciliation with God, the church, and themselves. Our churches should be filled to capacity with sinners who are saved by grace and reconciled to God, and who can then become Christ's agency for the salvation and reconciliation of others.

NOTE TO CHAPTER VII

1. S. Kenneth Chi and Sharon K. Houseknecht, "Protestant Fundamentalism and Marital Success," *Sociology and Social Research* 69 (1985): 351-375.